FRONTIERS

An Active Introduction to English Grammar

John Schmidt
Terry Simon

The University of Texas at Austin

 Addison-Wesley Publishing Company

*Reading, Massachusetts • Menlo Park, California • New York
Don Mills, Ontario • Wokingham, England • Amsterdam
Bonn • Sydney • Singapore • Tokyo • Madrid • Bogotá
Santiago • San Juan*

A Publication of the World Language Division

Sponsoring Editor: Kathleen Sands-Boehmer
Editorial: Kathleen Sands-Boehmer and Jennifer Bixby
Manufacturing/Production: James W. Gibbons
Photo Research: Merle Sciacca
Unit Opener Illustrations: Susan Avishai
Illustrations: Christopher Grieco and Len Shalansky
Design: Herb Caswell
Cover Design: Dick Hannus
Cover Photo: Cheryl Shepard / The New Image

Charts on pages 219 and 243 are from U.S. Office of Education, Digest of
Educational Statistics, 1972 (OE 73-19104).
Washington, D.C.: Department of Health, Education, and Welfare, page 35.

Photo Credits: p. 18, Xinhua News Agency/Yuan Ruxun (top), Salem High
School, NH (bottom); p. 19, Dominick N. Marcigliano; p. 40, N. Y.
Convention & Visitors Bureau; p. 60, Salem High School, NH; p. 77, British
Tourist Office; p. 101, Judith Bittinger; p. 102, Kathleen Robbins; p. 103, Print
from photograph in possession of the Louis A. Warren Lincoln Library and
Museum, Fort Wayne, Indiana; p. 137, Gallaudet College; p. 142, Northern
Essex Community College; p. 146, Ralph P. Turcotte; p. 153, Northeastern
University Photo by J. D. Levine; p. 191, Copyright 1987/Mike Fuger-Focus;
p. 194, Guenther Zuern; p. 221, Ralph P. Turcotte; p. 225, Vermont Travel
Division; p. 227, Smithsonian Institute (top), Courtesy of Air France (bottom);
p. 236, Government of Canada (left), British Tourist Office (right); p. 249,
Jennifer Bixby (top), Kent & Donna Dannen (bottom); p. 299, Courtesy of
Sears Roebuck and Co., Hedrich-Blessing; p. 303, Arizona Office of Tourism.

BCDEFGHIJ-AL-89
ISBN: 0-201-14990-7

Contents _____

Introduction

Frontiers: An Active Introduction to English Grammar is designed to provide a thorough program of beginning-level instruction to English as a second or foreign language (ESL/EFL) students. *Frontiers* is a communicative-based grammar text which provides instruction in the four language skills: listening, speaking, reading, and writing. The text introduces useful vocabulary and includes practice in English pronunciation. Grammatical points and vocabulary studied in previous chapters reappear in subsequent chapters, thus providing an opportunity for review and additional practice. The linguistic foundations of *Frontiers*, combined with a communicative approach to the instruction of introductory English grammar, provide the ESL/EFL student with the necessary elements for a successful entry into the English language.

Frontiers provides a thorough introduction to English within a grammatical framework. *Frontiers* guides students from controlled yet contextualized practice, to creative, meaningful, student-generated interaction, thus facilitating active use of basic English grammar. The communicative approach of the text combines teacher-centered and student-centered activities. Both the instructor and the student can personalize activities and exercises to the particular setting to stimulate meaningful communication within the classroom. The text provides opportunities for student production in whole class and in small group activities, particularly in paired practice. Although the overall tone of the text is pedagogically mature, humor is included, and opportunities for students to express themselves humorously are present.

In *Frontiers*, grammar is clearly introduced, explained, and illustrated with charts, formulas, dialogs, and example sentences. In addition to clarity, consistency from chapter to chapter is an important consideration in *Frontiers*. The chapters follow a similar outline in order to create a sense of familiarity and expectation. However, to maintain student interest, a wide variety of exercises and activities are provided within each chapter.

Flexibility and universality of use are major considerations in *Frontiers*. The text can be used with young adults or adults in intensive or non-intensive courses. *Frontiers* can be used to provide English instruction by native or non-native instructors in English-speaking countries or in non-English-speaking nations around the world. The text can be adapted to different teaching styles and learning styles. The flexibility of the text also includes its appropriateness for use by experienced or novice instructors, in large or small classes, and in classes with varying curricular emphases of language skills and degree of communicative performance.

Chapter Features

Introductory Dialogs and Reading Passages

Each chapter of *Frontiers* begins with a dialog or a reading passage which introduces most of the grammatical points of the chapter, yet requires only a passive understanding of the new grammar. The dialogs and passages often revolve around humorous, mysterious, or unanticipated situations. Comprehension exercises follow the dialogs and reading passages. The dialogs and reading passages are recorded on cassettes. The cassettes can be used in class or they can be used by students in a language laboratory or at home for additional, independent practice.

Pronunciation

Each chapter has a pronunciation section which focuses on an important phonemic distinction (e.g., [ā] vs. [e] vs. [a]), or on a morphophonemic variation (e.g., simple past tense endings). The pronunciation lessons are included on the cassettes.

Grammatical Introductions

Frontiers uses both deductive and inductive approaches to present grammar. Some grammar sections begin with a chart which clearly illustrates grammatical structures, followed by further explanation when necessary. Other sections begin with a short dialog or a series of example sentences, followed by an explanation or a rule. Grammar lessons sometimes include grammatical formulas. Explanations beyond charts and formulas are kept to a minimum and are written in simple language. Significant nuances follow as *Notes*. Complex grammar points are frequently divided into two or more parts within a chapter with practice and application following each part, and related aspects of a grammar topic are sometimes introduced in a later chapter.

Exercises and Activities

Practice and application of grammar range from exercises that are highly structured to exercises which allow for creative expression on the part of the student. Activities involve both oral and written application of the language in a wide variety of formats including interviews, dialogs, role plays, puzzles, riddles, guessing games, writing activities, cloze exercises, and listening activities.

Mini Conversations and Pairwork

Mini Conversations are included in every chapter. A conversational model and cue words are given. Students work in pairs or small groups with short, realistic conversations. The Mini Conversations facilitate acquisition of the structures and development of speaking fluency.

To further maximize oral practice, each chapter of *Frontiers* includes pairwork in which students work cooperatively in pairs cueing and correcting each other. The Mini Conversations and pairwork activities allow for student creativity at the end of the exercise.

Dictations and TOEFL-Like Chapter Quizzes

Each chapter in *Frontiers* concludes with a dictation, in which the major points of the chapter are checked. The dictation is followed by review quizzes. The quizzes are composed of a listening comprehension section (a sentence-level quiz in all chapters and a conversation-level quiz in Chapters 9–12) and a structure section (a sentence completion quiz and an error identification quiz). The quiz components are similar to the listening comprehension section and the structure and written expression section of the Test of English as a Foreign Language (TOEFL). The multiple-choice chapter quizzes introduce students to the format and question types of the TOEFL which many of the university-bound students eventually take. Instructors may use the dictations and quizzes as practice exercises or for diagnostic purposes. The dictations and the listening comprehension quizzes are a part of the cassette series.

Program Components

Student Text

In addition to the features previously mentioned which are found in all chapters of the text, *Frontiers* includes line drawings for charts, large sketches to accompany introductory dialogs and readings, and small sketches to accompany Mini Conversations, pairwork, and some of the other exercises and activities.

Teacher's Guide

The student text is accompanied by a teacher's guide which includes introductory explanations and instructions, scripts of dictations and quizzes, and notes. Answers to the exercises and quizzes are also provided.

Cassette Series

A tape cassette program accompanies the student text. It includes the introductory dialogs and reading passages, pronunciation lessons, and Mini Conversations.

Acknowledgments _____

We have received assistance and encouragement from our colleagues in the Intensive English Program at the University of Texas at Austin for which we are thankful. We particularly wish to thank Charlotte Gilman, Kay Summers, and James Hawkins for piloting *Frontiers* in their classes and for their insightful and valuable suggestions.

For their many helpful comments, we would also like to thank the following ESL and EFL professionals in the field who reviewed the *Frontiers* manuscript at various stages of completion:

Marie Elaine Aloise	State Department of Education, Gurabo School District, Gurabo, Puerto Rico
Larry Cisar	Athenée Français
Carol Houser Piñeiro	Center for English Language and Orientation Programs, Boston University, Boston, Massachusetts
María López de Adams Rose M. Hernández	Bayamón Technical University College, The University of Puerto Rico, Bayamón, Puerto Rico
John Petrimoulx	International Language Institute, University of South Florida, Tampa, Florida
Fredericka L. Stoller	English Department/Program of Intensive English, Northern Arizona University, Flagstaff, Arizona
Cathe Tansey	Addison-Wesley Publishers, Japan Ltd., Tokyo, Japan
Susan Taylor	University of Illinois at Urbana-Champaign, Urbana, Illinois
Julie Vernon-Edo	Tsukuba University, Japan

For their confidence in us and for their consummate professionalism, we owe special thanks to Robert Naiva, Judith Bittinger, and the other dedicated staff members of the World Language Division of Addison-Wesley Publishing Company.

We are particularly grateful to our talented and conscientious editor Kathleen Sands-Boehmer, who skillfully coordinated the various editing stages involved in the development and production of *Frontiers*.

We would like to thank our families, in particular our parents, Robert and Patricia Schmidt and Stanley and Alice Simon, for their continued encouragement and steady interest throughout the developmental stages of this project.

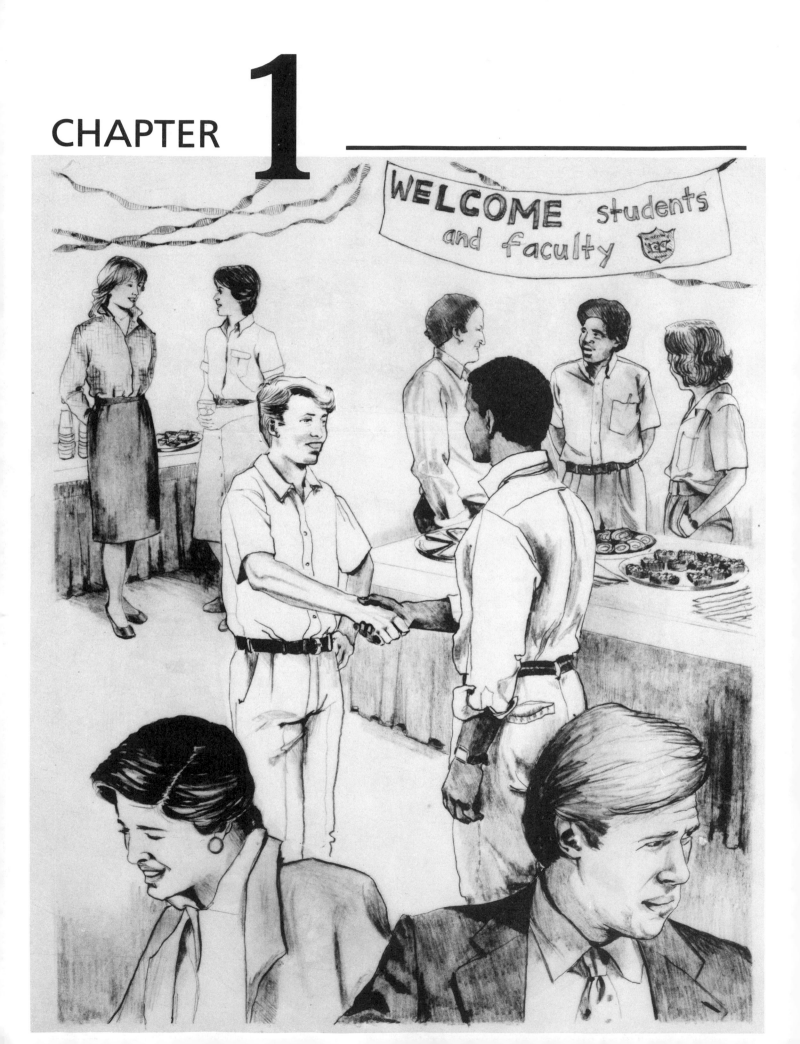

CHAPTER 1

Dialog

Chris Wilson:	Hi, my name is Chris Wilson.
Pat Miller:	I'm Pat Miller. Nice to meet you, Chris.
Chris Wilson:	Nice to meet you too. Where are you from, Pat?
Pat Miller:	I'm from Texas.
Chris Wilson:	Are you new at the university?
Pat Miller:	Yes, I am.
Chris Wilson:	I am too. What's your major?
Pat Miller:	Engineering. Are you in engineering?
Chris Wilson:	No, I'm not. I'm in the Business School. This is my first semester here.

Exercise 1. Answer the questions.

A. *True* or *False*?

1. Chris is a student.   *True* _____

2. Pat is from Texas.   _____

3. Chris is an engineer.   _____

4. Pat is a business student.   _____

5. Chris is a business student.   _____

6. Pat is new at the university.   _____

B. *Yes* or *No*?

1. Is Pat Miller an engineering student?   *Yes* _____

2. Is Chris Wilson a student?   _____

3. Is Chris Wilson an engineering student?   _____

4. Is Chris Wilson new at the university?   _____

5. Is Pat from the United States?   _____

C. About you.

1. Where are you from?   _____

2. What's your occupation?   _____

3. What's your major?   _____

Pronunciation of [ē] and [ĭ]

Exercise 2.

A. Listen to the difference between the pronunciation of [ē] and [ĭ]. Then repeat the words.

[ē]	[ĭ]
Jean	Chris
Keith	Jill
Jackie	Lynn
Peter	Linda
Steven	Victor

B. Listen to the sentences. Repeat the sentences. Then circle the [ē] sounds and underline the [ĭ] sounds.

1. Steve is from Greenville. He's in dentistry.
2. Kim is from Kansas City. She's in engineering.
3. Peter is British. He's a teacher.
4. Liz is Canadian. She's a singer.

Subject Pronouns

	SINGULAR	PLURAL
1st person	I	we
2nd person	you	you
3rd person	he she it	they

Subject pronouns often substitute for previous nouns.

Nouns	Pronouns	Nouns	Pronouns
John	he	John and I	we
Mrs. Fletcher	she	John and you	you
the dog	it	the students	they
the university	it	John and Mrs. Fletcher	they

Examples: **Mrs. Fletcher** is famous. **She** is a writer.
Texas and Florida are states. **They** are in the south.

Notes: 1. Singular means *one*.
2. Plural means *more than one*.
3. Examples of plural nouns: *students*, *schools*, *chairs*
4. The pronoun *I* is always a capital letter.

Exercise 3.
Give the correct subject pronoun. Choose from *he, she, it, we, you,* and *they.*

1. the mother   *she* _____
2. the cat _____
3. the radio _____
4. you and your friend _____
5. you and I _____
6. football and baseball _____

7. the doctor _____
8. he and his father _____
9. New York City _____
10. my sister and I _____
11. money _____
12. Mrs. Simon _____

Exercise 4.
Complete the sentences with subject pronouns.

1. My mother is a doctor. __*She*____ is Chinese.
2. Pat and James are dentists. __*They*____ are Canadian.
3. My father is a professor. _____ is British.
4. Charles and I are teachers. _____ are American.
5. Mr. and Mrs. Lee are musicians. _____ are Japanese.
6. Mr. Lara is a college student. _____ is Colombian.
7. His wife is an artist. _____ is French.
8. Miss Singh is a high school student. _____ is Indian.
9. My brother and I are soccer players. _____ are German.
10. She and her husband are factory workers. _____ are Vietnamese.
11. The Johnsons are farmers. _____ are Australian.
12. Her sister is an Arabic teacher. _____ is Egyptian.

Subject Pronoun + Present Tense of *be*

SINGULAR	PLURAL
I **am**	we **are**
you **are**	you **are**
he **is**	they **are**
she **is**	
it **is**	

FORMULA 1-1

Subject	am is are	a an	singular noun .

Examples: I **am** a secretary.
You **are** an engineer.
Barbara **is** an artist.
It **is** a computer.

FORMULA 1-2 | Subject | **are** | plural noun . |

Examples: We **are** professors.
You **are** students.
They **are** brothers.
Jane and I **are** sisters.

Exercise 5. Complete the sentences. Use *am*, *is*, or *are*.

1. Mr. and Mrs. Carter **are** teachers.
2. I _____ a student.
3. You _____ a student too.
4. We _____ students.
5. Mrs. Carter _____ a teacher.
6. She _____ an English teacher.
7. You _____ teachers.
8. It _____ an English book.
9. They _____ English books.
10. John and I _____ classmates.
11. Mary and Chris _____ classmates.
12. You and Mary _____ classmates too.

A and *an*

A and *an* mean one. Use *a* and *an* before *singular* nouns.

1. **a** + consonant sound
2. **an** + vowel sound

Examples: a book, a computer, a dollar
Examples: an apple, an engineer, an insect, an ocean, an umbrella

Exercise 6. Look at the pictures. Make a sentence for each picture.

Examples: She is a scientist.    He is an athlete.

1. police officer

2. office worker

3. banker

4. carpenter

5. dentist

6. airline pilot

7. lawyer

8. electrician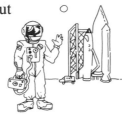

9. football player

10. astronaut

11. musician

12. soccer player

13. secretary

14. waitress

15. factory worker

Exercise 7.

Write *a* or *an* before a singular noun. Leave the space blank before a plural noun. Numbers 1–3 are examples.

1. Tom is __*an*____ engineer.
2. Tom and Mary are _____ artists.
3. Pat is __*a*____ teacher.
4. Chris is _____ actor.
5. Phil is _____ uncle now.
6. They are _____ brothers.
7. Susan is _____ nurse.
8. Lee is _____ athlete.
9. Lee and Mitch are _____ athletes.
10. Kathleen is _____ scientist.

11. I am _____ architect.
12. She is _____ dentist.
13. We are _____ actors.
14. He is _____ teacher.
15. He is _____ airline pilot.
16. They are _____ airports.
17. It is _____ hospital.
18. It is _____ apartment building.
19. They are _____ elevators.
20. It is _____ office building.

Exercise 8.

MINI CONVERSATIONS. Look at and listen to the Mini Conversations. Practice the Mini Conversations with a classmate.

Example: Bob / doctor
his
British

Pat: Bob is a doctor.
Lee: What's his nationality?
Pat: He is British.

1. Betty / nurse
her
Canadian

2. Marcos / student
his
Mexican

3. Maria / artist
her
Spanish

4. Robert / actor
his
American

5. Mayumi / teacher
her
Japanese

6. Ali / engineer
his
Lebanese

Exercise 9.

MINI CONVERSATIONS. Look at and listen to the Mini Conversations. Practice the Mini Conversations with a classmate.

Example: Lin / Chinese
her
architect

Pat: Lin is Chinese.
Lee: What's her occupation?
Pat: She is an architect.

1. Mr. Ritter / German
his
professor

2. Mrs. Calvin / French
her
writer

3. John / American
his
athlete

4. Sophia / Italian
her
actress

5. Mr. Kim / Korean
his
businessman

6. Silvia / Brazilian
her
singer

Capitalization

The first word in a sentence begins with a capital letter. The names of people, geographical locations, languages, and nationalities also begin with capital letters.

Examples: **Patricia Flores** is from **Los Angeles, California**.
She is **American**.

Exercise 10.   Copy the sentences. Use capital letters when necessary.

1. diana garza is mexican.   she is from acapulco, mexico.

   _____

2. mr. and mrs. ito are japanese.   they are from tokyo, japan.

   _____

3. mohamed abbas is from cairo, egypt.   he is egyptian.

   _____

4. my english teacher is british.   she is from london, england.

   _____

5. victor cardin is from paris, france.   he is french.

   _____

Exercise 11.   Complete the following sentences with subject pronouns, present tense forms of *be*, and nouns.

Occupations

1. _**We**_____ are gardeners.
2. She _*is*_____ a dentist.
3. I am an __*architect*___ .
4. _____ is an English teacher.
5. You _____ doctors.
6. Pat and I are _____ .
7. I _____ a _____ .
8. Terry _____ an _____ .
9. _____ are a student.

Relationships

10. We _____ sisters.
11. _____ are classmates.
12. They _____ friends.
13. Tom and Jim are _____ .
14. My family _____ from Brazil.

Places and Things

15. _____ is a small country.
16. _____ is a radio.
17. _____ are big cities.
18. Toyotas and Hondas _____ Japanese cars.

Exercise 12.   Complete the sentences.

_____ is from _____ . _____ is _____ .
(woman's name)   (country)   (pronoun)   (nationality)

_____ is _____ _____ . Her sisters are _____ and _____ .
(pronoun)   (a / an)   (occupation)   (name)   (name)

_____ are _____ .
(pronoun)   (occupation)

Exercise 13.   Complete the sentences.

I _____ from _____ , _____ . I _____ _____ .
                    (city)   (country)   (nationality)

_____ am _____ _____ . My mother and father's names are _____ and
              (a / an)   (occupation)   (woman's name)

_____ . _____ are _____ . My father _____ _____
(man's name)   are   (nationality)   (a / an)

_____ , and my mother _____ _____ _____ .
(occupation)   (a / an)   (occupation)

Negative with Verb *be*

FORMULA 1-3	Subject	am is are	not	a / an + singular noun . plural noun .

Examples: She **is not** an architect.
They **are not** gardeners.
I **am not** an artist.

Exercise 14.   Complete the sentences. Use subject pronouns, present tense forms of *be*, and the word *not*.

1. Mrs. Lee is a musician. __***She is not***___ a singer.

2. I am a student. _____ a teacher.

3. You and I are students. _____ teachers.

4. Mr. and Mrs. Chang are computer scientists. _____ engineers.

5. Her brother is an actor. _____ a singer.

6. She and her husband are farmers. _____ gardeners.

7. Mr. Sharif is a graduate student. _____ an undergraduate.

8. He and his brother are football players. _____ soccer players.

9. You are a nurse. _____ a doctor.

10. Eric and Pat are flight attendants. _____ pilots.

Cardinal Numbers

Exercise 15. Look, listen, and repeat. Pay attention to the pronunciation and the spelling of the numbers.

1. one	11. eleven	21. twenty-one
2. two	12. twelve	30. thirty
3. three	13. thirteen	33. thirty-three
4. four	14. fourteen	40. forty
5. five	15. fifteen	50. fifty
6. six	16. sixteen	60. sixty
7. seven	17. seventeen	70. seventy
8. eight	18. eighteen	80. eighty
9. nine	19. nineteen	90. ninety
10. ten	20. twenty	100. one hundred

254. two hundred fifty-four
1,000. one thousand
5,619. five thousand six hundred nineteen
1,000,000. one million

Exercise 16. Listen and write the numbers.

a. *12*

b. _____

c. _____

d. _____

e. _____

f. _____

g. _____

h. _____

i. _____

j. _____

k. _____

l. _____

m. _____

n. _____

Exercise 17. *How old are they?* Answer the questions with complete sentences.

1. How old is she? (36) ***She is thirty-six years old.***

2. How old is he? (13) _____

3. How old is it?   (89) _____

4. How old is he?   ( ) _____

5. How old is she?   ( ) _____

6. How old is it?   ( ) _____

7. How old are they?   ( ) _____

8. How old are you?   ( ) _____

Possessive Adjectives:
my, your, his, her, its, our, their

SINGULAR		PLURAL	
I am American.	**My** hometown is Dallas.	*We* are Venezuelan.	**Our** hometown is Caracas.
You are Taiwanese.	**Your** hometown is Taipei.	*You* are British.	**Your** hometown is London.
He is Canadian.	**His** hometown is Vancouver.	*They* are Algerian.	**Their** hometown is Algiers.
She is Saudi.	**Her** hometown is Jeddah.		
It is a German company.	**Its** office is in Hamburg.		

Possessive adjectives show possession. They go before the noun. They have the same form before singular and plural nouns.

Exercise 18. Complete the sentences with the correct possessive adjectives.

1. Mr. Ito is Japanese. *His* hometown is Osaka.

2. You are Panamanian. *Your* family is from Panama City.

3. I am Korean. _____ hometown is Seoul.

4. She is French _____ family is in Paris.

5. They are Chinese. _____ hometown is Beijing.

6. He is Moroccan. _____ family is in Casablanca.

7. We are Mexican. _____ hometown is Mexico City.

8. It is a Mexican company. _____ offices are in Monterrey.

9. Kathy and Mark are Australian. _____ parents are in Sydney.

10. Massoud and I are Iranian. _____ families are in Tehran.

11. You and Elena are Colombian. _____ hometown is Bogota.

12. Mrs. Singh is Indian. _____ hometown is Calcutta.

13. Patrick is Irish. _____ family is from Shannon.

14. You and I are Kenyan. _____ hometown is Nairobi.

15. Miss Pavlov is Russian. _____ parents are from Moscow.

16. Mr. and Mrs. Clark are British. _____ home is in London.

Affirmative Contractions with Pronouns + *be*

SINGULAR	PLURAL
I'm a secretary.	**We're** friends.
You're an artist.	**You're** classmates.
He's a taxi driver.	**They're** sisters.
She's a nurse.	
It's a thermometer.	

A contraction is a shortened form of two words joined together.
An apostrophe (') replaces the missing letter. Contractions are used in informal English. They are often used in speaking.

I am = **I'm**   you are = **you're**
he is = **he's**   we are = **we're**
she is = **she's**   they are = **they're**
it is = **it's**

Exercise 19. Fill in the blanks with a pronoun and *am, is,* or *are* with a contraction.

1. My car is from Sweden. *It's* _____ a Volvo.

2. I am an engineer. _____ an office worker.

3. We are Mexican. _____ tourists.

4. Jennifer is a parent. _____ twenty-four years old.

5. My mother and father are Mexican. _____ from Mexico City.

6. You are a police officer. _____ a captain.

7. He is an athlete. _____ a swimmer.

8. You and I are students. _____ undergraduates.

9. Montreal and Toronto are cities. _____ in Canada.

10. Sacramento is in California. _____ the capital of California.

Notes: 1. Contractions can be made with singular nouns and *is*. They are common in speaking and informal writing.

        Examples: Peter**'s** an office worker.
                      An engineer**'s** a scientist.
                      My television**'s** a Sony.

2. In writing, contractions cannot be made with plural nouns and *are*.

Correct	*Wrong*
The televisions are Sonys.	The televisions'~~is~~ Sonys.

Contractions in Negative Statements with *be*—Type 1

SINGULAR	PLURAL
I'm not an electrician.	**We're not** police officers.
You're not a cook.	**You're not** taxi drivers.
He's not a banker.	**They're not** carpenters.
She's not a travel agent.	
It's not a machine.	
Pat's not a dentist.	

Exercise 20. Complete the sentences. Use contractions and *not*. Write your own sentences for 11 and 12.

1. I am a banker.   *I'm not*_____ a lawyer.
2. They are lawyers.   _____ professors.
3. She is a musician.   _____ a singer.
4. We are nurses.   _____ doctors.
5. Joe is a guard.   _____ a police officer.
6. You are pilots.   _____ flight attendants.
7. He is an engineer.   _____ a scientist.
8. I am a student.   _____ a teacher.
9. California is a state.   _____ a city.
10. Madrid is the capital of Spain.   _____ the capital of Portugal.
11. _____   _____
12. _____   _____

Contractions in Negative Statements
with *be*—Type 2

SINGULAR	PLURAL
(No contraction with *am not*)	We **aren't** engineers.
You **aren't** the boss.	You **aren't** doctors.
He **isn't** a doctor.	They **aren't** insects.
She **isn't** a singer.	Ed and David **aren't** friends.
It **isn't** a vegetable.	My parents **aren't** from Chicago.
Nancy **isn't** an actress.	
Her car **isn't** a Cadillac.	

Note: are not = **aren't**   is not = **isn't**

Exercise 21.   Complete each sentence two ways. Make both sentences negative.

1. Jenny __*'s not*__ a secretary.
   Jenny __*isn't*__ a secretary.

2. We _____ English teachers.
   We _____ English teachers.

3. My sister _____ a student.
   My sister _____ a student.

4. You _____ athletes.
   You _____ athletes.

5. Joe _____ a baseball player.
   Joe _____ a baseball player.

6. They _____ carpenters.
   They _____ carpenters.

Exercise 22.   WRITING. Write six sentences about people and their occupations. Write about classmates, family members, or famous people. Make three sentences affirmative and three negative.

1. _____
2. _____
3. _____
4. _____
5. _____
6. _____

Subject + *be* + *(not)* + Adjective

SINGULAR	PLURAL
I am **cold.**	We aren't **hot.**
You aren't **late.**	You are **tired.**
He is **happy.**	They aren't **sad.**
Gold isn't **cheap.**	Lemons are **yellow.**
My dog is **thirsty.**	Bob and Jim aren't **hungry.**

FORMULA 1-4	Subject	am is are	not	adjective .

Notes: 1. *A* and *an* do not precede an adjective without a following noun.
2. Adjectives do not have a plural *-s* ending.

Correct

He is intelligent.
You are an intelligent student.
We are intelligent.

Wrong

He is an intelligent.
You are × intelligent student.
We are intelligents.

Exercise 23.

PAIRWORK. Work with a classmate. Make sentences which are meaningful and grammatically correct with words from the columns below.

Examples: English is easy.
My friends aren't famous.

SUBJECT	*be*		ADJECTIVE
Coffee A flower Oranges Superman I My classmate My friends London English Politicians The United States My country My mother The President _____	am is are	(not)	hungry intelligent big easy happy beautiful delicious important expensive strong round homesick hot famous single _____

Exercise 24.

Fill in the blanks with *is, are, isn't,* or *aren't.* Make correct statements.

1. Spain and Portugal __*aren't*__ in South America.

2. The United States _____ a small country.

3. Washington, D.C. _____ a state.

4. The Atlantic Ocean _____ east of North America.

5. The President of the U.S.A. _____ a woman.

6. Basketball players _____ usually tall.

7. Jet airplanes _____ cheap.

8. Ice _____ cold.

9. Diamond necklaces _____ expensive.

10. Discotheques _____ quiet.

11. Carrots _____ orange.

12. Apples _____ square.

13. The leader of my country _____ single.

14. The Pope _____ married.

Exercise 25. MINI CONVERSATIONS.

Example: Tom / hungry
Bob / thirsty

Pat: <u>Tom</u> is <u>hungry</u>.
Lee: <u>Bob</u> isn't <u>hungry</u>. He's <u>thirsty</u>.

1. Kathy / late
Patricia / early

2. Bill / scientist
Jim / engineer

3. Diana / nurse
Betty / doctor

4. Victor / sad
Bob / happy

5. Mrs. Allen / waitress
Mrs. Sharif / actress

6. Eric / married
John / single

Example: Mary / teacher
Sue / artist

Pat: <u>Mary</u> is <u>a teacher</u>.
Lee: <u>Sue</u> isn't <u>a teacher</u>. She's <u>an artist</u>.

7. Mohammad / strong
Ali / weak

8. Sophia / rich
Jenny / poor

9. Mr. Chang / old
Mr. Lee / young

10. Silvia / calm
Carmen / nervous

11. _____ / teacher

_____ / student

12. _____ / tall

_____ / short

Yes-No Questions with *be*

SINGULAR	PLURAL
Am I late?	**Are we** early?
Are you thirsty?	**Are you** hungry?
Is he sick?	**Are they** married?
Is she a doctor?	**Are Sue and Mike** busy?
Is it in Africa?	
Is the actress nervous?	

In questions with *be*, the form of *be* comes before the subject. In writing, a question mark (?) comes at the end of the sentence.

Am Is Are	subject	adjective phrase	?

FORMULA 1-5

Exercise 26. Write the questions.

Questions

1. ___*Are you happy?*___
2. ___*Is your father tall?*___
3. _____
4. _____
5. _____
6. _____
7. _____
8. _____
9. _____
10. _____

Answers

Yes, I'm happy.

No, he isn't tall.

Yes, they are hungry.

No, she isn't eighteen.

Yes, I'm married.

No, they're not cheap.

Yes, it's easy.

No, you're not late.

Yes, we are students.

No, it's not expensive.

Exercise 27. PAIRWORK. Student A: Read the first sentence.
Student B: Cover the left side of the page. Ask a question with the cue word.
Student A: Check Student B's question. Read the answer.

Examples: A: Madrid is in Spain. (Lisbon)
B: Is Lisbon in Spain?
A: No, it's in Portugal.

A: Toronto is in Canada. (Montreal and Quebec)
B: Are Montreal and Quebec in Canada?
A: Yes.

STUDENT A

1. Athens is in Greece.
   (Is *Rome* in Greece?)
   No, it's in Italy.

2. Seoul is in South Korea.
   (Are *Tokyo and Osaka* in South Korea?)
   No, they're in Japan.

3. Lima is in Peru.
   (Is *Caracas* in Peru?)
   No, it's in Venezuela.

4. France is in Europe.
   (Are *Norway and Denmark* in Europe?)
   Yes.

STUDENT B

(Rome)

(Tokyo and Osaka)

(Caracas)

(Norway and Denmark)

5. Cairo is in Egypt.   (Alexandria)
   (Is *Alexandria* in Egypt?)
   Yes.

6. New Delhi is in India.   (Bombay and Calcutta)
   (Are *Bombay and Calcutta* in India?)
   Yes.

7. Merida is in Mexico.   (Acapulco)
   (Is *Acapulco* in Mexico?)
   Yes.

8. Brazil and Argentina are in South America.   (Costa Rica and Panama)
   (Are *Costa Rica and Panama* in South America?)
   No, they're in Central America.

9. Iceland is in the Atlantic Ocean.   (Indonesia)
   (Is *Indonesia* in the Atlantic Ocean?)
   No, it's in the Pacific Ocean.

10. Cuba is in the Carribean Sea.   (Jamaica and Puerto Rico)
    (Are *Jamaica and Puerto Rico* in the Carribean Sea?)
    Yes.

Short Answers to *Yes-No* Questions with *be*

	LONG FORMS		CONTRACTIONS	
Question	*Affirmative*	*Negative*	*Negative*	*Negative*
Am I late?	Yes, you are.	No, you are not.	No, you're not.	No, you aren't.
Are you thirsty? (S)	Yes, I am.	No, I am not.	No, I'm not.	- - - - - - - - -
Are you hungry? (P)	Yes, we are.	No, we are not.	No, we're not.	No, we aren't.
Is she sick?	Yes, she is.	No, she is not	No, she's not.	No, she isn't.
Are we ready?	Yes, we are.	No, we are not.	No, we're not.	No, we aren't.
Are we early?	Yes, you are.	No, you are not.	No, you're not.	No, you aren't.
Are they married?	Yes, they are.	No, they are not.	No, they're not.	No, they aren't.

Notes: 1. There is no contracted form for an affirmative short answer.
English sentences never end in a contracted from of *be*.

Correct	*Wrong*
Yes, I am.	Yes, I'm.
Yes, she is.	Yes, she's.

2. Long answers are also possible, but short answers are more common.

Examples of long answers: Am I late?   Yes, you are late.
Yes, you're late.
No, you are not late.
No, you're not late.
No, you aren't late.

Exercise 28. MINI CONVERSATIONS. Practice the conversations. Then make up your own.

Example: China / Asia
             Shanghai

Chris: Is <u>China</u> in <u>Asia</u>?
Terry: Yes, it is.
Chris: Is <u>Shanghai</u> the capital?
Terry: No, it isn't.

1. Italy / Europe
   Florence

2. Mexico / North America
   Monterrey

3. India / Asia
   Bombay

4. Saudi Arabia / the Middle East
   Mecca

5. Brazil / South America
   Rio de Janeiro

6. Morocco / Africa
   Casablanca

7. Australia / the Pacific Ocean
   Sydney

8. _____

   _____

Exercise 29. MINI CONVERSATIONS.

Example: Sarah and Megan / sisters
             friends

Pat: Are <u>Sarah and Megan</u> sisters?
Jan: No, they aren't.
Pat: Are they <u>friends</u>?
Jan: Yes, they are.

1. Charles and Jack / brothers
   roommates

2. your roommates / football players
   soccer players

3. Liz and Emily / cousins
   classmates

4. Ivan and Nicolas / taxi drivers
   bus drivers

5. Marta and Ana / actresses
   singers

6. _____

   _____

Exercise 30. MINI CONVERSATIONS.

Example: hungry
thirsty

Jess: Are you <u>hungry</u>?
Fran: No, I'm not.
Jess: Are you <u>thirsty</u>?
Fran: Yes, I am.

1. finished
   busy

2. cold
   comfortable

3. nervous
   relaxed

4. sad
   happy

5. weak
   strong

6. _____
   _____

Exercise 31. PAIRWORK.

Student A: Read the question.
Student B: Answer the question with your book closed. Give true short answers, and use contractions if possible.
Student A: Correct wrong answers.

STUDENT A

1. Is Lebanon in Africa?
2. Are you an artist?
3. Are apples and bananas vegetables?
4. Is Albert Einstein dead?
5. Are you an athlete?
6. Are Alaska and Hawaii states?
7. Is a Rolls Royce very expensive?
8. Are you happy today?
9. Is Miami the capital of Florida?
10. Is Hawaii in the Atlantic Ocean?
11. _____

STUDENT B

No, it's not. / No, it isn't.
Yes, I am. / No, I'm not.
No, they're not. / No, they aren't.
Yes, he is.
Yes, I am. / No, I'm not.
Yes, they are.
Yes, it is.
Yes, I am. / No, I'm not.
No, it's not. / No, it isn't.
No, it's not. / No, it isn't.
_____

Exercise 32.

A. Answer the questions with short answers.

1. Is the teacher absent today? _____
2. Are you an artist? _____
3. Am I late? _____

4. Are your classmates British? _____

5. Are we finished with the exercise? _____

B. Complete the questions to match the answers.

6. _____ hungry?   Yes, I am.

7. _____ married?   No, they aren't.

8. _____ six o'clock?   No, it isn't.

9. _____ students?   Yes, we are.

10. _____ late?   No, you're not.

C. Complete the questions and answer them.

11. _____ from the United States?   _____

12. _____ a teacher?   _____

13. _____ Mexican?   _____

14. _____ ?   _____

15. _____ ?   _____

Wh-Questions with *be: where* and *what*

FORMULA 1-6	Where What	am is are	subject	(complement)	?

	Question	*Answer*
Examples:	**What is** your name?	Mohammed.
	Where are you from?	Malaysia.
	Where's Malaysia?	It's in southeast Asia.
	Where are your parents?	They're in Malaysia.
	What's your major?	Computer science.
	What are your favorite sports?	Soccer and tennis.

Notes: 1. *Where* asks about place. *What* asks about a thing or identity.

2. what is = **what's**
   where is = **where's**

3. In writing, *am* and *are* cannot be contracted with *wh*-question words.

Exercise 33. MINI CONVERSATIONS.

Example: Kathy
American
California
Los Angeles
mechanic

Bob: What's her name?
Pat: Her name is Kathy.
Bob: What's her nationality?
Pat: She's American.
Bob: Where's she from?
Pat: She's from California.
Bob: What's her hometown?
Pat: Her hometown is Los Angeles.
Bob: What's her occupation?
Pat: She's a mechanic.

1. Adam
American
Texas
Austin
painter

2. Amanda
Canadian
Ontario
Ottawa
computer programmer

3. Andrew
British
Kent
Canterbury
gardener

4. Hans
German
Bavaria
Munich
flight attendant

5. Anne
French
Provence
Cannes
travel agent

6. Maria
Spanish
Andalusia
Cordoba
cook

7. Mike
Australian
Queensland
Cooktown
tailor

8. _____
_____
_____
_____
_____

Exercise 34. MINI CONVERSATIONS

SINGULAR

Example: Lou
Chicago
biology

A: What's your name?
B: My name is Lou.
A: Where are you from?
B: I'm from Chicago.
A: What's your major?
B: My major is biology.
A: Are you an undergraduate?
B: Yes, I am.

1. Laura
   Washington, D.C.
   history

2. Mr. Li
   China
   economics

3. Paul
   France
   English

4. Abdulla
   Saudi Arabia
   engineering

5. _____
   _____
   _____

PLURAL

Example: Mary and Bob
Dallas
math / chemistry

A: What are your names?
B: Our names are Mary and Bob.
A: Where are you from?
B: We're from Dallas.
A: What are your majors?
B: My major is math and his major is chemistry.
A: Are you undergraduates?
B: Yes, we are.

1. Diana and Michael
   New York City
   dance / music

2. Amy and Eric
   Canada
   drama / education

3. Angel and Carlos
   Mexico
   computer science / accounting

4. Machiko and Toshio
   Japan
   business / architecture

5. _____
   _____
   _____

Prepositions of Place

Welcome to the Nelsons' neighborhood.

1. Where's Mrs. Nelson?   She's **in** the bedroom.

2. Where's the bedroom?   It's **above** the living room.

3. Where's Mr. Nelson?   He's **in front of** the house.

4. Where's Tom Nelson?   He's **in back of** the truck.   (or)
                             He's **behind** the truck.

5. Where's the truck?   It's **near** the Nelsons' home.

6. Where are the dogs?   They're **under** the car.

7. Where are the cats?   They're **on** the car.

8. Where's the Wilsons' home? It's **next to** the Nelsons' home.

9. Where's the garage?   It's **between** the Nelsons' home and the Wilsons' home.

10. Where's the school?   It's **across from** the Nelsons' home.

Exercise 35. Describe the location of the objects in the picture on page 23.

1. The sofa _is in_ _____ the living room.
2. The food _____ the dining room table.
3. The motorcycle _____ the garage.
4. The bicycle _____ the car and Mr. Nelson.
5. The tree _____ the house.
6. The birds _____ the garage.
7. The Nelsons' home _____ the Wilsons' home.
8. The bathroom _____ the dining room.
9. The car _____ the garage.
10. The chairs _____ the tree.
11. The hall _____ the bedroom and the bathroom.
12. The telephone pole _____ the Wilsons' home.
13. The Kleins' home _____ the Wilsons' home.
14. _____
15. _____

Exercise 36. PAIRWORK. Add more objects, animals, or people to the picture of the Nelsons' neighborhood on page 23.
Ask a classmate questions about the new picture.
Use "*Where is . . .?*" and "*Where are . . .?*"

Exercise 37. WRITING. Draw a picture of a room in your school. Then write a description of the room. Use prepositions of place (*in, on, above, under, in front of, in back of, behind, near, next to, between, across from*).

Activities

A. INTERVIEW. Ask a classmate the following questions.

1. Where are you from?
2. Are you an undergraduate?
3. What's your major? / What's your occupation?
4. Are you single?
5. Is your family large?
6. What's your favorite color? / food? / sport? / TV show? / holiday?
7. Are you fluent in Spanish? / Japanese? / French? / Arabic?
8. Are you _____ ?
9. What _____ ?
10. _____ ?

B. DIALOG. Practice the following dialog with a classmate.

Lynn: Hello, my name is Lynn Clark.
Jamal: I'm Jamal Al-Mashani. Nice to meet you.
Lynn: Where are you from, Jamal?
Jamal: I'm from Lebanon.
Lynn: My neighbor is Lebanese too. Are you new at the university?
Jamal: Yes, I am.
Lynn: I am too. What's your major?
Jamal: Computer science. Are you in computer science?
Lynn: No, I'm not. I'm in the English department. Are you a graduate student?
Jamal: No, I'm a freshman. This is my first semester here.

C. SENTENCE COMPLETION. Complete the dialog with a classmate. Use the dialog above as an example.

A: Hi, my name is _____ .

B: I'm _____ . Nice to meet you.

A: _____ you from, _____ ?

B: _____ from _____ .

A: Oh, my friend is from _____ . Are you _____ at _____ university?

B: Yes, _____ .

A: I am too. _____ your major?

B: _____ . Are you in _____ too?

A: No, _____ . I'm in the _____ department. _____ a graduate student?

B: No, I'm a _____ . This is _____ first semester here.

D. WRITING. Write a new dialog with a classmate. Use the dialog in Part B and the dialog at the beginning of Chapter 1 (page 1) as examples.

E. SENTENCE COMPLETION.   Complete the description of a family member. Fill in the blanks with appropriate words.

My Brother Steven

My brother _____ 25 years old. _____ name is Steven Nelson. _____ is in Chicago, Illinois. He's _____ accountant. He's short _____ thin. _____ hair is black. His eyes _____ brown. He _____ married. His wife _____ from Montreal. _____ is Canadian. _____ name is Marie. _____ house is big. _____ is old. Their family _____ large. _____ children are Elizabeth, Michael, Jennifer, and Nicolas. Steven and Marie _____ good parents.

F. WRITING.   Write a description of a member of your immediate family, a relative, or a friend. If possible, include a photograph of the person with the description.

G. GUESSING GAMES.

1. Describe a famous person. Then ask the class, *What's his name?* or *What's her name?*

   Example: She is tall and thin.
   She is beautiful.
   Her hair is blonde.
   Her eyes are blue.
   She is American.
   She is in Hollywood, California.
   She is an actress.
   What's her name?

2. Think of a famous person. Other students ask you *yes-no* questions. They try to guess the name of the famous person.

   Example: Is the person a man?   Yes, he is.
   Is he British?   Yes, he is.
   Is he tall?   No, he isn't.
   Is he old?   Yes, he is.
   Is he a politician?   No, he isn't.
   Is he an actor?   Yes, he is.

3. Write 5–8 sentences about yourself. Begin each sentence with *I am*. Pass in your papers. Your teacher will distribute them. Read the paper you receive. Guess who it's about.

4. Describe an object. Then ask the class, *What is it?*

   Example: It's round.
   It's red.
   It's delicious.
   It's in the kitchen.
   It's not expensive.
   It's a fruit.
   What is it?

H. PUZZLE. Put the words in the correct order.
Remember: a sentence begins with a capital letter.

Example: name / Jackson / is / my / Susan / .
My name is Susan Jackson.

1. New York / an / city / is / expensive / ?

_____

2. I / friends / are / and / Mary / .

_____

3. is / engineer / he / an / not / .

_____

4. is / from / father / where / her / ?

_____

5. and / you / sister / Spanish / are / your / in / fluent / ?

I. CAPITALIZATION AND PUNCTUATION. Rewrite the following sentences.
Use capital letters, periods, and question marks where needed.

1. is the canadian student from vancouver, british columbia

_____

2. my sister karen and i are students

_____

3. where are you from, miss martin

_____

4. is miami the capital of florida

_____

5. mr and mrs jackson are happy

_____

6. are french and spanish interesting languages

_____

J. DICTATION. You will hear each sentence two times. Write exactly what you hear.

1. _____
2. _____
3. _____
4. _____
5. _____
6. _____

Review Quizzes

A. LISTENING COMPREHENSION: SENTENCES

For each problem, you will hear a short sentence. You will hear each sentence two times. After you hear a sentence, read the four choices. Decide which written sentence is the closest in meaning to the spoken sentence. Circle the letter of the correct answer.

Example: You hear:

You read: (A) It isn't short.
(B) It's short.
(C) They're short.
(D) They aren't short.

Sentence (B) "It's short," is the closest in meaning to the sentence, "The sentence is short." Therefore, you should choose answer (B).

1. (A) The boy is Mexican.
   (B) The boys are Mexican.
   (C) The boy's in Mexico.
   (D) The boys are in Mexico.

2. (A) He is Canadian.
   (B) He isn't Canadian.
   (C) She is Canadian.
   (D) She isn't Canadian.

3. (A) She is early.
   (B) Linda is late.
   (C) Linda isn't a lady.
   (D) She isn't at the lake.

4. (A) Mrs. Anderson is a teacher.
   (B) Miss Anderson is a teacher.
   (C) Mr. Anderson is a teacher.
   (D) Mr. Anderson isn't a teacher.

5. (A) She's here.
   (B) She isn't here.
   (C) They aren't here.
   (D) They are here.

6. (A) California is the capital of Los Angeles.
   (B) The capital of California isn't Los Angeles.
   (C) Los Angeles is in California.
   (D) The capital of California is Los Angeles.

7. (A) It's on page 13.
   (B) It's on page 30.
   (C) They're on page 13.
   (D) They're on page 30.

8. (A) You're happy.
   (B) You aren't happy.
   (C) They're happy.
   (D) They aren't happy.

9. (A) He's single.
   (B) He's married.
   (C) She's single.
   (D) She's married.

10. (A) She is American.
    (B) She isn't American.
    (C) They are American.
    (D) They aren't American.

B. STRUCTURE: SENTENCE COMPLETION

Choose the *one* word or phrase that best completes the sentence. Circle the letter of the correct answer.

Example: "Are you hungry?"
"Yes, --------."

    (A) I hungry
    (B) I'm
    (C) I am
    (D) I'am

The correct sentence is "Yes, I am." Therefore, you should choose answer (C).

1. "Is Paris an old city?"
   "Yes, --------."

   (A) it's
   (B) it is
   (C) it old
   (D) is old

2. He -------- apartment manager.

   (A) are
   (B) is
   (C) is a
   (D) is an

3. "Are you thirsty?"
   "No, --------."

   (A) I not
   (B) I am
   (C) we're not
   (D) you're not

4. "Is your car small?"
   "No, -------- car is large."

   (A) her
   (B) their
   (C) our
   (D) your

5. "Is his name Charles?"
   "No, -------- is not."

   (A) he
   (B) it
   (C) name
   (D) Charles

6. "Are his roommates nice?"
   "Yes, --------."

   (A) he is
   (B) we are
   (C) they are
   (D) I am

7. "Are they Japanese?"
   "No, --------."

   (A) it is
   (B) it isn't
   (C) they are
   (D) they aren't

8. "Am I late?"
   "No, -------- not."

   (A) she's
   (B) I'm
   (C) you're
   (D) we're

9. "Are your friends married?"
   "No, -------- aren't."

   (A) you
   (B) they
   (C) we
   (D) my friend

10. She is --------.

    (A) hungry
    (B) a hungry
    (C) artist
    (D) a artist

11. -------- her favorite television programs?
    (A) What
    (B) What's
    (C) What are
    (D) Are they are

12. They are --------.
    (A) intelligent
    (B) intelligents
    (C) a intelligent
    (D) an intelligent

13. Mary and John are --------.
    (A) brothers
    (B) engineers
    (C) an engineer
    (D) an engineers

14. She -------- Korea.
    (A) from
    (B) from to
    (C) is from
    (D) is come from

15. -------- my books?
    (A) Where's
    (B) Where 'are
    (C) Where are
    (D) Are where

C. STRUCTURE: ERROR IDENTIFICATION

Each sentence has four underlined words or phrases. The four underlined parts of the sentence are marked (A), (B), (C), and (D). Circle the *one* underlined word or phrase that is not correct. Then correct the sentence.

Example: $\underset{A}{\underline{\text{Are}}}$ $\underset{B}{\underline{\text{your}}}$ father $\underset{C}{\underline{\text{an English}}}$ $\underset{D}{\underline{\text{teacher}}}$?

The correct sentence is, "Is your father an English teacher?" Therefore, you should choose (A).

1. $\underset{A}{\underline{\text{His}}}$ $\underset{B}{\underline{\text{old car}}}$ $\underset{C}{\underline{\text{is}}}$ not $\underset{D}{\underline{\text{a red}}}$.

2. Sandy $\underset{A}{\underline{\text{and}}}$ $\underset{B}{\underline{\text{my}}}$ brother $\underset{C}{\underline{\text{they are}}}$ $\underset{D}{\underline{\text{friends}}}$.

3. $\underset{A}{\underline{\text{His}}}$ family $\underset{B}{\underline{\text{are}}}$ $\underset{C}{\underline{\text{in the}}}$ United $\underset{D}{\underline{\text{States}}}$.

4. $\underset{A}{\underline{\text{They}}}$ in $\underset{B}{\underline{\text{their}}}$ $\underset{C}{\underline{\text{car}}}$ $\underset{D}{\underline{\text{now}}}$.

5. $\underset{A}{\underline{\text{I'am}}}$ $\underset{B}{\underline{\text{an}}}$ engineer $\underset{C}{\underline{\text{from}}}$ $\underset{D}{\underline{\text{Germany}}}$.

6. $\underset{A}{\underline{\text{Our}}}$ first $\underset{B}{\underline{\text{name}}}$ $\underset{C}{\underline{\text{are}}}$ Linda $\underset{D}{\underline{\text{and}}}$ Karen.

7. $\underset{A}{\underline{\text{Where're}}}$ $\underset{B}{\underline{\text{his}}}$ mother and $\underset{C}{\underline{\text{father}}}$ $\underset{D}{\underline{\text{from}}}$?

8. $\underset{A}{\underline{\text{Her}}}$ $\underset{B}{\underline{\text{eyes}}}$ $\underset{C}{\underline{\text{is}}}$ very $\underset{D}{\underline{\text{large}}}$.

9. $\underset{A}{\underline{\text{My}}}$ $\underset{B}{\underline{\text{new}}}$ shirt $\underset{C}{\underline{\text{it is}}}$ $\underset{D}{\underline{\text{blue}}}$.

10. $\underset{A}{\underline{\text{Her}}}$ $\underset{B}{\underline{\text{is not}}}$ $\underset{C}{\underline{\text{a university}}}$ $\underset{D}{\underline{\text{student}}}$ now.

11. Paul is $\underset{A}{\underline{\text{from Canada,}}}$ and $\underset{B}{\underline{\text{his native}}}$ $\underset{C}{\underline{\text{language is}}}$ $\underset{D}{\underline{\text{english}}}$.

12. $\underset{A}{\underline{\text{Her}}}$ $\underset{B}{\underline{\text{boyfriend}}}$ $\underset{C}{\underline{\text{is}}}$ $\underset{D}{\underline{\text{a}}}$ engineer.

13. $\underset{A}{\underline{\text{Its}}}$ $\underset{B}{\underline{\text{an}}}$ English $\underset{C}{\underline{\text{grammar}}}$ $\underset{D}{\underline{\text{book}}}$.

14. $\underset{A}{\underline{\text{I}}}$ $\underset{B}{\underline{\text{amn't}}}$ $\underset{C}{\underline{\text{very}}}$ $\underset{D}{\underline{\text{hungry}}}$ today.

CHAPTER 2

Dialog

Tommy: Good evening, ladies and gentlemen. My guest this evening is the famous movie star Lola Lovely. How are you tonight?
Lola: Oh, I'm fine, Tommy.
Tommy: You're very elegant tonight.
Lola Thank you, Tommy. This beautiful dress is from France.
Tommy Where are those enormous earrings from?
Lola: These lovely earrings are from Italy.
Tommy: Lola, what's the name of your new movie?
Lola: It's *Beautiful Lady*.
Tommy: Who is in the movie with you?
Lola: Two members of my family. My husband, Arthur, and my little Lucy. This is their first movie.
Tommy: How old is Lucy?
Lola: She's four years old. She is Lady in the movie.
Tommy: Lady? That's an unusual name for a little girl.
Lola: Lucy isn't a little girl. She's my dog, and here she is now.
Lucy: Woof! Woof!

Exercise 1. *True, False,* or *Unknown?*

1. Lola and Tommy are in California.   *Unknown*

2. Lola Lovely is the host of a television show.

3. Lola is a movie star.

4. Lola Lovely is from France.

5. Lola is single.

6. Her new movie is *Beautiful Lady*.

7. This is Lucy's first movie.

8. Lucy is five years old.

9. Lola has a daughter.

10. Lucy is a little girl.

Pronunciation of *th*

Exercise 2.

A. Listen to the two pronunciations of the letters *th*. Then repeat the words.

Pronunciation 1 (voiceless)	*Pronunciation 2* (voiced)
thanks	**th**is
thin	**th**e
theater	**th**ey
Thursday	**th**ere
three	wea**th**er
ma**th**	mo**th**er
four**th**	brea**th**e

B. Listen to the sentences. Repeat the sentences.

1. The movie *Beautiful Lady* is at the State Theater.
2. The State Theater is at 263 Third Street.
3. This afternoon the first show is at 3:30.
4. It's 3:13 now.
5. There are many people in line at the State Theater.

This and *That*

This wallet is Italian.
This purse is French.
Well, **this** belt isn't expensive.

That wallet is very small.
That purse is expensive.
That belt is perfect.

Note: *This* and *that* refer to singular nouns. *This* is for something at hand (here or near). *That* is for something not at hand (there or far).

Exercise 3.
Look around the room. Make sentences about objects in the room. Use *this* or *that*.

Examples: *That* tape recorder is new.
This watch is expensive.
That dictionary is my dictionary.
This book is interesting.

These and *Those*

These shirts are on sale.
These pants are on sale.
These shoes are Brazilian.

Those shirts are too big.
Those pants are ugly.
Those shoes are fine.

Note: *These* and *Those* refer to plural nouns. *These* is for things at hand (here or near). *Those* is for things not at hand (there or far).

Exercise 4. Complete the dialog below. Use *these* and *those*.

Salesclerk: *Customer:*

_____ sandals _____ .    _____

_____ socks _____ .   _____

_____ shoes _____ .   _____

_____ boots _____ .   _____

Exercise 5. Look at the picture. Complete the sentences with *this*, *that*, *these*, or *those*.

1. _____ telephone is new.

2. _____ pens are not cheap.

3. _____ clock is from Germany.

4. _____ tape recorders are Japanese.

5. _____ window is broken.

6. _____ computer is expensive.

7. _____ letters are important.

8. _____ chairs are from Mexico.

9. _____ typewriter is American.

10. _____ books are from Canada.

11. _____ radio is from Taiwan.

Telling Time

What time is it?

Honolulu

Caracas

London

Leningrad

It's 9 o'clock in the morning in Honolulu.   (It's 9 a.m.)
It's 3 o'clock in the afternoon in Caracas.   (It's 3 p.m.)
It's 7 o'clock in the evening in London.   (It's 7 p.m.)
It's 10 o'clock at night in Leningrad.   (It's 10 p.m.)

What time is it?

It's 1:15
It's one fifteen.
It's quarter past one.
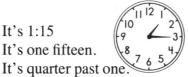

It's 3:30.
It's three thirty.
It's half past three.

It's 4:45.
It's four forty-five.
It's quarter to five.

It's 5:10
It's five ten.
It's ten minutes past five.

It's 6:50.
It's six fifty.
It's ten minutes to seven.

It's 12:00.
It's twelve o'clock.
It's noon.
It's midnight.

Exercise 6.   Say the time two ways. Write the time three ways.

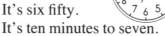

1.   `9:15`

ITs 9 15
ITs NINE FIFTEEN
ITs quARTeR PAST NINE

2.   `6:20`

ITs 6 20
ITs SIX TwENTY

3.   `7:45`

4.   `11:35`

5.   `10:30`

6.   `1:58`

Days of the Week

Listen and repeat.

Sunday	Monday	Tuesday	Wednesday	Thursday	Friday	Saturday

Exercise 7.   Answer the questions.

What day is it?   What day is today?

It's _____ .   It's _____ .

What day comes before Saturday?
What day comes after Monday?
What day comes before Friday?
What day comes after Wednesday?
What day is tomorrow?

Note: The days of the week begin with capital letters.

Months of the Year

Listen and repeat.

January	July
February	August
March	September
April	October
May	November
June	December

Exercise 8.   Answer the questions.

What month is it?

It's _____ .

What month comes after June?
What month comes before November?
What month comes after May?
What month comes before February?
What month comes after March?

Note: The months of the year begin with capital letters.

Years

Exercise 9.   Answer the questions.

What year is it?

It's _____ .

1. 30 AD   5. 1865
2. 1492   6. 1945
3. 1620   7. 1969
4. 1776   8. _____

This, that, these, those

Dialog

Tourist: **These** are photographs from my trip
to New York City. These are Broad-
way theaters, and **this** is Lincoln
Center.

Friend: Are **those** hotels?

Tourist: No, they're apartment buildings.

Friend: Is **that** the Empire State Building?

Tourist: Yes, it is.

Note: *This, that, these,* and *those* can be used alone
as the subject of a sentence.

Exercise 10.   Fill in the blanks with *this is, that is, these are,* or *those are*.

1. _____ the Leaning Tower of Pisa.

2. _____ the Rocky Mountains.

3. _____ the Eiffel Tower.

4. _____ the Golden Gate Bridge.

5. _____ the Pyramids.

6. _____ Greek statues.

7. _____ the Great Wall of China.

8. _____ Buckingham Palace.

9. _____

10. _____

Exercise 11. MINI CONVERSATIONS.

SINGULAR

A: Is this your <u>suitcase</u>?
B: No, it isn't. That's my <u>suitcase</u> over there.

1. suitcase
2. skis
3. umbrella
4. binoculars
5. purse
6. camera

PLURAL

A: Are these your <u>skis</u>?
B: No, they aren't. Those are my <u>skis</u> over there.

7. golf clubs
8. briefcase
9. tickets
10. keys
11. coat
12. _____

Exercise 12. Make sentences about people and objects in the room. Use *this*, *that*, *these*, and *those*.

Examples: *This is* my classmate Mohammed.
That is a map of the world.
These are new earrings.
Those are not my books.

Ordinal Numbers

Listen and repeat. (Note the spelling of the ordinal numbers in bold print.)

first	1st	eleventh	11th	twenty-**first**	21st
second	2nd	**twelfth**	12th	**thirtieth**	30th
third	3rd	thirteenth	13th	**fortieth**	40th
fourth	4th	fourteenth	14th	**fiftieth**	50th
fifth	5th	**fifteenth**	15th	**sixtieth**	60th
sixth	6th	sixteenth	16th	**seventieth**	70th
seventh	7th	seventeenth	17th	**eightieth**	80th
eighth	8th	eighteenth	18th	**ninetieth**	90th
ninth	9th	nineteenth	19th	one hundredth	100th
tenth	10th	**twentieth**	20th	one thousandth	1000th

Exercise 13. LISTENING. Write the numbers you hear in words.

Examples: **ninth**
              sixtieth

1. _____   7. _____   13. _____
2. _____   8. _____   14. _____
3. _____   9. _____   15. _____
4. _____   10. _____   16. _____
5. _____   11. _____   17. _____
6. _____   12. _____   18. _____

Exercise 14. Complete the ordinal numbers by adding two letters.

a. 35 *th*___   d. 41 _____   g. 24 _____
b. 52 _____   e. 63 _____   h. 11 _____
c. 12 _____   f. 128 _____   i. 21 _____

Notes: 1. Ordinal numbers are used to indicate position in an ordered sequence.

    Examples: I am the second child in my family.
                 April is the fourth month of the year.

   2. Ordinal numbers are also used with dates.

    Examples: My birthday is April 25th.
                 Today is the sixteenth of September.

Exercise 15.   Answer the questions.

1. What is the $\begin{bmatrix} \text{second} \\ \text{fifth} \\ \text{ninth} \\ \text{last} \end{bmatrix}$ month of the year?
2. What is the date today?
3. What is the date tomorrow?

Exercise 16.   Ask classmates the question, *When is your birthday?* Write down the answers.

A: When is your birthday?

B: My birthday is _____ , _____ .
                              (month)   *(date)*

Exercise 17.   Complete the sentences by writing the correct cardinal or ordinal form of the number in parentheses.

1. Today is the *first* _____ day of the rest of your life.   (1)
2. That jacket is _____ dollars.   (40)
3. Our baby girl is _____ days old.   (6)
4. She is our _____ child.   (3)
5. Independence Day in the U.S.A. is July _____ .   (4)
6. Our meetings are on the _____ Tuesday of every month.   (2)
7. His birthday isn't November _____ .   (21)
8. December is the _____ month of the year.   (12)
9. This is the _____ question of this exercise.   (9)
10. Is question _____ difficult?   (9)
11. Their wedding anniversary is the _____ of February.   (5)
12. Today is the _____ day of the month.   ( )
13. I am _____ years old.   ( )

Abbreviation of Dates

We can write dates using numbers and slashes. In the United States, the first number is the month, the second number is the day, and the last number is the year (usually the last two digits of the year).

Example: *4/6/52* = April 6, 1952 = April sixth, nineteen fifty-two

Remember: month / day / year

Exercise 18. Write each of the following dates two ways.

a. 7/4/1776 _____

b. 5/7/45 _____

c. 12/1/55 _____

d. 6/5/68 _____

e. 11/3/79 _____

f. 3/2/82 _____

Exercise 19. PAIRWORK.

Student A: Cover the left column. Ask questions about the pictures.
Student B: Cover the right column. Answer the questions about the pictures.

STUDENT A

STUDENT B

1. What's this?  It's a carrot.

2. What are these? They're peanuts.

3. What's this? It's an onion.

4. What are these? They're strawberries.

5. What's this? It's an egg.

6. What are these? They're mushrooms.

7. What's this?  It's a pumpkin.

8. What's this? It's an avocado.

9. What are these? They're raisins.

10. What's this? 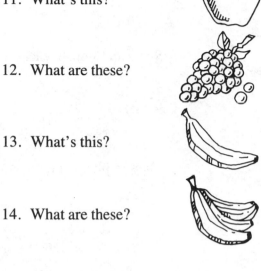 It's a pineapple.

11. What's this? It's an apple.

12. What are these? They're grapes.

13. What's this? It's a banana.

14. What are these? They're bananas.

Exercise 20. PAIRWORK.

STUDENT A   STUDENT B

1. What's her occupation?  She's an architect.

2. What's his occupation? He's a bus driver.

3. What's their occupation?  They're farmers.

4. What's his occupation?  He's an accountant.

5. What's their occupation?  They're pilots.

6. What's her occupation?  She's an English teacher.

7. What's their occupation?  They're plumbers.

8. What's his occupation?  He's a gardener.

9. What's her occupation?  She's an eye doctor.

10. What's their occupation?  They're photographers.

Adjective + Noun

SINGULAR	PLURAL
A Cadillac is an **expensive car**.	Cadillacs are **expensive cars**.
That **modern painting** isn't very valuable.	Those **modern paintings** aren't very valuable.
This **old coin** is rare.	These **old coins** are rare.
My **new vase** is from China.	My **new vases** are from China.
Is that **gold necklace** from Mexico?	Are those **gold necklaces** from Mexico?

Notes: 1. The same form of an adjective is used with a singular noun and a plural noun.
2. Adjectives can be used alone (without a following noun) when they come after the verb *be*.
3. Adjectives can also be used before a noun.
Examples above: *expensive, modern, old, new, gold.*

FORMULA 2-1	**a/an** **the** **this/that** **my/your/her**/*etc.*	adjective	singular noun

FORMULA 2-2	**∅** **the** **these/those** **my/your/her**/*etc.*	adjective	plural noun

Examples:

SINGULAR	PLURAL
It's **an old desk**.	They're **old desks**.
The brown sofa is cheap.	**The brown sofas** are cheap.
This new table isn't cheap.	**These new tables** aren't cheap.
Their old armchair is large.	**Their old armchairs** are large.

Exercise 21.

PUZZLE. Put the words in the correct order. Not all of the adjectives go before a noun.

Example: is / my / not / teacher / old / English / .

My English teacher is not old.

1. teacher / is / Rogers / a / Mr. / young / .

_____

2. students / are / busy / not / the / .

_____

3. are / their / books / where / new / ?

_____

4. easy / this / an / lesson / is / ?

_____

5. those / exercises / are / grammar / difficult / ?

_____

6. is / this / large / classroom / .

_____

Exercise 22. Use the words in parentheses to complete the sentences. Include *a* or *an* when necessary. Make the nouns plural when necessary.

1. (good friend)   She is _a good friend._

   Karen and Patricia are _good friends._

2. (famous musician) Beethoven is _____

   Mozart and Bach are _____

3. (Asian capital)   Manila and Beijing are _____

   Bangkok is _____

4. (fast reader)   I am _____

   My father and brother are _____

5. (expensive metal) Gold and silver are _____

   Platinum is _____

6. (American writer) Mark Twain is _____

   Pearl Buck and John Steinbeck are _____

Exercise 23. Describe the objects in the picture of the room below. Include some of the objects from the diamond below and adjectives from the box below.

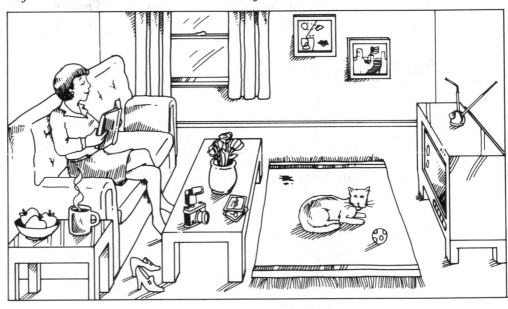

cup
roses   vase
room   television
frames   paintings   shoes
dress   table   coffee   woman
apples   walls   photograph
camera   earrings
sofa   book
cat

hot-cold	tired
big-little	modern
new-old	broken
sad-happy	delicious
ugly-pretty	red
clean-dirty	French
round-square	comfortable
cheap-expensive	rare

Examples: The **apples** are **red**.
             The **red apples** are **delicious**.

46   Frontiers

Exercise 24. WRITING. Write a description of a room in your house, apartment, or dormitory. Include some of the nouns and adjectives from Exercise 23.

_____

_____

_____

_____

_____

_____

_____

At, on, in with Time

AT	Use **at** with *hours* and *minutes*. The party is **at** 8 p.m. This class begins **at** 9 o'clock. This class ends **at** 10:15.
ON	Use **on** with *days* and *dates*. Queen Elizabeth II was born **on** the twenty-first. She was born **on** April 21, 1926. She was born **on** Wednesday, April 21, 1926.
IN	Use **in** with *months*, *seasons*, *years*, and *centuries*. She was born **in** April. She was born **in** the spring. She was born **in** 1926. She was born **in** the twentieth century.

Note: **in** the morning   **at** noon
       in the afternoon   **at** midday
       in the evening   **at** night
                              at midnight

Exercise 25. Fill in the blanks with *at, on, in, on the,* or *in the.*

1. His birthday is _____ February.

2. Isaac Newton was born _____ seventeenth century.

3. The party is _____ Friday.

4. Ronald Reagan was born _____ 1911.

5. The movie is _____ midnight.

6. Lucille Ball was born _____ August sixth.

7. Our meeting is _____ afternoon.

8. Michael Jackson was born _____ August 29, 1958.

9. The baseball game is _____ night.

10. Jerry Lewis was born _____ sixteenth of March.

11. The class begins _____ noon.

12. Paul McCartney was born _____ Thursday, June 18, 1942.

13. Our trip to Europe is _____ summer.

14. The show is _____ ten o'clock.

15. All classes are _____ morning.

16. Jacqueline Onassis was born _____ July, 1929.

Exercise 26. Answer the following questions. Note the words in parentheses.

1. When is your English class?

   (*time*) _____

   (*days*) _____

2. When is your English class finished?

   (*time*) _____

3. When is your English course finished?

   (*month*) _____

   (*month and date*) _____

4. When is your next exam?

   (*day*) _____

   (*day, month, and date*) _____

5. When is your favorite TV show?

   (*day and time*) _____

6. When is your favorite holiday?

   (*season*) _____

   (*month*) _____

   (*month and date*) _____

7. When is your birthday?

   (*season*) _____

   (*month*) _____

   (*month and date*) _____

8. When were you born?

   (*day, month, date, year*) _____

Exercise 27. INTERVIEW. Ask a classmate the questions in Exercise 26.

Weather: *It's* + Adjective

1. What's the weather like in Acapulco?   It's hot.

2. How's the weather in Casablanca?   It's warm.

3. What's the weather like in Paris?   It's mild.

4. How's the weather in Dublin?   It's cool.

5. What's the weather like in Toronto?   It's chilly.

6. How's the weather in Oslo?   It's cold.

7. What's the weather like in New Orleans?   It's humid.

8. How's the weather in Abu Dhabi?   It's sunny.

9. What's the weather like in Berlin?

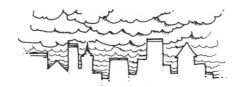

It's cloudy.

10. How's the weather in Sydney?

It's partly cloudy.

11. What's the weather like in Chicago?

It's windy.

12. How's the weather in Jakarta?

It's rainy.

13. What's the weather like in Moscow?

It's snowy.

14. What's the temperature in Caracas?

It's 75 degrees.

15. What's the climate like in Riyadh in the summer?

It's very hot and dry.

Note: Temperature Conversion

1. To convert Celsius to Fahrenheit, multiply by 9, divide by 5, and add 32°.

FORMULA $\dfrac{\text{Celsius} \times 9}{5} + 32 = \text{Fahrenheit}$

2. To convert Fahrenheit to Celsius, subtract 32°, multiply by 5, and divide by 9.

FORMULA $\dfrac{(\text{Fahrenheit} - 32) \times 5}{9} = \text{Celsius}$

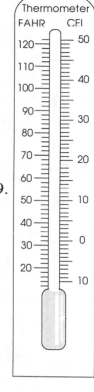

Exercise 28. INTERVIEW. Ask a classmate the following questions.

1. What is the weather like in your hometown in the summer?
2. What is the weather like in your hometown in the winter?
3. What are the high and low temperatures in your hometown in the summer and winter?
4. Are there four distinct seasons in your country?
5. What's your favorite season? Why?
6. What is the weather like today?
7. What is the temperature outside now?

Exercise 29.

A. LISTENING. Listen to the weather report and complete the sentences below.

Good morning. It's cold and _____ today in Boston. _____ 30 degrees now. It's _____ and partly _____ in Philadelphia. The temperature is _____ degrees. In Atlanta it's cool and _____ with a temperature of 54 _____ . In Orlando it's _____ and mild. The temperature _____ is 68 degrees.

B. Write questions about the weather in Boston, Philadelphia, Atlanta, and Orlando. Ask a classmate the questions.

1. What's _____ like _____ ?
2. Is _____ ?
3. How's the _____ ?
4. What's _____ temperature _____ ?
5. _____

Exercise 30.

Look at the map of the United States. Give the weather conditions for the cities below.

Be + Adverbs of Frequency

always	=	all of the time, at all times
usually	=	most of the time
often, frequently	=	much of the time, many times
sometimes, occasionally	=	some of the time
seldom, rarely	=	not often
never	=	at no time

Adverbs of frequency follow forms of *be*.

FORMULA 2-3	Subject	am is are	frequency adverb	complement.

Examples: I **am always** on time for class.
We **are never** late for class.
My teacher **is usually** happy.
It **is sometimes** hot in my classroom.
Tests **are seldom** fun.

Exercise 31. MINI CONVERSATIONS.

Example: absent from class
on time for class

Lee: How often are you absent from class?
Jan: I'm seldom absent from class.
Lee: Really? How often are you on time for class?
Jan: I'm usually on time for class.
Lee: Well, I'm never absent from class, and I'm always on time for class.

1. hungry at midnight
   thirsty at midnight

2. busy in the evening
   busy on weekends

3. at home in the afternoon
   at home at night

4. tired in the morning
   sleepy in the afternoon

5. cold in class
   warm in class

6. nervous before tests
   prepared for tests

7. in bed at 9:30 p.m.
   in bed at 12:30 a.m.

8. awake at 6:00 a.m.
   awake at 8:00 a.m.

Exercise 32. WRITING. Write six true sentences about classmates, friends, or family members. Use a form of *be* and an adverb of frequency in each sentence.

Note: The word *ever* is used in questions. *Ever* means at any time.

Examples: Are you **ever** late for class?

Yes, I'm **always** late for class.
Yes, I'm **usually** late for class.
Yes, I'm **often** late for class.
Yes, I'm **sometimes** late for class.
I'm **seldom** late for class.
I'm **rarely** late for class.
No, I'm **never** late for class.

Exercise 33. INTERVIEW. Ask and answer the following questions with a classmate. Use an adverb of frequency in each answer.

1. Are you ever late for class?
2. Are you ever hungry in class?
3. Are you ever tired in class?
4. Are you ever shy in class?
5. Are you ever sleepy after lunch?
6. Are you ever bored during vacation?
7. Are you ever sad on your birthday?
8. Are you ever afraid at night?
9. Are you ever nervous on airplanes?
10. Are you ever _____ ?
11. Are you ever _____ ?
12. Are you ever _____ ?

Activities

A. DIALOG. Practice the following dialog.

"Live from New York"

TV announcer:	Our guest this morning is Pat Conway. Welcome back to New York, Pat.
Pat:	Thank you, Chris.
TV announcer:	What's the name of your new TV show?
Pat:	It's called *Colorado Cool*. It's a police show.
TV announcer:	What's the weather like in Colorado now?
Pat:	It's snowy and very cold. It's 30° during the day and 10° at night.
TV announcer:	That's very cold! Who's in the show with you?
Pat:	My sons David and Ben are in the show. They are young police detectives.
TV announcer:	How old are they?
Pat:	David is twenty-one and Ben is nineteen. *Colorado Cool* is their first television show.
TV announcer:	Thank you, Pat. Good luck with your new show.
Pat:	Thanks.

B. WRITING. Write a new dialog. Use the TV interview above and the dialog at the beginning of the chapter as models.

_____

_____

_____

_____

_____

_____

_____

_____

_____

_____

C. SENTENCE COMPLETION. Fill in the blanks with appropriate words.

Houston, Texas

With over 2,000,000 people, Houston _____ the largest city in Texas, and

_____ is the fourth largest city in the United States. Houston is _____ young city.

It is approximately 150 years _____ . The average high temperature

_____ August is 92°, and the average low _____ 71°. The _____ in Hous-

ton is hot and humid _____ the summer. It is _____ cold in the summer. Winters

_____ cool and mild. Houston _____ the petroleum capital of

_____ United States. The Johnson Space Center _____ the Texas Medical Center

_____ in Houston. Houston is a _____ city.

D. WRITING. Write a description of your hometown or a different city.

_____

_____

_____

_____

_____

_____

_____

_____

_____

_____

_____

E. Draw a map of your country on another paper. Include several cities, weather symbols, and temperatures. Give the weather report for these cities.

F. RIDDLES. What are the answers?

1. What is the difference between here and there?
2. What's white when it's dirty and black when it's clean?
3. What's quiet when it's alive, but noisy when it's dead?

G. DICTATION. You will hear each sentence two times. Write what you hear.

1. _____
2. _____
3. _____
4. _____
5. _____
6. _____
7. _____

H. CROSSWORD PUZZLE. Complete the crossword puzzle with the words missing from the sentences below. The number of dashes (– – –) indicates the number of letters in the word.

Across

1. This is – – – twentieth century.
2. It's – – – – past eight.
4. I'm usually home – – midnight.
6. Is – – on July fourth?
7. My birthday is the twelfth – – November.
8. The exam is at two –'– – – – –.
10. It's twenty – – eleven.
13. September is the – – – – – month of the year.
15. The last day of the year is December – – – – – – – – – – –.
17. The party is – – Saturday.
18. The late show on TV is at – – – – – – – –.
21. – – – January and February winter months?
22. The month of – – – is before June.
24. The movie isn't in the afternoon. It's at – – – – – .

Down

1. It's – – – to two.
3. The – – – – – month of the year is May.
4. My English class isn't in the – – – – – – – – –.
5. Lunch is at – – – –.
9. It's a – – – – – – – to three.
11. – – – – – – – – – is after August.
12. February is not the – – – – – month of the year. March is.
14. It's seven – – – – – – – – in the evening. [7:13]
16. Is our meeting at nine – – – – – – ? [9:30]
19. I was born at – – – to four in the morning.
20. Supper is at six – –.
21. The basketball game is – – night.
23. Breakfast is at seven – –.
25. I was born – – 1959.
26. Was – – born in the spring?

Review Quizzes

A. LISTENING COMPREHENSION: SENTENCES

For each problem, you will hear a short sentence. You will hear each sentence two times. After you hear a sentence, read the four choices. Decide which written sentence is the closest in meaning to the spoken sentence. Circle the letter of the correct answer.

1. (A) It's at midnight.
   (B) It's at night.
   (C) It's at midday.
   (D) It's in the morning.

2. (A) Engineering is good.
   (B) Our major is engineering.
   (C) Engineers are good students.
   (D) You are good engineers.

3. (A) She was born in the winter.
   (B) She was born in 1925.
   (C) He was born in January.
   (D) He was born on the twenty-fifth.

4. (A) These boys are not hungry.
   (B) He isn't hungry.
   (C) This boy's not angry.
   (D) They aren't angry.

5. (A) It's very rainy here in the summer.
   (B) It's never rainy in the summer.
   (C) It's seldom rainy here in the summer.
   (D) It's frequently rainy here in the summer.

6. (A) It's on the 13th in Austin.
   (B) It's on August 13th in Boston.
   (C) It's on the 30th in Boston.
   (D) It's on the 30th in Austin.

7. (A) Those books are blue.
   (B) This book is blue.
   (C) The books on that table are blue.
   (D) The book on that table is blue.

8. (A) It's at quarter past nine.
   (B) It's at ten to ten.
   (C) It's at ten to nine.
   (D) It's at five to ten.

9. (A) Those cars are old.
   (B) These cars are old.
   (C) Those cars are new.
   (D) These cars are new.

10. (A) It's here.
    (B) It's there.
    (C) They're here.
    (D) They're there.

B. STRUCTURE: SENTENCE COMPLETION. Choose the *one* word or phrase that best completes the sentence. Circle the letter of the correct answer.

1. -------- my shoes?
   - (A) Where
   - (B) Where's
   - (C) Where're
   - (D) Where are

2. It is --------.
   - (A) black shirt
   - (B) shirt black
   - (C) a black shirt
   - (D) a shirt black

3. "Is this car new?"
   "Yes, --------."
   - (A) it's
   - (B) this is
   - (C) it's new car
   - (D) it is

4. Are -------- your books?
   - (A) these
   - (B) that
   - (C) it
   - (D) this

5. They are --------.
   - (A) student
   - (B) students
   - (C) a student
   - (D) a students

6. "How old is she?"
   "-------- twenty-five."
   - (A) It's
   - (B) She's
   - (C) Its
   - (D) It

7. "Are you busy?"
   "No, -------- not."
   - (A) we're
   - (B) they're
   - (C) you're
   - (D) I

8. -------- Terry and Charles.
   - (A) Our name is
   - (B) We names are
   - (C) Our name are
   - (D) Our names are

9. "Is his hair black?
   "Yes, -------- black."
   - (A) it
   - (B) it's
   - (C) he
   - (D) he's

10. -------- in her office.
    - (A) Lawyer
    - (B) Lawyer is
    - (C) The lawyer
    - (D) The lawyer's

11. "Are your sister and Jess in Miami?"
    "Yes, --------."
    - (A) they are
    - (B) you are
    - (C) we are
    - (D) he is

12. He isn't --------.
    - (A) hot
    - (B) a hot
    - (C) banker
    - (D) a bankers

13. My class is -------- .
    - (A) in night
    - (B) at night
    - (C) in the night
    - (D) at the night

14. -------- my coat over there.
    - (A) Those are
    - (B) These are
    - (C) That's
    - (D) This is

15. Bill Cosby was born -------- July 12, 1937.
    - (A) at
    - (B) on
    - (C) in
    - (D) in the

C. STRUCTURE: ERROR IDENTIFICATION

Each sentence has four underlined words or phrases. Circle the *one* underlined word or phrase that is not correct. Then correct the sentence.

1. This earrings are from my grandmother.
   A   B   C   D

2. Is the dentist's in the office?
   A   B   C   D

3. Is the Mrs. Smith fifty-five years old?
   A   B   C   D

4. These aren't your grammar book.
   A   B   C   D

5. Our Jane and Mary famous movie actresses?
   A   B   C   D

6. It's eleven o'clock in the night in New York.
   A   B   C   D

7. What's time is it now?
   A   B   C   D

8. Those dresses are not very cheaps.
   A   B   C   D

9. They rarely are absent from their English class.
   A   B   C   D

10. He is not usually a busy on Sunday evenings.
    A   B   C   D

11. Those are very beautiful paintings from France?
    A   B   C   D

12. Its nine thirty-five in the morning in Tokyo.
    A   B   C   D

13. March is third month of the year.
    A   B   C   D

14. This painting over there is a famous painting by Van Gogh.
    A   B   C   D

15. Is it a hot in Montreal in the summer?
    A   B   C   D

CHAPTER 3

Dialog

Mrs. Graves:	Neal Import Export Company. May I help you?
Mr. Neal:	Mrs. Graves, this is Mr. Neal. I'm calling from Hong Kong.
Mrs. Graves:	Oh, hello, Mr. Neal. How are you?
Mr. Neal:	I'm fine, but I'm very busy.
Mrs. Graves:	What's the weather like in Hong Kong?
Mr. Neal:	It's warm and sunny here. There isn't a cloud in the sky. How's the weather there?
Mrs. Graves:	It's very rainy. One minute it's drizzling, and the next minute it's pouring.
Mr. Neal:	Are you busy at the office today?
Mrs. Graves:	Yes. We're working very hard.
Mr. Neal:	How many new contracts are there this week?
Mrs. Graves:	There are four new contracts. Elizabeth is typing them now.
Mr. Neal:	Who's preparing the boxes of hospital supplies for South America?
Mrs. Graves:	Donna and Tom are.
Mr. Neal:	Is Jim at work today?
Mrs. Graves:	Yes, he is.
Mr. Neal:	What's he doing?
Mrs. Graves:	He's leaving the office right now.
Mr. Neal:	Where's he going?
Mrs. Graves:	He's going to the post office. When are you returning?
Mr. Neal:	I'm flying home on Sunday. I'm in a hurry now. My next meeting is in five minutes. I'm working day and night here in Hong Kong. See you at the office on Monday.
Mrs. Graves:	Have a good trip home, Mr. Neal. Good-bye.
Mr. Neal:	Bye.

Exercise 1.   Answer the questions.

1. Where's Mr. Neal calling from?
2. What's his occupation?
3. What's the weather like back home?
4. How's the weather in Hong Kong?
5. What is Mrs. Graves doing?
6. How many new contracts are there?
7. Is Elizabeth typing the contracts?
8. Are Donna and Tom preparing boxes?
9. Where's Jim going?
10. What is Mr. Neal doing?

Pronunciation of [n] and [ŋ]

Exercise 2. A. Listen to the pronunciations of [n] and [ŋ]. Then repeat the words.

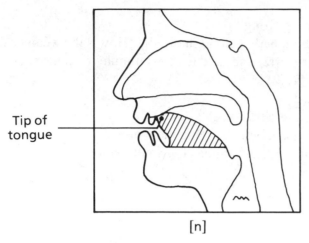

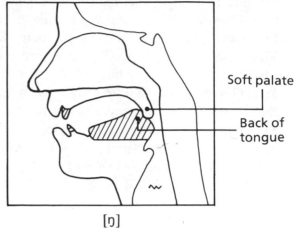

[n]

[ŋ]

[n]	**[ŋ]**
no	thi**ng**
pla**nt**	tha**nk**
e**nd**	u**n**cle
cha**n**ge	E**n**glish
noo**n**	si**nging**

B. Listen to the sentences. Repeat the sentences.

1. Elizabeth is typing the new contracts.
2. Jim isn't going to the bank now.
3. Mr. Neal is working in sunny Hong Kong.
4. His next meeting is in five minutes.

Present Continuous: Affirmative Statements

SINGULAR	PLURAL
I **am** writ**ing** a letter. You **are** wear**ing** golf clothes. He **is** call**ing** a client. She **is** talk**ing** on the telephone. It **is** rain**ing**.	We **are** work**ing**. You **are** mak**ing** noise. They **are** typ**ing**.

FORMULA 3-1	Subject	**am** **is** **are**	verb +**ing**	(complement) .

Notes:
1. In the present continuous, forms of the verb *be* (*am, is, are*) are used with a main verb. The main verb always ends in *-ing*.
2. The present continuous generally expresses a temporary, incomplete action that is progressing or continuing now.
3. Use the present continuous with *now, right now, at the moment, at this moment*.

Exercise 3.

What is happening in the pictures? Describe what the people below are doing. For each picture, use the subject and the present continuous form of the verb in parentheses.

1. (He / play tennis)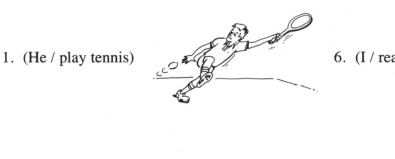

6. (I / read)

2. (They / listen to records)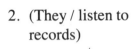

7. (The students / learn English)

3. (We / study)

8. (Najib and Carmen / speak)

4. (She / eat)

9. (The baby / cry)

5. (They / drink)

10. (It / sleep)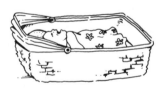

-*ing* Forms: Spelling Rules

Study the rules. Write the **-ing** forms.

Rule 1:	consonant + vowel + consonant →
	consonant + vowel + consonant + consonant + **ing**
	<u>same</u>

Base Form	-*ing* Form
run	*running*
shop	*shopping*
put	_____
swim	_____
begin	_____
occur	_____

Notes:
1. When a verb ends in a single consonant preceded by a single ***stressed vowel***, double the final consonant and add **-ing**.
2. Do not double final *w, x,* or *y*. Examples: *drawing, fixing, buying.*

| **Rule 2:** | consonant + **e** → consonant + **ing** |
| | **u** + e → **u** + **ing** |

Base Form	-*ing* Form
dance	*dancing*
continue	*continuing*
live	_____
write	_____
glue	_____

| **Rule 3:** | ie → y + **ing** |

Base Form	-*ing* Form
lie	*lying*
tie	_____
die	_____

Rule 4:	all other verb endings → word + **ing**

Base Form	-*ing* Form
ski	*skiing*
open	*opening*
eat	_____
listen	_____
study	_____
agree	_____

Exercise 4.   Write the -*ing* form of each verb.

1. buy _____
2. come _____
3. cry _____
4. sit _____
5. shout _____
6. visit _____
7. drive _____
8. read _____
9. snow _____
10. smoke _____
11. drop _____
12. sleep _____
13. study _____
14. make _____
15. relax _____

16. dream _____
17. play _____
18. die _____
19. happen _____
20. swim _____
21. write _____
22. argue _____
23. agree _____
24. rain _____
25. plan _____
26. wait _____
27. give _____
28. help _____
29. rob _____
30. dry _____

Exercise 5.   Write the base form of each verb.

1. writing _____
2. tying _____
3. hurrying _____
4. smiling _____
5. hugging _____

6. adding _____
7. riding _____
8. hoping _____
9. kissing _____
10. saving _____

Present Continuous: Affirmative Contractions

SINGULAR	PLURAL
I'm drying the dishes. **You're** reading the newspaper. **He's** cleaning the kitchen. **Anna's** studying for an exam. **It's** lying on the floor.	**We're** doing our homework. **You're** watching TV. **They're** making supper.

Notes: 1. Contractions are common in present continuous sentences. The subject (a pronoun or a singular noun) combines with a form of *be* to make a contraction. The *-ing* form of the base verb follows the contraction.
2. Do not make contractions with plural nouns.

Exercise 6.

Complete the story using the present continuous. Fill in the blanks with *am, is* or *are*, and the *-ing* form of the verbs in parentheses. Use contractions where possible.

It's eight o'clock Monday evening. The Martin Family _____ the evening at
(spend)
home. Mrs. Martin _____. She _____ her favorite TV program,
(relax)   (watch)
and she _____ popcorn. Mr. Martin is a high school math teacher. He
(eat)
_____ homework and he _____ his lessons for tomorrow.
(correct)   (plan)
Lisa Martin is in her room. She _____ her homework, and she
(do)
_____ for a spelling quiz. Rick Martin is hungry. He _____ a
(study)   (cut)
piece of cheese.

The Martin grandparents _____ their son and his family. They
(visit)
_____ with the Martins for one week. Grandmother Martin _____
(stay)   (play)
with the baby and Grandfather Martin _____ a letter. They _____
(write)   (listen)
to the radio. It's a busy evening at the Martin house.

Exercise 7.

WRITING. Think of a famous person. Where is he or she? Who is he or she with? What is this person doing now? Write six or more sentences. Use contractions.

_____

_____

_____

_____

_____

Weather: *It's* Verb + *ing*

1. What's the weather like in Boston now?   It's drizzling.

2. What's the weather like in Bogota today?   It's raining.

3. What's the weather like in Jakarta today?   It's pouring.

4. What's the weather like in Quebec today?   It's snowing.

5. What's the weather like in Vienna now?   It's hailing.

6. What's the weather like in San Juan now?   It's thundering and lightning.

Exercise 8.
Ask and answer questions with another student about the current weather conditions in various cities around the world. Use the weather words above.

At, on, in with Place

AT	addresses with building numbers
ON	street names
IN	cities, states, provinces, countries, continents

Examples: My sister lives **at** 345 Oak Street.
My sister lives **on** Oak Street.
My sister lives **in** Miami.
My brother lives **in** California.
My parents live **in** Canada.
My family lives **in** North America.

Exercise 9. Fill in the blanks with *at, on,* or *in*. Finish the last four sentences.

1. The White House is _____ Washington, D.C.
2. It is _____ Pennsylvania Avenue.
3. It is _____ 1600 Pennsylvania Avenue.
4. Canada is _____ North America.
5. Ottawa is _____ Ontario.
6. The Mexican Embassy _____ Ottawa, Canada is _____ Albert Street.
7. The home of the British Prime Minister is _____ London _____ 10 Downing Street.
8. The National Theater _____ Tokyo is _____ Hayabusacho Street.
9. The Oriental Hotel _____ Bangkok is _____ 48 Oriental Avenue.
10. The Metropolitan Museum of Art is _____ 82nd Street _____ New York City.
11. The Museum of Modern Art is _____ 11 West 53rd Street.
12. My home is in _____
13. My family is in _____
14. My school is on _____
15. My house is at _____

Present Continuous:
Yes / No Questions and Short Answers

Am Is Are	subject	verb + **ing**	(complement) **?**

FORMULA 3-2

	QUESTIONS	ANSWERS

Examples:

Am I do**ing** the correct exercise?

Yes, you are.
No, you are not.
No, you're not.
No, you aren't.

Is the teacher speak**ing** English?

Yes, she is.
No, she is not.
No, she's not.
No, she isn't.

Are they tak**ing** notes now?

Yes, they are.
No, they are not.
No, they're not.
No, they aren't.

Exercise 10. PAIRWORK.

Student A: Ask the question.
Student B: Cover the right column. Answer the questions.

1. Are they answering questions?

Yes, they are.

2. Is she reading a magazine?

No, she's not. / No, she isn't.
She's reading a newspaper.

3. Am I sitting in your seat?

Yes, you are.

4. Is he doing his homework?

Yes, he is.

5. Are the students listening to
    grammar exercises?

No, they're not. / No, they aren't.
They're listening to music.

6. Are you taking notes?

Yes, we are.

7. Are they speaking Spanish?

No, they're not. / No, they aren't.
They're speaking English.

8. Are you writing a composition?

No, I'm not.
I'm writing a letter.

9. Is Maria taking a grammar quiz?

No, she's not. / No, she isn't.
She's taking a math quiz.

10. Are Pat and Chris practicing
    a dialog?

Yes, they are.

11. _____ ?

_____

Exercise 11.
Make *yes-no* questions. Use the present continuous.

1. John / play volleyball   *Is John playing volleyball?*
2. Bob and Mary / swim at the beach   _____
3. the football players / rest   _____
4. Anna / run in the park   _____
5. you / exercise now   _____
6. your roommate / lift weights   _____
7. Mr. Kowalski / ride his bike   _____
8. _____   _____
9. _____   _____

Present Continuous: Negative Statements

FORMULA 3-3	Subject	am is are	not	verb + ing	(complement) .

Examples: I am not typing.
You are not working.
She is not calling a client.
We are not mailing letters.
They are not reading reports.

Exercise 12.
Make negative statements. Use the present continuous.

Example: the boss / plan a meeting   *The boss is not planning a meeting.*

1. I / mail letters   _____
2. you / send a telegram   _____
3. the clerk / tie up packages   _____
4. we / listen to the news   _____
5. you / type a contract   _____
6. the accountant / write checks   _____
7. the managers / begin their meeting   _____
8. the secretaries / photocopy documents   _____
9. the receptionist / make a long distance call   _____
10. _____ / _____   _____

Present Continuous: Negative Contractions

FORM 1	FORM 2
I**'m not** working.	------------------
You**'re not** working.	You **aren't** working.
He**'s not** working.	He **isn't** working.
My father**'s not** working.	My father **isn't** working.
Diana**'s not** working.	Diana **isn't** working.
We**'re not** working.	We **aren't** working.
They**'re not** working.	They **aren't** working.

Exercise 13. PAIRWORK. First time — Student A: Ask the questions.
Student B: Answer the questions.
Second time — Student A: Ask the questions again.
Student B: Cover the answers and answer the questions.

1. Where's Michael?
   Is he watching TV?
   What's he doing?

He's at home.
No, he isn't.
He's listening to records.

2. Where are Nora and Anna?
   Are they playing volleyball?
   What are they doing?

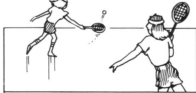

They're at the gym.
No, they aren't.
They're playing racketball.

3. Where are you?
   Are you shopping?
   What are you doing?

I'm downtown.
No, I'm not.
I'm working.

4. Where's Professor Williams?
   Is she studying in Paris?
   What's she doing in Paris?

She's in Paris.
No, she isn't.
She's teaching in Paris.

5. Where are you and Jeff?
   Are you playing football?
   What are you doing?

We're at the football stadium.
No, we aren't.
We're watching a football game.

6. Where are your parents?
   Are they shopping?
   What are they doing?

   They're on Fifth Avenue.
   No, they aren't.
   They're eating lunch at
   Simon's Cafe.

7. Where's Kathy?
   Is she studying?
   What's she doing?

   She's at the library.
   No, she isn't.
   She's reading French
   magazines.

8. Where are Mr. and Mrs. Carter?
   Are they cating?
   What are they doing?

   They're in the kitchen.
   No, they aren't.
   They're washing the dishes.

9. _____

   _____

   _____

10. _____

    _____

    _____

Regular Plural Nouns: Spelling Rules

Rule 1: consonant + **y** → consonant + **ies**

la**dy**   _ladies_

secreta**ry**   _____

ba**by**   _____

supp**ly**   _____

Rule 2:	s → ses
	x → xes
	ch → ches
	sh → shes

business _____ *businesses*

box _____

wat**ch** _____

di**sh** _____

(Exception: *stomach*)

| **Rule 3:** | f(e) → ves |

lea**f** _____ *leaves*

wi**fe** _____

shel**f** _____

li**fe** _____

(Exceptions: *chiefs, roofs*)

| **Rule 4:** | all other endings → + s |

day _____ *days*

radio _____

shoe _____

price _____

page _____

mosquito _____

(Exceptions: *tomatoes, potatoes*)

Exercise 14. Write the plural forms.

1. class _____

2. potato _____

3. knife _____

4. tax _____

5. photocopy _____

6. boy _____

7. zoo _____

8. monkey _____

9. library _____

10. sandwich _____

11. thief _____

12. dictionary _____

13. tomato _____

14. photo _____

15. college	_____	18. scarf	_____
16. wife	_____	19. church	_____
17. piano	_____	20. day	_____

Exercise 15. Write the singular forms.

1. watches	_____	6. knives	_____
2. horses	_____	7. oranges	_____
3. noises	_____	8. plates	_____
4. stories	_____	9. classes	_____
5. trees	_____	10. circles	_____

There is and *there are*

SINGULAR	PLURAL
There is a calculator on the table. **There's** a stamp on the table. **There isn't** an envelope on the desk.	**There are** two calculators on the desk. **There are** four stamps on the desk. **There aren't** three envelopes on the desk.

QUESTIONS	SHORT ANSWERS
Is there a typewriter in that office?	Yes, there is. No, there is not. No, there's not. No, there isn't.
Are there paperclips?	Yes, there are. No, there are not. No, there aren't.
QUESTIONS WITH HOW MANY	ANSWERS
How many stamps **are there?** **How many** envelopes **are there?**	There is one stamp. There are two envelopes.

Notes: 1. *There is* and *there are* are expressions that indicate existence.
2. In questions with *how many*, the subject is always plural.

Exercise 16.
PAIRWORK. Look at the picture of the desktop. Then ask and answer the questions below.

STUDENT A	STUDENT B
1. Is there a calculator on the desk?	No, there isn't.
2. Are there pens on the desk?	Yes, there are.
3. How many pens are there?	There are five pens.
4. Is there a ruler?	Yes, there is.
5. Are there books on the desk?	Yes, there are.
6. How many books are there?	There are two books.
7. Is there a calendar on the desk?	No, there isn't.
8. Is there a cup?	Yes, there is.
9. Are there cigarettes on the desk?	No, there aren't.
10. Is there paper on the desk?	Yes, there is.
11. How many staplers are there?	There is one stapler.
12. How many pencils are there?	There are three pencils.

Exercise 17.
Complete the sentences with the correct words from the box.

their	there	they're	there's	there are

Example: Mr. and Mrs. Allen have two daughters. ***Their*** daughters are students at Howard University in Washington, D.C. ***They're*** studying law. ***There's*** a very good law school ***there***. ***There are*** approximately 500 students in the law school at Howard University.

Cambridge is an old university city in England. In Cambridge _____ approximately 11,000 students. _____ from all over the United Kingdom. Also, _____ many international students. _____ far from _____ homes, but _____ glad to be at this world famous university. _____ 29 colleges. Peter House, one of the colleges _____, is from the year 1284. _____ not many modern buildings at Cambridge University. _____ a famous church named King College Chapel at the university. _____ a wonderful panoramic view of the town of Cambridge from Gagmagog Hills.

Wh-Questions with the Present Continuous

	Who What Where When Why	am are is	subject	verb + **ing**	(complement) **?**
FORMULA 3-4					

	QUESTION	ANSWER
Examples:	1. Who are you talking to on the telephone?	My sister.
	2. What is Tom doing?	He's studying.
	3. Where are Lee and Chris living now?	In Chicago.
	4. When are you going to the bank?	This afternoon.
	5. Why is Pat leaving now?	Because she's tired.

	Who	is	verb + **ing**	(complement) **?**
FORMULA 3-5				

Examples: Who is coming to the party?
Who is living in apartment 201?

FORMULA 3-6	How many	plural subject	are	verb + **ing**	(complement) **?**

Examples: How many students are studying English at your school?

How many teachers are coming to the school party?

Exercise 18. PAIRWORK. Ask and answer questions about the picture.

STUDENT A

STUDENT B

1. What is the barber doing?   He's cutting hair.
2. Where are the reporters working?   They're working in the newspaper office.
3. How many people are waiting for the bus?   Three people are waiting for the bus.
4. Who is carrying a briefcase?   A businessman is carrying a briefcase.
5. What is the mail carrier delivering?   He's delivering a package.
6. Where is the bus going?   It's going to Lincoln Avenue.
7. Who is directing traffic?   Two police officers are directing traffic.
8. Why are the police officers directing traffic?   Because the traffic lights aren't working.
9. How many workers are fixing the roof?   Two workers are fixing the roof.
10. Who is the mail carrier talking to?   He's talking to a businessman.
11. Who are the girls helping?   They're helping an old woman.

Exercise 19.

Write *wh*-questions. Use *who, what, where, how many*. Then write your own questions and answers.

1. *Who is selling tickets?*   *The ticket agent* is selling tickets.

2. _____   A customs agent is checking *passports*.

3. _____   *Sixty* passengers are taking flight 31.

4. _____   They are waiting *at Gate 6*.

5. _____   The flight attendants are greeting *the passengers*.

6. _____   *A steward* is collecting tickets.

7. _____   The mechanics are *inspecting the engines*.

8. _____   *The pilot* is talking to an air traffic controller.

9. *Where* _____   _____

10. *When* _____   _____

Activities

A. ROLE PLAY INTERVIEW. Interview another student. The other student is an actor or actress, a famous athlete, or an old friend. Below are some questions to use in your interview. Add other questions. Use the verb *be* or the present continuous tense.

1. Where are you living now?
2. Where are you working?
3. (Actor) Who are you starring with?
   (Athlete) What team are you playing for? Who are you playing against?
   (Old friend) Who are you working with? Who are you working for?
4. Are you happy with your job?
5. What else are you doing?
6. _____
7. _____

B. PUZZLE. How's your memory? Cover the questions on page 81 and look at the picture on this page for two minutes. Then cover this picture and answer the questions on page 81.

Answer the questions from memory. Don't look back at the picture.

1. Where is the scene?
2. How many floors are there in the building?
3. Is the travel agency open?
4. Where's the bus going?
5. Are there any other public vehicles?
6. Are there any mailboxes on Pine Avenue?
7. How many telephone booths are there on Pine Avenue?
8. What is above the travel agency?
9. Is there a sign for a bus stop on Pine Avenue?
10. Is there a clock on the street?
11. What time is it?
12. What is between the travel agency and the barber shop?
13. When is the barber shop open?
14. How many cars are there on the street?
15. What is the name of the local newspaper?
16. Is Pine Avenue a one-way street or a two-way street?
17. How many passengers are there on the bus?
18. Who works above the newspaper office?
19. How many people are working in the newspaper office?
20. Who is standing under the street sign?

C. LISTENING. Listen to the story about Mr. Neal's trip home from Hong Kong. Then listen again and answer the questions.

1. It's Friday. What's Mr. Neal doing?
2. Who is waiting for Mr. Neal at the Honolulu International Airport?
3. It's Saturday. What are Mr. Neal and Phil Spencer doing?
4. What's Martha doing?
5. What are Gary and Cindy doing?
6. It's Monday. Where is Mr. Neal and what is he doing?
7. What are Mrs. Graves and Elizabeth doing?
8. What are Donna and Tom doing?
9. What's Jim doing?
10. Is it a typical day at Neal Import Export Company?

D. LISTENING. Listen again to the story and complete it. Fill in the blanks with the words that you hear.

It's Friday morning. Mr. Neal _____ returning home from Hong Kong. He's _____ in Hawaii. Now he is flying from Hong Kong to Honolulu. _____ traveling to Hawaii to visit his sister Martha, her husband Phil Spencer, and _____ children, Cindy and Gary. The Spencers _____ waiting for Mr. Neal at the Honolulu International Airport.

It's Saturday. Mr. Neal is _____ Waikiki Beach with the Spencer family. _____ enjoying the warm weather. Mr. Neal and Phil are _____ in the sun. Martha _____ swimming in the ocean. Gary _____ along the beach and Cindy is playing volleyball _____ the beach.

It's Monday. Mr. Neal is _____ work in his office. He's _____ at his desk and _____ reading his mail. Mrs. Graves is _____ the phone. Elizabeth is _____ a letter. Donna and Tom _____ packing boxes. Jim is _____ stamps on the boxes. _____ a typical day at Neal Import Export Company.

E. WRITING. Imagine you are on a dream vacation. Where are you? Who are you with? What are you doing? Write about your vacation. Use the present continuous tense.

F. INTERVIEW AND ROLE PLAY. Your friend is on vacation. Your friend is calling you long distance. Write questions to ask your friend about the vacation. Use the words below to form questions in the present continuous tense.

1. Where / vacation
2. What / do
3. Are / have a good time
4. Where / stay
5. Who / travel with
6. Is / rain
7. When / come back
8. _____

You are on vacation. You are calling a friend at home. Your friend is asking you questions about your vacation. Answer the questions.

G. RIDDLES. What are the answers?

1. You are my sister, but I am not your brother. Who am I?
2. What is everyone around the world doing now?

H. DICTATION. You will hear each sentence two times. Write exactly what you hear.

1. _____
2. _____
3. _____
4. _____
5. _____
6. _____
7. _____

Review Quizzes

A. LISTENING COMPREHENSION: SENTENCES
For each problem, you will hear a short sentence. You will hear each sentence two times. After you hear a sentence, read the four choices. Decide which written sentence is the closest in meaning to the spoken sentence. Circle the letter of the correct answer.

1. (A) She's typing.
   (B) She's not typing.
   (C) They're typing.
   (D) They're not typing.

2. (A) There are 14 pens.
   (B) There are 14 pencils.
   (C) There are 40 pens.
   (D) There are 40 pencils.

3. (A) They're looking at the dog.
   (B) They're cleaning the dog.
   (C) He's looking at the dog.
   (D) He's cleaning the dog.

4. (A) They're working.
   (B) You're working.
   (C) We're working.
   (D) She's working.

5. (A) She's in the water.
   (B) She's not in the water.
   (C) They're in the water.
   (D) They're not in the water.

6. (A) They are living in London.
   (B) Their houses are in London.
   (C) There are houses in London.
   (D) There are horses in London.

7. (A) He's a waiter.
   (B) He's on Main Street.
   (C) He isn't on Main Street
   (D) He's waiting at home.

8. (A) They're in class.
   (B) They're not in class.
   (C) We're in class.
   (D) We're not in class.

9. (A) It's raining a little.
   (B) It's raining a lot.
   (C) It isn't pouring.
   (D) It isn't raining in Miami.

10. (A) How's the new president?
    (B) What's the name of the president?
    (C) Where's the new president?
    (D) When's the new president coming?

B. STRUCTURE: SENTENCE COMPLETION

Choose the *one* word or phrase that best completes the sentence. Circle the letter of the correct answer.

1. What -------- doing?
   - (A) are
   - (B) he
   - (C) are you
   - (D) is they

2. She's buying --------.
   - (A) television
   - (B) a television
   - (C) a televisions
   - (D) an television

3. -------- pants over there are expensive.
   - (A) This
   - (B) These
   - (C) That
   - (D) Those

4. When -------- coming?
   - (A) she
   - (B) she's
   - (C) is she
   - (D) is she's

5. Where --------?
   - (A) are you live
   - (B) you live
   - (C) you living
   - (D) are you living

6. The White House is -------- 1600 Pennsylvania Avenue.
   - (A) at
   - (B) in
   - (C) on
   - (D) to

7. What -------- reading?
   - (A) is the boys
   - (B) is the boy's
   - (C) are the boy's
   - (D) are the boys

8. My parents --------.
   - (A) is not old
   - (B) is not olds
   - (C) are not old
   - (D) are not olds

9. Her office is -------- Congress Avenue.
   - (A) on
   - (B) in
   - (C) at
   - (D) at the

10. They're -------- now.   (*spelling*)
    - (A) swimming
    - (B) shoping
    - (C) studing
    - (D) writting

11. -------- clean towels in the closet.
    - (A) There's
    - (B) There are
    - (C) They're
    - (D) Their are

12. They are --------.   (*spelling*)
    - (A) boys
    - (B) tomatos
    - (C) citys
    - (D) churchs

13. -------- a post office near our house.
    - (A) It isn't
    - (B) They aren't
    - (C) There isn't
    - (D) There aren't

14. I am -------- now.
    - (A) teacher
    - (B) thirsty
    - (C) a sick
    - (D) work

C. STRUCTURE: ERROR IDENTIFICATION

Each sentence has four underlined words or phrases. Circle the *one* underlined word or phrase that is not correct. Then correct the sentence.

1. $\underset{A}{\underline{Were}}$ $\underset{B}{\underline{at}}$ $\underset{C}{\underline{the}}$ drugstore $\underset{D}{\underline{on}}$ the corner.

2. $\underset{A}{\underline{Where's}}$ $\underset{B}{\underline{Mr.}}$ and Mrs. Ewing $\underset{C}{\underline{going}}$ $\underset{D}{\underline{on\ their}}$ vacation?

3. $\underset{A}{\underline{Its}}$ not $\underset{B}{\underline{eating}}$ $\underset{C}{\underline{its}}$ $\underset{D}{\underline{dog\ food}}$ now.

4. $\underset{A}{\underline{Jennifer's}}$ going $\underset{B}{\underline{at}}$ $\underset{C}{\underline{the}}$ bank $\underset{D}{\underline{on}}$ First Street.

5. $\underset{A}{\underline{There\ are}}$ two $\underset{B}{\underline{window}}$ in $\underset{C}{\underline{the}}$ bedroom on $\underset{D}{\underline{the\ second}}$ floor.

6. $\underset{A}{\underline{David's}}$ $\underset{B}{\underline{take}}$ $\underset{C}{\underline{a}}$ $\underset{D}{\underline{hot}}$ shower now.

7. $\underset{A}{\underline{Where's}}$ are $\underset{B}{\underline{the}}$ $\underset{C}{\underline{girls}}$ $\underset{D}{\underline{living}}$ now?

8. $\underset{A}{\underline{There}}$ $\underset{B}{\underline{are}}$ $\underset{C}{\underline{a}}$ letter for you $\underset{D}{\underline{on}}$ your desk.

9. $\underset{A}{\underline{Susan}}$ wearing $\underset{B}{\underline{a}}$ $\underset{C}{\underline{new,}}$ $\underset{D}{\underline{red\ blouse}}$ today.

10. $\underset{A}{\underline{What's}}$ $\underset{B}{\underline{the}}$ child $\underset{C}{\underline{is\ doing}}$ $\underset{D}{\underline{in\ the}}$ bedroom?

11. $\underset{A}{\underline{Pat's}}$ is $\underset{B}{\underline{writing}}$ $\underset{C}{\underline{a\ letter}}$ $\underset{D}{\underline{to\ the}}$ telephone company.

12. $\underset{A}{\underline{Melissa's\ studing}}$ for $\underset{B}{}$ $\underset{C}{\underline{a\ history}}$ test $\underset{D}{\underline{at\ the}}$ library.

13. $\underset{A}{\underline{What're}}$ you $\underset{B}{\underline{doing}}$ $\underset{C}{\underline{in}}$ the classroom with $\underset{D}{\underline{that\ dog}}$?

14. The Prime Minister $\underset{A}{\underline{is}}$ $\underset{B}{\underline{staying}}$ $\underset{C}{\underline{at\ a}}$ hotel $\underset{D}{\underline{on\ the}}$ State Street.

15. $\underset{A}{\underline{Her}}$ father $\underset{B}{\underline{isn't}}$ $\underset{C}{\underline{wash}}$ his $\underset{D}{\underline{new\ car}}$ now.

16. $\underset{A}{\underline{Who}}$ standing $\underset{B}{\underline{in\ front\ of}}$ $\underset{C}{\underline{the}}$ store $\underset{D}{\underline{across\ the}}$ street?

CHAPTER 4

Dialog

Faith: Ellen, where were you last night? Were you late for the movie?

Ellen: No, Faith, I wasn't late. I was at the movie theater on time. I was looking for you outside the theater and in the lobby.

Faith: That's strange. I was in the lobby from 7:30 until the start of the movie at 8:00. I was sitting by the popcorn stand.

Ellen: Well, I was standing by the ticket window.

Faith: Were you at the Empire Theater?

Ellen: Yes, of course. Where were you?

Faith: I was at home until 6:50. I was at the bus stop at 7:00, and I was on the 89th Street bus at 7:05. I was at the theater by 7:30.

Ellen: Why were you on the 89th Street bus?

Faith: Because the Empire Theater's on the corner of 87th Street and Sherman Avenue.

Ellen: No, Faith, the Empire Theater's on Third Street.

Faith: Ellen, that's the old Empire Theater downtown. I was at the new Empire Theater on 87th Street.

Ellen: Oh, no! I was at the Empire Theater downtown!

Exercise 1.   *True, False, or Unknown?*

1. Faith was at the Empire Theater last night.   _____

2. Ellen was at the Empire Theater last night.   _____

3. The Empire Theater downtown is on the corner of Third Street and Empire Avenue.   _____

4. Faith was on the 89th Street bus at 7:05.   _____

5. Ellen was on a different bus.   _____

6. The movie was at 7:30 *p.m.*   _____

7. Faith and Ellen were on time for the movie.   _____

8. Ellen was looking for Faith in the lobby of the theater.   _____

9. Faith was eating popcorn in the lobby.   _____

Exercise 2.   Answer the questions with short answers.

1. Who was at the Empire Theater last night?
2. Were Ellen and Faith late for the movie?
3. When were Faith and Ellen at the theater?
4. Is the new Empire Theater downtown?
5. Was Ellen eating popcorn in the lobby?
6. Was Faith drinking coffee in the lobby?
7. What was Ellen doing at 7:45 last night?
8. Where was Ellen standing?

---

9. Were you at a movie theater last night?
10. Where were you last night?
11. What were you doing at 8:00 p.m.?

Pronunciation of [ā], [e], and [a]

 Exercise 3. Listen to the pronunciation of [ā], [e], and [a]. Then repeat the words.

A.

[ā]	[e]	[a]
wait	when	at
late	next	that
eight	friend	last
strange	weather	stand

B. Listen to the sentences. Repeat the sentences. Then circle the [ā] sounds, underline the [e] sounds, and put a box around the [a] sounds.

1. Faith was waiting for her friend at the theater last night.
2. Ellen was standing next to the ticket window.
3. Ellen was waiting for Faith at the theater downtown.
4. Faith wasn't late yesterday.

Past Tense of *be*

SINGULAR	PLURAL
I **was** at the movie theater.	We **were** in Hollywood two years ago.
You **were** on time for the movie.	You and your friend **were** at different theaters.
Faith **was** in the lobby last night.	They **were** hungry after the movie.
He **was** a good actor.	
It **was** a very funny movie.	

Time Words in the Past

Yesterday	**Last** _____	_____ _____ **ago**
yesterday	last night	ten minutes ago
yesterday morning	last week(end)	five hours ago
yesterday afternoon	last month	four days ago
yesterday evening	last semester	two weeks ago
	last summer	a / one month ago
		three semesters ago
		six years ago

Exercise 4.   Fill in with *was* or *were*.

Last night my family _____ busy. My mother and my father _____ downtown.
They _____ at a business meeting until 9:00. My brother _____ at a basketball game.
He _____ with his girlfriend. My cousin and I _____ at the university. My cousin
_____ at the library. The library _____ very crowded. I _____ at the language
lab.

Exercise 5.   Complete the sentences with *was* or *were*, time words, and any other necessary words.

> *Examples:*   My parents and I ***were*** at the airport ***yesterday evening.***
> The planes from Chicago ***were late last night.***
> I ***was*** in Chicago ***two years ago***.

1. My friend and I _____ at school yesterday _____ .
2. You _____ late for class _____ _____ ago.
3. My sister _____ sick last _____ .
4. Her boyfriend _____ last _____ .
5. My aunt and uncle _____ yesterday _____ .
6. The classroom _____ yesterday _____ .
7. I _____ ago.
8. Our teacher _____ last _____ .
9. We _____ ago.

Location: *∅, in, at, on*

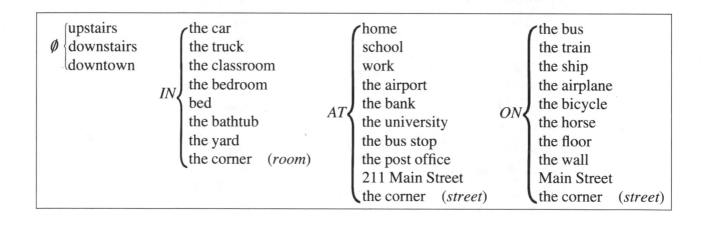

Exercise 6. Complete with *in, at, on, in the, at the, on the,* or leave the space blank.

Yesterday morning I was sick. I was _____ home _____ bed. My wife was _____ work. My daughter was _____ school. My son was _____ downstairs _____ living room with his grandmother. My father was _____ downtown _____ bus station _____ Washington Avenue. My cousin was _____ bus from New Orleans.

Exercise 7. PAIRWORK.
Student A: Ask the question.
Student B: Look only at the cue word(s) and answer the question.
Student A: Look at the answer and correct Student B if necessary.

STUDENT A	STUDENT B
1. Where was the nurse? (She was *at* work.)	work
2. Where was the party? (It was *in the* yard.)	yard
3. Where were Mr. and Mrs. Ford? (They were *on the* airplane.)	airplane
4. Where were you? (I was *at* school.)	school
5. Where was the calendar? (It was *on the* wall.)	wall
6. Where was the old bus station? (It was downtown.)	downtown
7. Where was your aunt? (She was *at* home.)	home
8. Where was his son? (He was *at the* university.)	university
9. Where was the car? (It was *on* Second Avenue.)	Second Avenue
10. Where was the TV? (It was *in the* living room.)	living room
11. Where were you at 8:00? (I was *at the* bus stop.)	bus stop
12. Where was Uncle George? (He was *in the* kitchen.)	kitchen

Past Tense of *be:* Negative

FORMULA 4-1

Subject	was were	not	complement .

Contractions: **wasn't**
weren't

Examples: I **was not** absent two days ago.
My grandmother **wasn't** in the hospital last month.
My parents **were not** sick last week.
We **weren't** tired yesterday morning.

Exercise 8.
Complete the past tense sentences. Use *was, were, wasn't,* or *weren't.*
Also use a past time expression and other necessary words. Study the example
sentences.

1. I __was__ at home yesterday, but ___I wasn't at home two days ago___ .
2. We __were__ sick last week, but ___we weren't sick yesterday___ .
3. My roommate _____ tired last night, but _____ .
4. James and Lucy _____ at work yesterday morning, but _____ .
5. My TV _____ broken yesterday, but _____ .
6. You _____ ready for the exam yesterday, but _____ .
7. I _____ on time last Friday, but _____ .
8. You and I _____ in class yesterday, but _____ .
9. I _____ , but _____ .
10. _____ , but _____ .

Past Tense of *be:*
Yes-No Questions and Short Answers

FORMULA 4-2

Was Were	subject	(complement) ?

Examples:

QUESTION	SHORT ANSWER
Was John F. Kennedy from California?	No, he **wasn't.**
Was he from Massachusetts?	Yes, he **was.**
Were Isaac Newton and Charles Darwin Canadian?	No, they **weren't.**
Were they British?	Yes, they **were.**

Exercise 9. MINI CONVERSATIONS.

Examples: Sigmund Freud German
Austrian

Pat: Was <u>Sigmund Freud German</u>?
Lee: No, <u>he</u> wasn't. <u>He</u> was <u>Austrian</u>.

you late for history class
on time

Bob: Were <u>you late for history class</u>?
Tom: No, <u>I wasn't. I was on time.</u>

1. the homework difficult
easy

2. the professor in her office
at home

3. the answers in the textbook
workbook

4. Abraham Lincoln born in Illinois
Kentucky

5. I correct
wrong

6. the history map in the bookstore
in the library

7. the final exams in Clark Hall
in Dexter Hall

8. we on page twenty-nine
on page thirty-three

9. the geography exam long
short

10. _____

_____

Exercise 10. INTERVIEW. Ask a classmate the questions.

1. When was your last vacation?
2. How long was your vacation?
3. Where were you during your vacation?
4. Who were you with?
5. What was the weather like?

6. _____

Past Tense of *be:* *Wh*-Questions

FORMULA 4-3	*Wh*-word	was were	subject	(complement) ?

Study the questions in Exercises 10 and 11.

Exercise 11. INTERVIEW. Ask a classmate the questions.

1. Where were you born?
2. When was your last birthday?
3. How old were you?
4. Where were you on your birthday?
5. Who were you with?

Exercise 12.

Read the answers. Then write the *Wh*-questions about the underlined parts of the answers. Use *who, what, when, where, how old,* and *how many*.

1. ___When were your grandparents married?___ My grandparents were married in 1936.
2. _____ Their wedding was in Japan.
3. _____ They were nineteen years old in 1936.
4. _____ My grandfather was a businessman.
5. _____ Their fiftieth wedding anniversary party was on June 30, 1986.
6. _____ The party was at a large restaurant.
7. _____ There were one hundred people at the party.
8. _____ Mr. Ito was the chef.

Regular Plural Nouns: Pronunciation

1. The plural ending (spelled **-s**) is pronounced [s] after voiceless consonant sounds.

banks	months	minutes
boats	shops	photographs

There are twelve month**s** and fifty-two week**s** in a year.
The check**s** and deposit**s** from these account**s** are good.
There were many old book**s** in those shop**s**.

2. The plural ending (spelled **-s** or **-ies**) is pronounced [z] after vowels and voiced consonant sounds.

animals	bags	days
gloves	songs	shoes
chairs	pens	cities

How many day**s** are there in two year**s**?
There were four pair**s** of shoe**s** in those bag**s**.
The downtown building**s** in large cit**ies** are often tall.

3. The plural ending (spelled **-s** or **-es**) is pronounced [ĭz] after the sounds [s] class, box; [sh] dish; [ch] lunch; [z] nose; [zh] garage; [j] page.

places	bushes	surprises
houses	churches	garages
taxes	sizes	colleges

The tax**es** in those place**s** are high.
These watch**es** are different size**s** and price**s**.
The class**es** at those college**s** are easy.
These dish**es** and glass**es** are beautiful.

Exercise 13. Indicate the pronunciation of the plural nouns. For each noun, write an X in the correct column.

	s	z	ĭz
1. cars		X	
2. dishes			X
3. suits	X		
4. horses			
5. parties			
6. rooms			
7. trucks			
8. schools			
9. classes			
10. kitchens			
11. walls			
12. offices			
13. maps			
14. universities			
15. things			
16. buses			
17. tickets			
18. windows			
19. boxes			
20. pages			
21. years			
22. pizzas			

Going (to) (the) + **Place**

going	going to	going to the
home	class	(living) room
downtown	school	park
downstairs	work	bus stop
upstairs	church	airport
inside	Sears (Department Store)	(train) station
outside	France	(post) office
	Paris	bank
	England	hospital
	London	(grocery) store
	Bond Street	supermarket
	700 Bond Street	United States
		U.S.S.R.

Exercise 14.

PAIRWORK. Student A: Ask the question.
Student B: Look only at the cue word(s) and answer the question.
Student A: Look at the answer and correct Student B if necessary.

STUDENT A

1. Where are you going?
   (I'm going home.)

2. Where is your father going?
   (He's going *to the* bank.)

3. Where are Pat and Tom going?
   (They're going *to* school.)

4. Where are you going?
   (I'm going *to the* supermarket.)

5. Where's the fire truck going?
   (It's going *to* 619 Park Avenue.)

6. Where's Mom going?
   (She's going downtown.)

7. Where's Dad going?
   (He's going *to* work.)

8. Where is this bus going?
   (It's going *to* Market Street.)

9. Where's Patricia going?
   (She's going *to the* library.)

10. Where are her brother and sister going?
    (They're going *to the* airport.)

11. Where are you going?
    (I'm going upstairs.)

12. Where's Miss Kelly going?
    (She's going *to* class.)

13. Where is your uncle going?
    (He's going *to* McDonald's.)

14. Where are William and Sue going?
    (They're going *to the* drugstore.)

15. Where is that plane going?
    (It's going *to* San Francisco.)

STUDENT B

home

bank

school

supermarket

619 Park Avenue

downtown

work

Market Street

library

airport

upstairs

class

McDonald's

drugstore

San Francisco

Exercise 15.   Fill in the blank spaces with *to* or *to the*, or leave the spaces blank.

It's Monday morning. Residents of the Newport Apartment Building are leaving the building. Mr. Stevens is going _____ outside for a newspaper. Mrs. Klein is going _____ downtown. She's going _____ hospital on Mayfair Avenue. Mrs. Harder is also going _____ Mayfair Avenue. Her children Bill and Jack are going _____ bus stop. They're going _____ class. Ms. Granger is a flight attendant. She's going _____ airport. She's going _____ Dallas today. Mr. and Mrs. Erickson are going _____ park to run.

I'm not going _____ school. I'm not going _____ work. I'm not going _____ downstairs. I'm staying here, and I'm watching everybody from my apartment window.

Plural Nouns: Irregular Forms

SINGULAR	PLURAL	SINGULAR	PLURAL
one man	six men	a foot	two feet
a woman	five women	one tooth	many teeth
one child	four children	a mouse	three mice
a person	several people	a fish	twelve fish
		that sheep	those sheep

Note: The following nouns are always plural:
police, pants, trousers, slacks, jeans, shorts, pajamas, scissors.

Police has a singular form — *policeman, policewoman,* or *police officer.*

Exercise 16.   MINI CONVERSATIONS.

Example: young man (2)

A: Was there one young man?
B: No, there wasn't.
A: How many young men were there?
B: There were two young men.

1. foreign woman (3)
2. fish (5)
3. new tooth (2)
4. gray mouse (4)
5. sick child (2)
6. angry person (3)

7. black sheep (6)
8. businesswoman (3)
9. goldfish (5)
10. salesman (2)
11. broken tooth (2)
12. foot of snow (2)

Exercise 17.   Write the plural forms of the words below.

1. lady   _____
2. fish   _____
3. watch   _____
4. day   _____
5. knife   _____
6. mouse   _____
7. man   _____
8. potato   _____
9. roof   _____
10. child   _____

11. secretary   _____
12. person   _____
13. tooth   _____
14. dish   _____
15. foot   _____
16. tax   _____
17. boy   _____
18. stomach   _____
19. wife   _____
20. saleswoman   _____

Possessive Forms of Nouns

SINGULAR NOUNS	PLURAL NOUNS	
	Regular plural nouns	*Irregular plural nouns*
Add **'s**	Add **'**	Add **'s**
the student**'s** teacher the boy**'s** mother the boss**'s** office the secretary**'s** desk	the students**'** teacher the boys**'** mother the bosses**'** offices the secretaries**'** desks	
a woman**'s** shoes a policeman**'s** uniform a child**'s** toys		women**'s** shoes policemen**'s** uniforms those children**'s** toys
Jess**'s** apartment Sandra**'s** address Alex**'s** bicycle		
Sandra Lee**'s** address Mr. Jackson**'s** car	the Lees**'** address the Jacksons**'** car	
today**'s** newspaper Canada**'s** economy the earth**'s** atmosphere		

Exercise 18. Read the two passages below and complete the sentences. Make the underlined nouns possessive. Add **'s** or **'**.

This is the office of Meyer Construction Company. Paul Meyer is the president. The _president_ office is large. His _secretary_ desk is in the lobby. It is near the _ladies_ room. The _men_ room is in the back corner. Mr. _Meyer_ assistant is Nicholas Dunning. _Nicholas_ office is next to the Conference Room. _Yesterday_ meeting was in the Conference Room.

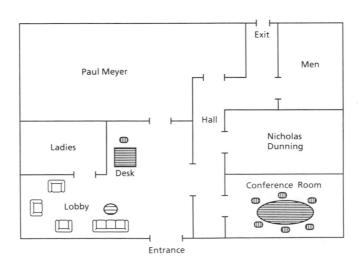

Parents Weekend at the university is this weekend. The Meyers are visiting their _children_ campus. Mr. Meyer is staying at his _son_ dormitory. _James_ dorm is near the football stadium. The _Meyers_ two daughters live in an apartment on Langdon Street. Mrs. Meyer is staying at her _daughters_ apartment.

Exercise 19. MINI CONVERSATIONS.

Note: _Whose_ is a question word. It asks who the possessor or owner of something is.

Examples: Amanda's watch   Andrew's shoes
            Joan's   George's

Lynn:	Is this Amanda's watch?	Mac:	Are these Andrew's shoes?
Kim:	No, it isn't.	Pam:	No, they aren't.
Lynn:	Whose watch is it?	Mac:	Whose shoes are they?
Kim:	It's Joan's watch.	Pam:	They're George's shoes.

1. Tom's car
   Carlos's

2. Bess's gloves
   Mary's

3. the Carters' house
   the Carsons'

4. your umbrella
   my sister's

5. the Hildreths' children
   the Windsors'

6. your glasses
   my roommate's

7. your cup
   Nancy's

8. _____

    _____

Exercise 20.
Collect objects from your classmates. Find out who the objects belong to by asking questions with _whose_.

Exercise 21.
Write sentences combining terms from each column.

The children		truck		brown
The actress		car		large
The woman		office		short
The dog		bed	is	red
Charles		house		new
That businessman	's	meeting	are	expensive
Last night		sons		silver
Liz	'	leg	was	boring
Those women		toys		round
Mr. and Mrs. Garza		room	were	broken
The babies		party		clean
Those firefighters		eyes		fun
The Petersons		jackets		beautiful

_____ _____ _____

Example: The children's toys were broken.

Past Continuous: Statements

There was a robbery last night in our neighborhood around 9:30. What was everyone doing between nine and ten p.m.?

SINGULAR	PLURAL
I **was** study**ing**.	We **were** prepar**ing** for an exam.
You **were** read**ing** the newspaper.	You and Bob **were** work**ing**.
Mr. Baker **was** watch**ing** TV.	Mr. and Mrs. Loren **were** shopp**ing**.
Sonia Durland **was** bak**ing** a cake.	The police **weren't** driv**ing** around
The watchdog **was** sleep**ing**.	the neighborhood.

FORMULA 4-4

Subject	was were	(not)	verb + ing	(complement) .

The past continuous tense generally describes an incomplete activity occurring or in progress in the past.

Exercise 22.
Complete the following sentences about last night. Use the past continuous form of a verb in the box. Add words to form a complement.

work	cook	study	eat	visit
clean	sleep	read	play	watch

Last night a friend was visiting me during the storm. My friend and I were playing cards.

My parents _____

My brother _____

My two sisters _____

My grandfather _____

My grandmother and my aunt _____

As usual, my dog _____

Past Continuous: Questions

FORMULA 4-5

(Wh-word)	was were	subject	verb + ing	(complement) ?

Exercise 23. Answer the questions.

1. Were you sleeping in class yesterday?
2. Were your classmates speaking only English in class yesterday?
3. Was your teacher speaking only English in class yesterday?
4. Were you paying attention during class?
5. What were you doing before yesterday's class?
6. Where were you sitting during class?
7. Who was sitting next to you?
8. What was your teacher doing at the beginning of class?
9. What were we studying at the end of class?

Exercise 24. MINI CONVERSATIONS.

Example: Alexis
make breakfast

Lou: What <u>was</u> Alexis doing during the earthquake?
Ben: <u>She was making breakfast.</u>

1. Christopher and Emily
drive to work

2. you
sleep

3. Carmen
take a bath

4. you and Pat
walk to school

5. Terry Moto
shave

6. _____
_____

Exercise 25. MINI CONVERSATIONS.

Example: you / New York
read magazines

Kazumi: What <u>were</u> you doing during the flight to <u>New York</u>?
Carmen: <u>I was reading magazines.</u>

1. the flight attendant / Stockholm
serve meals

2. Jim and Sam / Las Vegas
play cards

3. you and your secretary / Manila
write a business report

4. you / Santo Domingo
watch a movie

5. Joan's baby / Glasgow
cry

6. _____
_____

Exercise 26. MINI CONVERSATIONS.

Example: the bride
                smile
                happy

Mona: What <u>was the bride</u> doing during the wedding?
Lisa: <u>She was smiling.</u>
Mona: Why <u>was she smiling</u>?
Lisa: Because <u>she was happy</u>.

1. the groom
   shake
   nervous

2. the bride's mother and father
   cry
   happy and sad

3. the groom's father
   perspire
   hot

4. the groom's aunt and uncle
   smile
   happy

5. the bride's little brother
   sleep
   tired

6. _____
   _____
   _____

Activities

A. INTERVIEWS. Work with a classmate.

1. Childhood

   When were you born?
   Where were you born?
   What was your favorite toy?
   What was your favorite game?
   What was your favorite food?
   What was your first school?
   Were you happy at school?

2. High School

   Where was your high school?
   Was it a large school?
   How many students were there in your school?
   What were your courses during your last year?
   Were you on any high school teams?
   Were you in any clubs in high school?

3. Recently

   Where were you last Saturday?
   Were you busy?
   What were you doing?
   Who were you with?

   What were you doing two hours ago?
   What were you doing four hours ago?
   What were you doing eight hours ago?

B. WRITING. Write a composition about the past year. Answer the questions below in your composition.

Where were you living last year?
Were you working last year? Where? What was your job?
or
Were you studying last year? Where? What?
What was your favorite movie last year? What language was it in?
What was your favorite song last year? Was it in English?
What was your favorite TV show last year? What language was it in?

C. SENTENCE COMPLETION. Read the passage below about Abraham Lincoln. Fill in the spaces with appropriate words.

Abraham Lincoln _____ born in Kentucky _____ February 12, 1809. He _____ from _____ very poor family. He _____ a tall, thin man. Lincoln was six _____ four inches tall. He _____ married to Mary Todd. _____ marriage was generally happy. Their four children's names _____ Robert, Edward, William, and Wallace. Lincoln _____ against slavery. He was President of _____ United States _____ 1861 to 1865. He was _____ great president and _____ important American during the nineteenth century.

D. GUESSING GAME: Famous Person of the Past.

Think of a very famous person from the past. Your classmates will ask you *yes-no* questions with the past tense of *be*. They will try to guess the identity of your famous person.

Examples: Was the mystery person female?
Was the person from the twentieth century?
Was the person from Europe?
Was the person German?
Was the person tall? / blond? / etc.
Was the person a politician? / a scientist? / etc.

Was the person married to _____ ?

E. WRITING. Write about a famous person of the past. See Part C. SENTENCE COMPLETION for an example.

F. PUZZLE.
The letters in the seven words below are in the wrong order. Write the letters in the correct order in the boxes.

1. S L E E P A
   ⬚⬚⬚⬚⬚⬚

2. D O Y A T
   ⬚⬚⬚⬚⬚

3. G R I N N N U
   ⬚⬚⬚⬚⬚⬚⬚

4. F C O E E F
   ⬚⬚⬚⬚⬚⬚

5. W O D T N N O W
   ⬚⬚⬚⬚⬚⬚⬚⬚

6. B E A L T
   ⬚⬚⬚⬚⬚

7. L I C G A N L
   ⬚⬚⬚⬚⬚⬚⬚

What was he doing yesterday?

ANSWER: ⬚⬚⬚⬚⬚⬚⬚ ⬚⬚⬚⬚⬚⬚⬚⬚

Put the circled letters in the boxes under the picture to find the answer to the question.

G. DICTATION. You will hear each sentence two times. Write exactly what you hear.

1. _____
2. _____
3. _____
4. _____
5. _____
6. _____
7. _____
8. _____

Review Quizzes

 A. LISTENING COMPREHENSION: SENTENCES
For each problem, you will hear a short sentence. You will hear each sentence two times. After you hear a sentence, read the four choices. Decide which written sentence is the closest in meaning to the spoken sentence. Circle the letter of the correct answer.

1. (A) Their children were happy.
   (B) Their children were sad.
   (C) His children weren't happy.
   (D) His children weren't sad.

2. (A) The shoes are next to the door.
   (B) There's a shoe near the door.
   (C) The shoes are near the door.
   (D) There isn't a shoe near the door.

3. (A) They were going to class.
   (B) They're going to class.
   (C) We were going to class.
   (D) We're going to class.

4. (A) They aren't preparing exams.
   (B) They're preparing for an exam.
   (C) They're not studying for a test.
   (D) They aren't examining tests.

5. (A) They were not studying last week.
   (B) They were studying a week ago.
   (C) They were studying two weeks ago.
   (D) They weren't studying two weeks ago.

6. (A) She was born in 1980.
   (B) She was born eighteen years ago.
   (C) She is eighty years old.
   (D) It's her eighteenth birthday.

7. (A) My aunt's name was Pat.
   (B) Her husband was Pat Brown.
   (C) My aunt's name was Mary Pat Brown.
   (D) Her husband wasn't married to Pat Brown.

8. (A) Her uncle was in Europe.
   (B) Her uncle was French.
   (C) Her father's brother wasn't in France last week.
   (D) Her father was in France last week.

9. (A) Women's clothes are on the fifth floor.
   (B) There are women's clothes on the first floor.
   (C) The woman's clothes are on the floor.
   (D) The women's clothes are on the floor.

10. (A) That student's class is in room 308.
    (B) This student's English class is in room 308.
    (C) Their class is in room 308.
    (D) His English class is in room 308.

B. STRUCTURE: SENTENCE COMPLETION.

Choose the *one* word or phrase that best completes the sentence. Circle the letter of the correct answer.

1. -------- your brother in the hospital yesterday?

   (A) Is
   (B) Are
   (C) Was
   (D) Were

2. -------- some eggs in the refrigerator.

   (A) There's
   (B) There are
   (C) They're
   (D) Their are

3. The boys -------- playing football last night.

   (A) was
   (B) is
   (C) are
   (D) were

4. Her brother is --------.

   (A) write
   (B) hungry
   (C) dentist
   (D) a tall

5. That store sells -------- shoes.

   (A) women's
   (B) woman's
   (C) womens'
   (D) womans'

6. Who -------- to?

   (A) are you talking
   (B) you are talking
   (C) are you talk
   (D) you are talk

7. Their office is -------- Commerce Street -------- London.

   (A) on ... at
   (B) on ... in
   (C) at ... at
   (D) at ... in

8. There --------.

   (A) are one child
   (B) are two children
   (C) is one children
   (D) are two childrens

9. When -------- coming home?

   (A) is your father
   (B) your father is
   (C) are your father
   (D) your father are

10. Your mother -------- at 5:00 yesterday afternoon.

    (A) was cook
    (B) was cooking
    (C) were cook
    (D) were cooking

11. I was -------- yesterday afternoon at 3:00.

    (A) at post office
    (B) at the living room
    (C) at work
    (D) at the downstairs

12. Why --------?

    (A) Mary's cry.
    (B) is Mary cry
    (C) Mary is crying
    (D) is Mary crying

13. I -------- thirsty.

    (A) isn't
    (B) weren't
    (C) wasn't
    (D) not have

14. "Were you hungry?" "No, --------."

    (A) I wasn't
    (B) I weren't
    (C) I'm wasn't
    (D) I'm not

15. What's -------- doing?

    (A) he's
    (B) are they
    (C) you
    (D) she

C. STRUCTURE: ERROR IDENTIFICATION

Each sentence has four underlined words or phrases. Circle the *one* underlined word or phrase that is not correct. Then correct the sentence.

1. Pat and Chris <u>was</u> <u>doing</u> their homework <u>at 7:00</u> <u>last night</u>.
               A   B   C   D

2. <u>How many</u> <u>childrens</u> <u>were</u> <u>there</u> at the birthday party?
    A   B   C   D

3. It's <u>Mrs.</u> <u>Seltzer's</u> <u>new</u> <u>cars</u>.
     A   B   C   D

4. <u>Johns'</u> parents <u>were</u> not <u>at home</u> <u>last</u> Friday night.
   A   B   C   D

5. <u>Who</u> <u>are</u> those <u>mens</u> standing <u>next to</u> the door?
   A   B   C   D

6. <u>Who's</u> jacket <u>is</u> <u>on</u> the floor <u>near the</u> armchair?
   A   B C   D

7. <u>What</u> <u>she</u> <u>doing</u> with <u>that</u> <u>old newspaper</u>?
   A   B   C   D

8. <u>Was</u> <u>you</u> <u>watching</u> TV <u>last night</u> at <u>eight thirty</u>?
   A   B   C   D

9. The <u>boys'</u> were <u>going</u> <u>home</u> <u>at three o'clock</u> this afternoon.
      A   B   C   D

10. My <u>grandmother's</u> birthday <u>was</u> <u>a week ago</u> <u>in</u> October 21.
        A   B   C   D

11. Our two <u>children</u> <u>were</u> <u>in</u> Mexico City one <u>weeks</u> ago.
         A   B C   D

12. Your father <u>was</u> <u>at bank</u> <u>on</u> First Street <u>thirty minutes ago</u>.
         A   B   C   D

13. I <u>was</u> not <u>write</u> a letter to <u>him</u> <u>yesterday</u> afternoon at 2 o'clock.
    A   B   C   D

14. <u>Her</u> uncle <u>is living</u> <u>on</u> 213 Fremont Street <u>in</u> Monterey, California.
   A   B   C   D

15. <u>They</u> <u>were</u> only two <u>tomatoes</u> <u>in the</u> refrigerator.
   A   B   C   D

16. My <u>uncle</u> <u>wife</u> <u>was born</u> <u>in</u> Algeria <u>forty-five years ago</u>.
       A   B   C   D

CHAPTER 5

Dialog

Linda:	Hello, Jeff.
Jeff:	Oh hi, Linda. How are you?
Linda:	Fine. What are you doing here at the airport?
Jeff:	I'm flying to Washington on business. Where are you going?
Linda:	I'm going to a medical convention in Los Angeles. What's new with you?
Jeff:	Not much. Every month my boss sends me to Washington. I have to work six days a week. I don't have much free time, and my wife always complains about my job. She doesn't like my work schedule and she . . .
Linda:	How are your children?
Jeff:	Paul is a college freshman now, but he wants to quit school. He doesn't like his classes. Karen lives in Florida now. She teaches math at Florida International University. She seldom calls or writes us, and we . . .
Airline announcer:	This is the final call for flight 470 to Los Angeles.
Linda:	That's my flight. I need to go.
Jeff:	My flight doesn't leave for an hour. This airline is always late. It was nice seeing you, Linda.
Linda:	Yeah. Have a good trip to Washington.

Exercise 1. *True, False, or Unknown?*

1. Linda is flying to Los Angeles.
2. Linda is going on vacation.
3. Jeff's boss sends him to Washington every week.
4. Jeff works every day of the week.
5. Linda has a lot of free time.
6. Jeff's wife complains about his work schedule.
7. Jeff's son Paul lives in Los Angeles.
8. Paul doesn't like his university classes.
9. Jeff's daughter frequently calls him and his wife.

Exercise 2. Answer the questions.

1. In your opinion, is Jeff happy?
2. What problems does Jeff have?

The Simple Present Tense: Affirmative Statements

SINGULAR	PLURAL
I work six days a week. You seldom **call** us. He **lives** in Boston. She always **complains** about his job. The plane **leaves** at 8:30.	We **go** to Washington every month. You and your wife **travel** a lot. They often **travel** by plane.

The simple present tense expresses an action that occurs habitually. It also expresses a fact.

Examples: Habit: I brush my teeth every morning.
Pepe sleeps late on Saturdays.

Fact: Water boils at 100 degrees Centigrade.
Pineapples grow in Hawaii.
The sun sets in the west.

Simple Present Tense: Forms

SUBJECT	VERB	SUBJECT	VERB
I You We They	**work** [base form]	He She It	**works** [base form + s]

Exercise 3. Complete each sentence with the correct form of the verb in parentheses.

1. (work)   I _____ in a small company.

2. (make)   The company _____ computer parts.

3. (begin)   The secretaries _____ work at 8:00.

4. (arrive)   Our boss usually _____ at 9:00.

5. (work)   My assistant and I _____ in the accounting department.

6. (prepare)   Our department _____ bills.

7. (close)   The company _____ at 5:00.

Third Person Singular Present Tense: Pronunciation

English uses the same pronunciation rules for the final sound of the following:

1. plural nouns (*books, pens, watches*)
2. possessive of nouns (*Pat's, Tom's, Chris's*)
3. third person singular present tense verb forms (*stops, sends, dances*)

 ## Exercise 4. Listen and repeat.

/s/
Paul wants to leave school.
Jeff's daughter seldom writes to him.
He works six days a week.

/z/

His daughter seldom calls.
His wife complains about his job.
He needs to work on weekends.
She lives in Florida.

/ĭz/

Jeff catches a plane to Washington every month.
The airport closes at midnight.
Linda changes planes in Chicago.

Adverbs of Frequency

Adverbs of frequency go *after* forms of the verb *be*.
Adverbs of frequency go *before* all other main verbs.

FORMULA 5-1

Subject	adverb of frequency	verb	(complement) .

Examples: **I always take** a shower in the morning.
My roommate **usually listens** to music at night.
You **seldom eat** lunch at home.

Exercise 5.

Select words from each column to make sentences. Use the third person singular form of the verb when necessary. You may expand the complement. See the example sentences above.

SUBJECT	ADVERB OF FREQUENCY	VERB	COMPLEMENT
I	always	arrive	my friends
My classmate	almost always	wake up	breakfast
You	usually	take	a shower
My roommate	often	eat	a nap
Linda	frequently	listen	a bus
My parents	sometimes	write	late
____ and I	seldom	drive	before class
My mother	rarely	call	on weekends
____ and ____	almost never	visit	to work
	never	_____	early
_____			to music
			in the evening
			alone
			_____

The Simple Present Tense:
Yes-No Questions and Short Answers

FORMULA 5-2	Do	I you we they	(frequency adverb)	verb [base]	(complement) ?

Examples:

Question	Short Answer
Do I know your boss?	Yes, you do.
Do you live in Chicago?	No, I don't.
Do they frequently travel to Canada?	No, they do not.

FORMULA 5-3	Does	he she it	(frequency adverb)	verb [base]	(complement) ?

Examples:

Question	Short Answer
Does he speak Spanish?	Yes, he does.
Does she play tennis?	No, she does not.
Does it often rain in Las Vegas?	No, it doesn't.

Note: The verb is in the base form. It does *not* end with an -s.

Exercise 6.   INTERVIEW. Ask and answer the following questions with a classmate. Give true short answers.

1. Do you smoke?
2. Do you often exercise?
3. Does your father work six days a week?
4. Do your parents drink coffee?
5. Does your mother play a musical instrument?
6. Do you play a musical instrument?
7. Do you have a car?
8. Do you have any pets?
9. Does it sometimes snow in your hometown in the winter?
10. Do you like chocolate?
11. Do you usually eat a big breakfast?
12. Does your English teacher always give you homework?
13. Do you often speak English outside of class?
14. Does your father do housework?
15. Do you study a lot?
16. _____

Exercise 7. Complete the questions. Use *do* or *does* and the correct forms of the verbs in parentheses. Then complete the short answers.

1. (like)   _**Does**_ she _like_ fish?   Yes, _she does._
2. (want)   _____ you _____ an orange?   No, _____
3. (smoke)   _____ your brother _____ ?   No, _____
4. (eat)   _____ you always _____ breakfast?   Yes, _____
5. (need)   _____ they _____ some water?   No, _____
6. (drink)   _____ Mrs. Yamaura _____ coffee?   No, _____
7. (cook)   _____ Husscin _____ ?   Yes, _____
8. (help)   _____ Mr. Esparza _____ his wife?   Yes, _____

Exercise 8. Complete the questions. Write *am*, *is*, *are*, *do*, or *does*. Then answer the questions with short answers.

1. _**Do**_ you drink coffee every morning?   _No, I don't._
2. _**Are**_ you studying English?   _Yes, I am._
3. _____ today Wednesday?   _____
4. _____ I late?   _____
5. _____ wc have a test today?   _____
6. _____ your classroom have a map?   _____
7. _____ it raining now?   _____
8. _____ our teacher speak Arabic?   _____
9. _____ we practicing the past tense now?   _____
10. _____ you often get up early?   _____
11. _____ you busy today?   _____
12. _____ it often rain here in April?   _____
13. _____ you usually sleep at least seven hours? _____

Object Pronouns: *me, you, him, her, it, us, them*

SINGULAR	PLURAL
They know **me.** They often visit **me.** I like **you.** I respect **you.** I know **Ted.** I frequently visit **him.** I work with **Pam.** I see **her** every day. I have a new **car.** I drive **it** every day.	They know **Jim and me.** They often visit **us.** I admire **you and your boss.** I respect **you** both. I know **Ted and Bob.** I often talk to **them.**

Object pronouns substitute for nouns. They follow a verb or a preposition.

Exercise 9.
Rewrite the sentences about an anniversary dinner.
Substitute object pronouns for the underlined words.

1. Call your mother.   *Call her.*
2. Invite your parents to a restaurant.   *Invite them to a restaurant.*
3. Call the restaurant.
4. Make a reservation for five people.
5. Go to the restaurant with your parents.
6. Meet your brother and me at the restaurant.
7. Give your name to the hostess.
8. Follow the waiter to your table.
9. Ask for menus.
10. Order your meal.

Exercise 10.   MINI CONVERSATIONS.

Examples: Tom love Sue

Does Tom love Sue?
Yes, he does. He loves her a lot.

you like strawberries

Do you like strawberries?
Yes, I do. I like them a lot.

1. you admire your father
2. you study English
3. your sister watch TV
4. you like me

5. your boss respect you
6. you and your brother visit your cousins
7. he take his girlfriend to movies
8. your teacher help you and your classmates

Third Person Singular Present Tense: Spelling Rules

Rule 1:   consonant + **y** → consonant + **ies**

cry   _____

study   _____

fly   _____

Rule 2:   s → s**es**
                 x → x**es**
                 ch → ch**es**
                 sh → sh**es**

miss   _____

fix   _____

catch   _____

finish   _____

> **Rule 3:** all other endings → + **s**

stay   _____

tie   _____

run   _____

rob   _____

Exceptions: *does, goes, is, has.*

Exercise 11.   Write the third person singular forms.

1. have __*has*__
2. ski _____
3. crash _____
4. mix _____

5. stand _____
6. go _____
7. play _____
8. try _____

9. pass _____
10. enjoy _____
11. watch _____
12. hurry _____

Exercise 12.   Write the base forms.

1. flies __*fly*__
2. is _____
3. rushes _____

4. prepares _____
5. does _____
6. carries _____

7. dries _____
8. teaches _____
9. has _____

Exercise 13.   Complete the passage. Fill in the blanks with the correct present tense forms of the verbs in parentheses.

Kathy's Day

On weekday mornings after breakfast, Kathy _____ (prepare) her lunch. She usually _____ (fix) a sandwich and a salad. She _____ (pack) them in her lunchbox. She _____ (hurry) to the bus stop. She often _____ (catch) the 8:30 bus. It usually _____ (come) on time, and Kathy seldom _____ (miss) it.

Kathy _____ (have) three classes in the morning. Then she _____ (eat) lunch. After lunch she frequently _____ (study) in the library until 4:00. Her professors _____ (give) a lot of homework. She _____ (take) the bus home. At home she often _____ (watch) the news on television. Then she and her roommate _____ (eat) supper. After supper Kathy _____ (finish) her homework. She usually _____ (go) to bed before midnight.

Exercise 14.

Write about the weekday routine of a friend or a relative.

Every morning _____

_____

_____

_____

_____

_____

A and *an*

Use **a** before words that begin with a *consonant sound*.	Use **an** before words that begin with a *vowel sound*.
a young man a university, a European a woman a new car a one-bedroom apartment a gift a hundred dollars, a history test	an animal an evening an idea an old car an uncle an x-ray an hour, an honest person* *h is silent

Exercise 15.

Write *a* or *an* in each blank.

1. _____ wonderful day
2. _____ one-dollar bill
3. _____ umbrella
4. _____ European country
5. _____ used car

6. _____ hospital
7. _____ hour
6. _____ ounce
9. _____ university
10. _____ apple tree

11. _____ island
12. _____ honor
13. _____ year
14. _____ elevator
15. _____ uniform

Would like + Noun Phrase

Would like is a polite way to say "want." *Would like* indicates a want or a desire at the present time or in the future. Compare the sentences with *want* and *would like*:

Want

I want a hamburger.
Mary wants some chicken.
Do you want some coffee?
What does Tom want?

Would Like

I would like a hamburger.
Mary would like some chicken.
Would you like some coffee?
What would Tom like?

FORMULA 5-4

Subject	**would like**	noun phrase .

| FORMULA 5-5 | Would | subject | like | noun phrase ? |

| FORMULA 5-6 | What (kind of ...) | would | subject | like ? |

Exercise 16.
Look at the sentences above with *want* and *would like*. Then complete the two statements below about the grammatical differences.

1. In third person singular statements, there is a final _____ on *want*, but there is not a final _____ on *would* or *like*.

2. Questions with *would like* do not have the auxiliary words _____ or _____ .

Exercise 17.
In writing, there are only seven contractions with *would*. Complete the list of contractions.

I would   = *I'd* _____   we would   = *we'd* _____

you would = _____   they would = _____

he would   = _____   would not   = *wouldn't* _____

she would = _____

Exercise 18.
PAIRWORK.   Student A: Read the statement.
                              Student B: Ask the question. Use *would like*.
                              Student A: Respond.

STUDENT A	STUDENT B
1. I'm hungry.	*Would you like* a sandwich?
Yes, please.	
2. This is a good sandwich.	*Would you like* some dessert?
No, thank you.	
3. The children are thirsty.	What *would they like*?
They'd like some milk.	
4. It's my sister's birthday.	What _____ ?
_____	
5. I need a new watch.	What kind of watch _____ ?
_____	
6. My son's thirsty.	What _____ ?
_____	
7. I have a headache.	_____ some aspirin?
_____	

8. These boxes are heavy. _____ some help?

_____

9. _____ _____ ?

_____

Count / Non-Count Nouns

Dialog (In a cafeteria line)

Server: May I help you?
Customer: I would like some roast beef and some rice.
Server: What else?
Customer: Some beans and a roll. What's that?
Server: It's spinach. Would you like some?
Customer: No, thank you.

	SINGULAR	PLURAL
Count:	I'd like ⎡a roll. ⎣an apple.	I'd like (some) ⎡rolls. ⎣apples.
Non-count:	I'd like (some) ⎡rice. ⎣beef.	------------

Notes: 1. A count noun has a singular form and a plural form. (Example: *roll, rolls*)

2. A non-count noun has a singular form, but it does not have a plural form.
(Example: *rice, ⌀*).

3. A number (or *a* or *an*) can go before a count noun. (Examples: *an apple, one apple, five apples*)

4. A number (or *a* or *an*) can not go before a non-count noun.

Exercise 19.   MINI CONVERSATIONS.

Example: roast beef / rice
            beans / roll

Server: May I help you?
Customer: I'd like some <u>roast beef</u> and some <u>rice</u>.
Server: What else would you like?
Customer: Some <u>beans</u> and a <u>roll</u>.

1. chicken / broccoli
   potatoes / salad

2. meat / soup
   French fries / hamburger

3. cereal / milk
   strawberries / banana

4. bread / butter
   potato chips / sandwich

5. fruit / cheese
   crackers / cookie

6. lamb / corn
   peas / baked potato

7. coffee / juice
   pancakes / muffin

8. toast / jelly
   fried eggs / cup of tea

Exercise 20.

Write *a* or *an* before singular count nouns. Write *some* before non-count nouns and before plural nouns.

Server: What would you like?
Customer: I'd like ——————— .

1. *an* —— egg
2. *some* —— milk
3. *some* —— cookies
4. ——— carrot
5. ——— lettuce
6. ——— popcorn
7. ——— sugar

8. ——— tomato
9. ——— meat
10. ——— lemon
11. ——— grapes
12. ——— yogurt
13. ——— ketchup
14. ——— candy

15. ——— raisins
16. ——— ice
17. ——— salt
18. ——— honey
19. ——— cherries
20. ——— water
21. ——— olive

Exercise 21. MINI CONVERSATIONS.

Example: banana / cereal
            grape juice

Server: What would you like?
Customer: I'd like a banana and some cereal. What's that?
Server: It's grape juice.

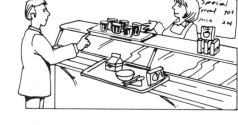

1. baked potato / beans
   spinach

2. soup / crackers
   banana bread

3. lettuce / vinegar and oil
   mushroom

4. orange / grapes
   avocado

5. lamb / rice
   pineapple juice

6. hot dog / mustard
   potato salad

7. omelette / toast
   cereal

8. ———— / ————
   ————

Exercise 22.
Follow the example sentences and use the words below to make sentences about the picture of the kitchen. Use the expressions from Exercise 23.

Examples: There is some fruit on top of the refrigerator.
There is a round table in the kitchen.
There are some cups in the cupboard.

1. _____ mushrooms _____ .
2. _____ juice _____ .
3. _____ apple _____ .
4. _____ glasses _____ .
5. _____ meat _____ .
6. _____ pears _____ .
7. _____ avocado _____ .
8. _____ vinegar _____ .
9. _____ watermelon _____ .
10. _____ frying pan _____ .

Exercise 23.
WRITING. Describe your kitchen. Use the sentences above as models. Include some of these expressions:

on the floor
on the counter
on the table
on the stove
on (top of) the refrigerator

on the wall
in the oven
in the cupboard
in the refrigerator
in the freezer

_____
_____
_____
_____
_____

Simple Present Tense: *Wh*-Questions

FORMULA 5-7	Wh-question word	do does	subject	verb [base form]	(complement) **?**

SINGULAR	PLURAL
How **do I** get to the main office? Who **do you** study with? Why **does Ed** often come to class late? How **does Carol** get to school? What time **does your class** begin?	Where **do we** buy our textbooks? What **do you and Rob** study? When **do they** do their homework?

Exercise 24. PAIRWORK.

Student A: Ask the questions above.
Student B: Respond with the correct answer from the list below.

He frequently misses the bus.
You buy them at the university bookstore.
It starts at 8:30.
We study business administration.
Her husband always gives her a ride.
Go upstairs. It's the first door on the left.
They usually do it in the afternoon.
I study with my roommate.

Exercise 25. INTERVIEW. Ask a classmate the following questions.

1. What time do you usually get up?
2. What do you usually do on weekday mornings?
3. When do you do your homework?
4. Where does your family live?
5. How do you spell your last name?
6. Where do you often go on Saturdays?
7. What kind of music do your parents like?
8. What kind of music do you enjoy?
9. What does your family usually do on Sundays?
10. What do you do in your free time?
11. How often do you go to movies?
12. What kind of movies do you like?
13. What languages do you speak?
14. What languages does our English teacher speak?
15. _____ ?

Exercise 26.

Make questions using terms from the columns below. Include verbs and complements. Ask a classmate your questions.

Question Word	Auxiliary	Subject	Verb (Base Form)	(Complement) ?
What		I	------------	------------
Where		you	------------	------------
When	do	we	------------	------------
Who		they	------------	------------
Why		------	------------	------------
How		he	------------	------------
What time	does	she	------------	------------
How often		it	------------	------------
What kind of . . .		------	------------	------------

Examples: Where do you eat lunch?
What kind of food do you like?
How often does it rain here this time of year?
What does your roommate do on weekends?

Expressions of Definite and Indefinite Quantity

FORMULA 5-8	a	measurement, container, or section word	of	food or substance noun

Examples: a pound of potatoes
a bowl of soup
a piece of chicken

Some count and non-count nouns combine with quantity expressions. The combination indicates a measurement, a container, or a section of a whole.

DEFINITE QUANTITY	
Measures	
gallon	liter
quart	pound
ounce	kilo
cup	teaspoon

INDEFINITE QUANTITY		
Containers		*Sections*
bowl	bottle	piece
glass	jar	slice
bag	tube	
can	carton	
sack	pitcher	
box	package	

Notes: 1. Other common quantity expressions: *loaf (of bread), head (of lettuce), bunch (of carrots, of grapes), ear (of corn), stick (of butter), bar (of soap), roll (of film).*

2. Examples of quantity expressions in the plural form: *two gallons of milk, many cans of beans*

3. An exception to FORMULA 5-8 and to Note 2 above: *a dozen eggs*

Exercise 27. Complete the shopping list. Write four or more items in each column.

SHOPPING LIST					
a bottle of *shampoo*	three cans of *soup*	a gallon of *water*	a box of *cereal*	two kilos of *coffee*	a jar of *face cream*

Exercise 28. PAIRWORK. You're at the grocery store. Your shopping list is at home on the kitchen table. Call home and ask your roommate to read your shopping list to you. Include the expressions of quantity for each item. For example: *Buy a bottle of shampoo, three cans of soup, a gallon of water, a box of cereal, . . .*

The Simple Present Tense: Negative Statements

FORMULA 5-9	Subject	**do** **does**	**not**	verb [base form]	(complement) .

Contractions: do not = **don't**
does not = **doesn't**

Examples: France and Italy **do not** have kings.
The king of Spain **doesn't** live in Barcelona.

Exercise 29.
Complete the sentences with *don't* or *doesn't* and with the appropriate forms of the verbs in parentheses.

(go)   1. The Amazon River _**goes**_ through Brazil, but it _**doesn't go**_ through Argentina.

(grow)   2. Coffee beans _____ in Mexico, but they _____ in the United States.

(have)   3. Austria _____ a president, but Norway _____ a president.

(rain)   4. It _____ a lot in Central Africa, but it _____ a lot in North Africa.

(border)   5. Turkey _____ on the Soviet Union, but Syria and Lebanon _____ on the Soviet Union.

(snow)   6. It _____ in China and Japan, but it _____ in Malaysia and Indonesia.

Exercise 30.
Complete the sentences with *isn't, aren't, doesn't,* or *don't.*

1. The geography students _____ taking a test now.
2. Penguins _____ live in Canada.
3. Peru _____ border on the Atlantic Ocean.
4. Bahrain _____ have any mountains.
5. Costa Rica and Panama _____ in South America.
6. Japan _____ export petroleum.
7. Paraguay and Bolivia _____ have a sea coast.
8. Colombia and Venezuela _____ import coffee.
9. Switzerland _____ produce cotton.
10. The geography professor _____ giving a lecture today.

Exercise 31.
Complete the sentences. For each pair of sentences use the appropriate negative form of the verb in the first sentence and the affirmative form in the second sentence.

(be)   1. Australia _____ a small island. It _____ a continent.

(have)   2. The United States _____ forty-eight states. It _____ fifty states.

(border)   3. Canada _____ on the Soviet Union. It _____ on the United States.

(be)   4. Guatemala and Honduras _____ in North America. They _____ in Central America.

(have)   5. Spain and Portugal _____ very cold winters. They _____ mild winters.

(   )   6. _____

Infinitives After Verbs: *have, like, need, want*

SUBJECT	VERB	INFINITIVE
I You We They	have like need want	to study
He She	has likes needs wants	to study

Notes: 1. An infinitive = **to** + the base form of a verb.
2. These infinitive expressions are simple present tense expressions. They are not used in the present continuous tense.
3. **have** + infinitive and **need** + infinitive are expressions of necessity.

Another infinitive expression is **know how** + infinitive. It expresses ability.

Examples: I **know how** to speak English.
Maria **knows how** to play the guitar.
My brothers **know how** to fly an airplane.

Exercise 32. Match the questions and short answers.

QUESTIONS

*D*____ 1. When do you want to eat lunch?

_____ 2. Where does Frank like to study?

_____ 3. Why do we need to leave now?

_____ 4. What do Tim and Ed want to do after class?

_____ 5. Do you know how to play the piano?

_____ 6. Does your brother need to see a doctor?

_____ 7. How do you like to travel?

_____ 8. When do you have to catch a plane?

_____ 9. What languages does your teacher know how to speak?

SHORT ANSWERS

(A) Because it's late.

(B) By train.

(C) Yes, we do.

(D) Now. I'm very hungry.

(E) In the library.

(F) Play tennis.

(G) Only English.

(H) No, he's fine now.

(I) At eight o'clock.

Exercise 33.   PAIRWORK. Ask and answer the questions.

STUDENT A   STUDENT B

1. What do you want to eat?   I want to eat a hamburger.

2. What does your mother need to buy?   My mother needs to buy a coat.

3. What do we have to study?   We have to study Chapter 5.

4. What does your sister like to read?   My sister likes to read business
                                                     magazines.

5. What do you want to watch?   I want to watch the news.

6. What does your roommate have to type?   My roommate has to type a letter.

7. What do your parents need to send you?   My parents need to send me some
                                                     money.

8. What do you like to cook?   I like to cook spaghetti.

Exercise 34.   PAIRWORK. Tell a classmate three things that you *need to* do today. Also tell your classmate three things that you *want to* do this weekend.

Exercise 35. Complete the sentences below with infinitive expressions.

This evening I have _____ , and I also have _____

_____ . After that I want _____ .

This weekend I need _____ . On Sundays I like _____

_____ , and I like _____ .

Exercise 36. INTERVIEW/WRITING. Complete the nine questions below. Use a variety of verbs. Ask a classmate your questions. Then write sentences about your classmate using his or her answers.

1. What do you like _____ ?
2. What do you need _____ ?
3. What do you want _____ ?
4. What do you have _____ ?
5. Where do you like _____ ?
6. Where do you want _____ ?
7. When do you need _____ ?
8. When do you have _____ ?
9. Do you know how _____ ?

Wh- Question Review

Exercise 37. PAIRWORK. Complete with a question word (*who, what, when, where,* or *how*), and *is, are, does,* or *do.* Ask and answer the questions with a classmate.

Wh-QUESTIONS	SHORT ANSWERS
1. ***Where are*** _____ you going?	To school.
2. _____ the train arrive?	At 9:45.
3. _____ you leaving?	At 12:30.
4. _____ I need for the trip?	A passport and a visa.
5. _____ you usually eat dinner with?	My roommate.
6. _____ your notebook?	At home.
7. _____ Mr. Seltzer teach?	Mathematics.
8. _____ your family usually go on vacation?	To the coast.
9. _____ her students doing now?	They're taking a test.
10. _____ your brother admire?	Our grandfather.
11. _____ the Summer Olympics begin?	In July.
12. _____ Pat talking to on the phone?	Her mother.
13. _____ you today?	I'm fine.
14. _____ "glad" mean?	It means "happy."

Exercise 38.

Read the answers below. Write *Wh*-questions with *who, what, when,* and *where* that correspond to the underlined parts of the answers. Use *do, does, is,* or *are.*

1. ___*When do you do your laundry?*___   I do my laundry on Mondays.
2. _____   James and William play football.
3. _____   My boyfriend lives in Osaka.
4. _____   My family eats out on Saturdays.
5. _____   She calls her sister every weekend.
6. _____   I usually play tennis with Mike.
7. _____   Mark is calling his boss.
8. _____   My brothers work in a bank.
9. _____   Mrs. Rose goes to work at 8:00.
10. _____   The secretaries are typing letters.
11. _____   Pat's brother plays the violin.
12. _____   The scientists are working in their laboratory.

Exercise 39.

INTERVIEW. Make *Wh*-questions using some of the expressions below. Ask a classmate your questions.

Examples: Where do you usually eat lunch?
             What do you do on weekends?

live	eat lunch	come to class	go on vacation
work	exercise	make supper	go swimming
study	go to bed	do on weekends	have for breakfast

Exercise 40.

WRITING. Use your classmate's answers in **Exercise 39** to write about him or her.

Activities

A. RIDDLES. What are the answers?

1. In what English word does the letter *o* sound like the letter *i*?
2. When does Friday come before Thursday?
3. Where do cows go on dates?
4. Why do cows wear bells?
5. If your uncle's sister is not your aunt, what relation is she to you?

B. PARAGRAPH COMPLETION. Complete the passage below. In each sentence write the correct form of the verb and another appropriate word. Use each verb from the box below only once.

go	wake	eat	have	ride	discuss
live	give	like	meet	attend	

The President's Day

The President of _the_ United States _lives_ in the White House in Washington, D. C. He usually _____ up _____ 6:30. He _____ breakfast _____ his family. The President frequently _____ to the Capitol in _____ limousine. At the Capitol he _____ the economy with senators _____ representatives. _____ President occasionally _____ a speech to the Congress. The President and foreign officials often _____ lunch at _____ White House.

Every afternoon the President _____ with _____ advisors in the Oval Office. The President sometimes _____ to receptions at embassies _____ Washington, D.C. The President _____ to listen _____ music. After dinner he and his _____ occasionally _____ concerts at the Kennedy Center for the Performing Arts.

C. ROLE PLAY / INTERVIEW.
Student A: Play the role of the leader of a country.
Student B: Play the role of a TV reporter. Interview the leader about his or her daily routine, interests, and other topics. Use some of the question types below.

Do you (and your wife / advisors / vice president)_____?

What do you _____?

When do you _____?

Where do you _____?

How frequently do you _____?

Do you (sometimes / often) _____?

What do you like to / want to / need to / have to_____?

D. WRITING.
1. Write about the daily routine of a real or a fictitious political leader.
2. Write about an animal. Describe it and write about its habits.
3. Write about the perfect/ideal job for you. What do you do in your perfect job?

E. GUESSING GAME. Think of an animal. Classmates ask you *yes-no* questions using verbs in the box below or other verbs. They try to guess the animal.

have	walk	swim	run	climb	attack
fly	live	eat	drink	sleep	weigh

Examples: Does it __walk__ ? Yes, it does.
Does it __have four legs__? No, it doesn't.
Is it a(n) _____ ? No, it isn't.

F. PUZZLE.

GROCERY PRICES	
a quart of orange juice = $.89	a carton of yogurt = $.54
a gallon of milk = $1.15	a loaf of bread = $.98
a pound of hamburger = $2.00	a dozen eggs = $1.12
a bottle of ketchup = $.99	a box of cereal = $1.60
a can of soup = $.64	a tube of toothpaste = $1.95

On Saturday Scott Morgan goes to the supermarket. He buys the groceries on his list below. How much does Scott spend (total)? $_____.

SHOPPING LIST	
4 cartons of yogurt	3 cans of soup
1 box of cereal	1/2 dozen eggs
2 gallons of milk	2 loaves of bread
3 1/2 pounds of hamburger	1 tube of toothpaste
2 bottles of ketchup	5 quarts of orange juice

G. DICTATION. You will hear each sentence two times. Write exactly what you hear.

1. _____ .
2. _____ .
3. _____ .
4. _____ .
5. _____ .
6. _____ .
7. _____ .
8. _____ .
9. _____ .

Review Quizzes

A. LISTENING COMPREHENSION: SENTENCES

For each problem, you will hear a short sentence. You will hear each sentence two times. After you hear a sentence, read the four choices. Decide which written sentence is the closest in meaning to the spoken sentence. Circle the letter of the correct answer.

1. (A) They rarely work late.
   (B) They usually work late.
   (C) They seldom arrive late.
   (D) They usually arrive late.

2. (A) He phones him every week.
   (B) He phones her every week.
   (C) He phones them every week.
   (D) He phones us every week.

3. (A) She never gets bad grades.
   (B) She never gets good grades.
   (C) She always gets bad grades.
   (D) She often gets good grades.

4. (A) We need to make dinner.
   (B) They have to cook dinner.
   (C) We have to cook lunch.
   (D) They need to make lunch.

5. (A) There isn't milk in the kitchen.
   (B) We have some milk.
   (C) There's some milk in the chicken.
   (D) We don't have milk.

6. (A) I don't want to live here.
   (B) I want to leave here.
   (C) I want to stay here.
   (D) I don't want to stay here.

7. (A) She rarely arrives late.
   (B) She usually arrives late.
   (C) He rarely arrives late.
   (D) He usually arrives late.

8. (A) We give her a present.
   (B) We give him a present.
   (C) We give you a present.
   (D) We give them a present.

9. (A) They swim in the lake every day.
   (B) They go to the lake every day.
   (C) They aren't swimming in the lake now.
   (D) They're at the lake now.

10. (A) She needs to work.
    (B) She has to work.
    (C) She doesn't need to work.
    (D) She doesn't want to work.

B. STRUCTURE: SENTENCE COMPLETION.

Choose the *one* word or phrase that best completes the sentence. Circle the letter of the correct answer.

1. My sister -------- to school every day.
   (A) walk
   (B) walks
   (C) walking
   (D) is walk

2. People in my hometown --------
   German.
   (A) speak
   (B) speaks
   (C) speaking
   (D) is speaking

3. Those are Richard's gloves. Please give
   -------- to --------.
   (A) it ... him
   (B) it ... you
   (C) them ... you
   (D) them ... him

4. When -------- your airplane --------?
   (A) do ... leave
   (B) does ... leave
   (C) does ... leaves
   (D) is does ... leave

5. When do you -------- lunch?

   (A) usually eats
   (B) eats usually
   (C) usually eat
   (D) eat usually

6. -------- to her now?

   (A) Does he talking
   (B) Does he talks
   (C) Is he talks
   (D) Is he talking

7. She has --------.

   (A) a ice cream cone
   (B) an university class at night
   (C) a uncle in Montreal
   (D) an hour to finish the exam

8. What --------?

   (A) does mean "throw"
   (B) does means "throw"
   (C) means "throw"
   (D) does "throw" mean

9. My mother and father are sick.
   I'm helping --------.

   (A) them
   (B) they
   (C) their
   (D) me

10. -------- you happy with your new car?

    (A) Is
    (B) Are
    (C) Do
    (D) Does

11. My parents -------- not like loud music.

    (A) do
    (B) does
    (C) is
    (D) are

12. What -------- he doing now?

    (A) is
    (B) are
    (C) do
    (D) does

13. She -------- on weekends.

    (A) isn't work
    (B) isn't works
    (C) doesn't work
    (D) doesn't works

14. Where --------?

    (A) is he live
    (B) do he lives
    (C) does he live
    (D) does he lives

15. My father -------- the newspaper every
    morning.

    (A) read
    (B) reads
    (C) reading
    (D) is read

16. It -------- today.

    (A) snow
    (B) snows
    (C) snowing
    (D) is snowing

17. She -------- to class every day.

    (A) hurrying
    (B) is hurrying
    (C) hurrys
    (D) hurries

18. She needs -------- tonight.

    (A) study
    (B) studies
    (C) to study
    (D) to studying

19. -------- your husband -------- at night?

    (A) Is ... work
    (B) Do ... works
    (C) Does ... work
    (D) Does ... works

C. STRUCTURE: ERROR IDENTIFICATION

Each sentence has four underlined words or phrases. Circle the *one* underlined word or phrase that is not correct. Then correct the sentence.

1. She <u>wants</u> <u>to study</u> at <u>an</u> university <u>in</u> Paris.
        A   B   C   D

2. He <u>dosen't</u> <u>like</u> <u>to clean</u> his apartment <u>every week</u>.
        A   B   C   D

3. <u>Do</u> <u>your</u> new car <u>have</u> <u>a radio</u>?
    A   B   C   D

4. I <u>usually</u> <u>gets</u> up early <u>on</u> Saturday <u>mornings</u>.
       A   B   C   D

5. <u>Do</u> you want <u>go</u> <u>to a</u> movie <u>with me</u> tonight?
    A   B   C   D

6. They <u>washes</u> <u>their</u> <u>clothes</u> once <u>a week</u>.
          A   B   C   D

7. <u>Where</u> <u>does</u> <u>she</u> eating lunch <u>this</u> afternoon?
     A   B   C   D

8. <u>My grandmother</u> <u>is cleaning</u> <u>her house</u> every <u>Friday afternoon</u>.
         A   B   C   D

9. <u>Are</u> you <u>usually</u> <u>watch</u> television <u>on</u> Tuesday evenings?
    A   B   C   D

10. I <u>work</u> <u>at</u> night, and they <u>also</u> <u>are work</u> at night.
       A   B   C   D

11. <u>Does</u> he busy <u>this semester</u> with <u>his</u> classes <u>at the</u> university?
      A   B   C   D

12. My friends Carol and Pat are <u>basketball players</u>, but <u>they're</u> not <u>very</u> <u>talls</u>.
                          A   B   C D

13. I <u>am looking</u> for <u>a</u> umbrella because <u>it</u> <u>is raining</u> now.
         A   B   C   D

14. I <u>have go</u> <u>to bed</u> <u>early tonight</u> because I have <u>an important test</u> at 8:00 tomorrow
        A   B   C   D
    morning.

15. I'm taking the records to my boyfriend. <u>I'm</u> giving <u>it</u> to <u>him</u> for <u>his</u> birthday.
                                         A   B   C   D

CHAPTER 6

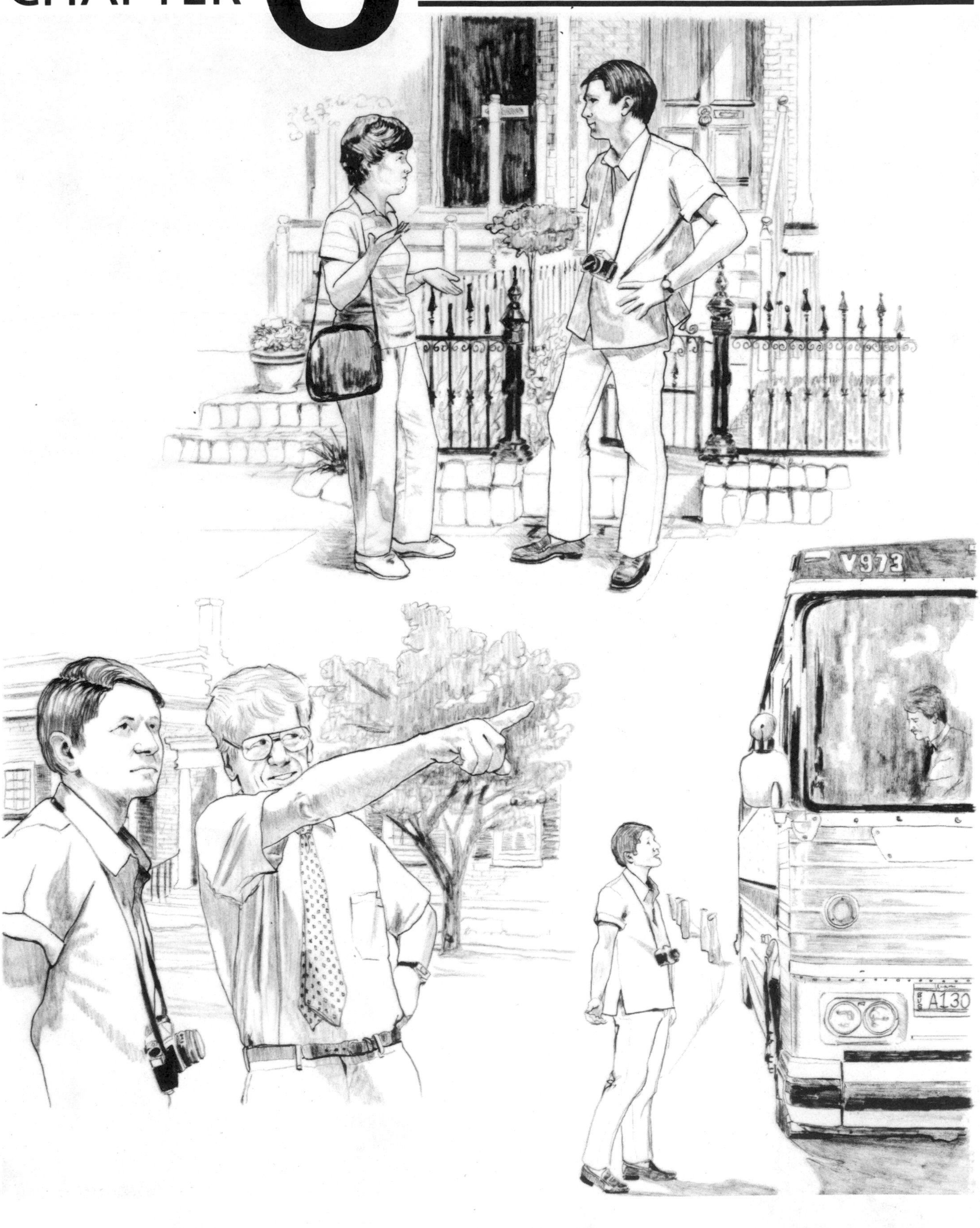

A tourist stops a woman on a street in San Antonio, Texas.

Tourist: Excuse me. Can you tell me how to get to the Witte Museum
on Broadway?

Woman: I'm sorry. I'm not from San Antonio. I'm new in town.

Tourist: Thanks, anyway.

The tourist walks to the corner and asks a businessman for directions.

Tourist: Excuse me. I'm looking for the Witte Museum on Broadway. Can you tell me how
to get there?

Businessman: I don't have any idea. I'm just visiting San Antonio. But I'm going to catch a bus
here to the zoo. You can ask the bus driver for directions. The bus is going to be
here in a few minutes.

Tourist: That's a good idea. I'm from Houston, and I don't know my way around
San Antonio.

Businessman: How long are you going to be in San Antonio?

Tourist: Only a few days. I'm going to return home next Tuesday.

Businessman: Are you enjoying your visit here?

Tourist: Yes, I am. What do you think of San Antonio?

Businessman: I like it a lot. This is my first visit to Texas. I'm attending a business convention,
but I have a little free time this afternoon. I'm from Detroit, and it's cold and
snowy there now. I like the warm weather here. Oh, here comes the bus.

The businessman gets on the bus. The tourist stands outside the bus and looks up at the bus driver.

Bus Driver: Can I help you?

Tourist: I'm going to the Witte Museum. Can you give me directions?

Bus Driver: This bus goes to the Witte Museum.

Tourist: How far is it?

Bus Driver: It's ten minutes from here by bus.

Tourist: How much is the fare?

Bus Driver: It's seventy-five cents. Exact change only.

Tourist: Okay, thanks.

The tourist boards the bus, puts three quarters in the fare box, and takes a seat.

Bus Driver: Attention, everyone. There is something wrong with the engine. You have to get
off this bus and wait for the next bus.

Exercise 1. Answer the questions.

1. Where is the Witte Museum?
2. Can the woman give directions to the museum?
3. Where is the businessman going?
4. How is he going to get there?
5. What is the businessman doing in San Antonio?
6. When is the tourist going to return to Houston?
7. What is the problem with the bus?
8. What do the passengers have to do?

- -

9. Do you often visit museums?
10. What's your favorite museum?
11. Do you know your way around town?
12. Do you frequently take a city bus?
13. How much is the bus fare where you live?

Pronunciation of [ü] and [u̇]

 Exercise 2. **A.** Listen to the difference between the pronunciation of [ü] and [u̇]. Then repeat the words.

[ü]	[u̇]
new	**book**
museum	**cook**
usually	**look**
Tuesday	**goo**d
z**oo**	f**u**ll

B. Listen to the sentences. Repeat the sentences. Then circle the [ü] sounds and underline the [u̇] sounds.

1. San Antonio has a good zoo, a few museums, and many restaurants.
2. You can look in the guide book for some good restaurants.
3. The new restaurant on Houston Street has a full menu and a good cook.
4. It's open on Tuesdays, and dinner for two is usually under twenty dollars.

Can: Ability and Possibility

One use of *can* is to express ability. Another use of *can* is to express possibility. *Can* is not a verb; it is an auxiliary. It never ends with *-ing* or *-s. Do* and *does* are not used as auxiliaries with *can* in negative statements or in questions. The verb after *can* is always in the base form.

FORMULA 6-1	Subject	**can (not)**	verb [base]	(complement) .

Examples: I **can** fly a plane.   (ability)
Sandy **cannot** drive a car.   (ability)
I **can** wash your car today.   (possibility)
I **can't** buy a new car this year.   (possibility)
We **can't** watch TV because the TV is broken.   (possibility)

Note: can not = cannot = can't
$\left(\text{formal} \longleftrightarrow \text{informal}\right)$

In formal writing use **can not.**

FORMULA 6-2

(Wh-word [+ noun])	**can**	subject	verb	(complement) **?**

Examples: **Can** you cook?   (ability)
What **can** you make?   (ability)
What desserts **can** you make?   (ability)
Can you help me now or are you busy?   (possibility)
Where **can** we buy tickets for the concert?   (possibility)

QUESTIONS	SHORT ANSWERS	
	Affirmative	*Negative*
Can you type?	Yes, I can.	No, I can't.
Can she type?	Yes, she can.	No, she can't.
Can they type?	Yes, they can.	No, they can't.

Exercise 3. MINI CONVERSATIONS.

Example: you go to a movie with me on Friday
on Sunday

Mark: Can you go to a movie with me on Friday?
Chris: No, I can't, but I can go to a movie with you on Sunday.

1. you play the guitar
   play the drums

2. your mother cook Italian food
   cook Mexican food

3. you run five miles
   run three miles

4. you and your sister speak German
   speak French

5. you have lunch with me on Wednesday
   have dinner with you on Wednesday

6. Tom fix a TV
   fix a radio

7. Yoko and Akiro play basketball
   play volleyball

8. Silvia ride a motorcycle
   ride a bicycle

9. _____

_____

Exercise 4. MINI CONVERSATIONS.

Example: you speak Chinese
speak Korean

Terry: Can you speak Chinese?
Jan: Yes, I can.
Terry: Oh, come on. Can you really speak Chinese?
Jan: Yes, and I can speak Korean too.

1. you type 100 words per minute
   take shorthand

2. Mr. and Mrs. Cheng read Arabic
   read Persian

3. you run a mile in four minutes
   run three miles in twelve minutes

4. Khalid do 100 push-ups
   do 100 push-ups

5. Ana fly a plane
   fly a helicopter

6. _____

   _____

Exercise 5.   INTERVIEW. Interview a classmate. Your classmate will also interview you.

1. Can you cook?
2. Can you make a pizza?
3. What kind of food can you cook?
4. Can you eat with chopsticks?
5. Can you ride a bicycle?
6. Can your mother drive a car?
7. Can your father ride a horse?
8. Can you play a musical instrument?
9. What sports can you play?
10. How many languages can you speak?
11. What can you do well?
12. Can _____ ?
13. What _____ ?

Exercise 6.   Complete the sentences. Use *can* or *can't* and an appropriate verb from the box.

| play   cook   go   drive   type   remember   ride   speak |

Example: I _**can play**_ the violin.

1. I _____ _____ French.

2. My mother _____ _____ a truck.

3. I _____ _____ 60 words a minute.

4. My father _____ _____ a bicycle.

5. _____ Mr. Li _____ Chinese food?

   Yes, he _____ _____ Chinese food very well.

6. I _____ _____ my third birthday.

7. Carmen _____ _____ to school today. She is very sick.

Count / Non-Count Nouns

A and *an* can come before a singular count noun (*a lemon, an orange*).

A and *an* cannot come before a plural count noun (*oranges*), or before a non-count noun (*sugar*).

Use *some* before a plural count noun (*some oranges*), or before a non-count noun (*some sugar*).

There are many nouns in English that are usually or always non-count.

Some common non-count nouns are in the box below.

Materials	Abstractions	Generalities	Activities/Subjects
gold	help	luggage	shopping
oil	advice	furniture	dancing
water	information	clothing	skiing
air	hunger	jewelry	tennis
paper	intelligence	money	chess
wood	love	mail	writing
corn	happiness	traffic	music
salt	peace	machinery	math
beef	luck	pollution	chemistry
blood	beauty	garbage	homework

Exercise 7. Write *a, an,* or *some* before each word.

1. I see ___*a*___ woman.
2. I see ___*some*___ women.
3. I need ___*some*___ advice.
4. I have _____ silver.
5. I attend _____ university.
6. I have _____ homework.
7. I need _____ information.

8. I need _____ bread.
9. I have _____ money.
10. I have _____ dollar.
11. I have _____ hour.
12. I have _____ luggage.
13. I have _____ mail.
14. I see _____ people.

Exercise 8. Add a plural ending to the count nouns in the sentences.

1. My dad is going to buy some magazine__*s*__ , some milk___ , some bread___ , some beef___ , and some jar___ of jelly at the supermarket.

2. To make the salad, Cindy is combining some lettuce___ , some carrot___ , some cheese___ , some tomato___ , and some vinegar___ and oil___ .

3. Before going on the trip I need to get some guide book___ , some luggage___ , some film___ , and some flash cube___ for my camera.

4. The secretary is ordering some furniture___ , some ink___ , some pencil___ , and some paper___ for the office.

5. The boss is asking his employees for some help___ , some information___ , some idea___ , and some hard work___ .

Exercise 9.

Complete the sentences. Write *a* or *an* before singular count nouns, but not before plural count nouns or before non-count nouns. Capitalize the first word of each sentence. Write the correct forms of the verbs in parentheses. Use singular verb forms after non-count nouns and after singular count nouns.

Examples: **A**   king **rules** (rule) for life.

          M   ~~m~~oney sometimes **causes** (cause) problems.

          D   ~~d~~ogs **have** (have) a good sense of smell.

1. _____ engineering _____ (be) my favorite subject.
2. _____ rain on roads can _____ (cause) auto accidents.
3. _____ emerald _____ (be) an expensive jewel.
4. _____ piece of cake _____ (have) many calories.
5. _____ skiing _____ (be) an enjoyable sport.
6. _____ American dollar bills _____ (be) green.
7. _____ paper _____ (be) usually cheap.
8. _____ hunger _____ (be) a serious problem in the world.
9. _____ countries without petroleum _____ (need) to import oil.
10. _____ big boat _____ (cost) a lot of money.

Exercise 10.

Make sentences using the following words.

Examples: coffee   *American coffee is not strong.*
                            I like coffee.
                            Coffee can be bad for you.
                            Colombia exports coffee.

1. money
2. love
3. homework
4. music
5. rice
6. orange juice
7. snow
8. gold
9. diamonds
10. oil
11. swimming
12. roses

Future Tense: *Be* + *Going* + Infinitive

Dialog

Pat: What are you going to do during vacation?
Nick: I'm going to go to Mexico.
Pat: Are you going to go alone?
Nick: No, I'm not. My brother is going to travel with me.
Pat: Where are you going to go in Mexico?
Nick: We're going to visit Mexico City and Acapulco.
Pat: Are you going to fly to Mexico?
Nick: Yes, we are.
Pat: Have a nice trip.
Nick: Thanks.

FORMULA 6-3	Subject	am is are	(not)	going to	verb [base]	(complement) .

Examples: I'**m going to** travel to Miami tomorrow morning.
My brother and I **are going to** go to the beach.
We'**re going to** buy some presents for our parents.
Pat **isn't going to** leave town during vacation.
Nick and his brother **aren't going to** drive to Mexico.

FORMULA 6-4	(Wh-word)	am is are	subject	going to	verb [base]	(complement) ?

Examples:

Is Nick **going to** miss any classes?
Are Nick and his brother **going to** see a bullfight?

What is Pat **going to** do next week?
When are Nick and his brother **going to** return?

Short Answers

No, he isn't.
Yes, they are.

Answers

She's going to study.
They're going to
return next Sunday night.

Exercise 11.

Complete the sentences with the correct words to express future time. Some blanks need more than one word.

1. I _____ going _____ visit friends tomorrow night.

2. My brother _____ going _____ at the library this afternoon.

3. Is _____ going _____ study here next year?

4. Pat and I are _____ complete our term papers next month.

5. _____ your teacher going _____ give you homework during vacation?

6. Nick's brother _____ not _____ miss class next Monday.

7. What _____ you _____ to do next semester?

Exercise 12.

Complete the dialog. Use the words in parentheses with forms of *be* and *going to*.

Chris: _____ ?
(you / graduate in May)

Lee: No, _____ .

Chris: _____ ?
(When / you / graduate)

Lee: _____ .
       (I / graduate / next December)

Chris: _____ ?
       (What / you / do after graduation)

Lee: _____ .'
       (I / look for a job in my hometown)

Future Time Expressions

tomorrow_____	*next_____*	*in_____*	*_____ from_____*
tomorrow	next week	in five minutes	five minutes from now
tomorrow morning	next Monday	in an hour	an hour from now
tomorrow afternoon	next month	in two days	two days from now
tomorrow evening	next winter	in three weeks	three weeks from now
tomorrow night	next year	in four months	a month from now
tomorrow at 8:00	the week after next	in a year	five years from now
the day after tomorrow		in a few minutes	in a few days from now
		in a little while	a week from tomorrow
		in a couple of hours	two weeks from today

Exercise 13.   MINI CONVERSATIONS.

Example: we / have a test this week
               next week

Ian: Are we going to have a test this week?
Lee: No, we aren't.
Ian: When are we going to have a test?
Lee: We're going to have a test next week.

1. we / play cards tonight
   tomorrow night

2. you / play golf tomorrow
   the day after tomorrow

3. Susan / travel to South America
      next summer
   next fall

4. you / buy a new car this year
   in two years

5. Tom and Cher / get married this month
   next month

6. Mohammed / graduate two years from now
   a year from now

7. you / practice the piano now
   in a little while

8. you and your family / go to the zoo next
      Saturday
   next Sunday

9. _____ / _____

   _____

Exercise 14. INTERVIEW / WRITING.

A. On a piece of paper write six or more questions for an interview with a classmate. Use *Formula 6-4* to make *Wh-* and *yes-no* questions.

B. Ask a classmate your questions. Take notes.

C. Use your classmate's answers to write complete sentences in the third person (*he, she, they*).

Some and any

Affirmative (+)	I have **an** eraser. I have **some** pencils. I have **some** paper.
Negative (−) (**not**)	I don't have **a** stamp. I don't have **any** envelopes. I don't have **any** money.
Interrogative (?)	Do you have **a** stamp? Do you have **any** envelopes? Do you have **any** money? Do you have **some** envelopes? Do you have **some** money?

Notes: 1. Use *a(n)* with singular count nouns (*stamp, eraser*).
2. Use *some* and *any* with non-count nouns (*paper, money*) and with plural count nouns (*pencils, envelopes*).
3. In questions you can use either *any* or *some*. *Any* is more frequent in questions than *some*, but they have similar meanings.

Exercise 15. MINI CONVERSATIONS.

Jamal: Do you have any coffee or tea?
Abdul: I have some coffee, but I don't have any tea.

  1. milk or cream
  2. lemons or limes
  3. rice or potatoes

  4. butter or margarine
  5. sugar or honey
  6. _____

Exercise 16. Complete the sentences with *a, an, some,* or *any*.

  1. We need _____ groceries.

  2. We don't have _____ tomatoes.

  3. There isn't _____ lettuce.

  4. We need to buy _____ bottle of ketchup.

  5. We need _____ meat.

  6. Do you want _____ strawberries?

7. Do you want _____ juice?

8. Do we need to buy _____ onion?

9. We don't need to buy _____ bread or _____ cheese.

Very + **Adjective**

Very is an intensifier. It can emphasize adjectives. It cannot emphasize nouns.

Examples: He is **very short.**
He is **very handsome.**
He is **very popular**.

Exercise 17. Complete the following passage about South Texas. Use the correct present tense form of *be, very,* and an adjective from the box. Use each adjective only once.

hot	big	dry
delicious	cold	sunny
✔long	friendly	

South Texas

The Rio Grande River separates the state of Texas from the Republic of Mexico. The Rio Grande _**is very long**_. It extends 1885 miles from northern New Mexico to the Gulf of Mexico. The region north of the Rio Grande River near the Gulf of Mexico is called South Texas.

Summer daytime temperatures in South Texas are frequently over 100° Fahrenheit. Summers _____ and very long in South Texas. Summer days are long and the sun shines a lot, so it _____ . Because it rarely rains in South Texas during the summer, this region _____ in August.

Temperatures rarely go below 35° in South Texas during the winter. Winters there _____ not _____ . Grapefruits are an important winter crop in South Texas. Grapefruits from there _____ , and they _____ also _____ .

The mild winter climate attracts many older visitors to South Texas from northern states. They often stay in South Texas for several months during the winter. Because the visitors come from cold places, people in South Texas call them "Snow Birds." Texans welcome the winter visitors. The people in South Texas _____ .

Exercise 18.

Use *very* before adjectives. Use *a lot of* before nouns in affirmative statements. Use *much* or *many* before nouns in negative statements.

1. He has *a lot of* money.

   He is *very* rich.

2. She has _____ friends.

   She doesn't have _____ enemies.

   She is _____ nice.

3. Their teachers give them _____ homework.

   They are _____ busy this semester.

   They don't have _____ free time.

4. This coffee is _____ hot, but it's not _____ fresh.

5. I'm _____ hungry.

   I hope there is _____ food.

6. He can't lift _____ weight.

   He isn't _____ strong.

7. There are _____ Mexicans in the United States. There aren't _____ Mexicans in Japan. Japan is _____ far from Mexico.

8. This exercise is not _____ difficult.

Could: Ability in the Past

George Marshall is seventy-four years old. When he was fourteen he **could** play football, but he **can't** play football now. He **could** also climb trees, but he **can't** climb trees now. George **can** speak three languages now, but he **couldn't** speak three languages when he was young. He **can** also play the piano, but he **couldn't** sixty years ago.

Exercise 19. Answer the questions.

1. What could George do before, but he can't do now?
2. What couldn't George do before, but he can do now?
3. What could you do before, but you can't do now?
4. What couldn't you do five years ago, but you can do now?

 ## Exercise 20. MINI CONVERSATIONS.

Example: you roller skate

Marie: Can <u>you roller skate</u>?
Alex: I could <u>roller skate</u> when <u>I was</u> young, but <u>I</u> can't now.

1. you run fast
2. your uncle swim across the lake
3. your parents play tennis
4. you stay up all night

5. your sister do gymnastics
6. you do fifty sit-ups
7. your friends play football
8. _____

Exercise 21. Fill in each blank with *can, could,* or *couldn't* and one of the verbs in the following box. Use some of the verbs more than once.

understand	speak	read	write

Last year I ___*could speak*___ only a little English. I _____ very easy books, but I _____ newspapers or magazines. I _____ English movies. I _____ short personal letters in English, but I _____ compositions.

Now I _____ a lot of English with my American friends. I _____ movies in English, and I _____ newspapers and magazines.

Could: **Possibility in the Past**

Rita Lopez is from Guadalajara, Mexico. She was studying in Grenoble, France last year. In France she **could** eat French food every day, but she **couldn't** eat Mexican food very often. Rita **could** practice French every day, but she **couldn't** use Spanish very often. Telephone calls to Mexico were very expensive. Rita **couldn't** call her family very often, but she **could** write to her family every week.

Exercise 22. Answer the questions.

1. Where was Rita studying last year?
2. What could she do there every day?
3. What couldn't she do there every day?
4. Think about Rita's situation. What are some other things (not in the passage) that Rita could do in France?
5. What are some other things that Rita couldn't do in France?

Exercise 23. MINI CONVERSATIONS.

Example:　Silvia go to the class party last Saturday
　　　　　　out of town

Marie:　Could Silvia go to the class party last Saturday?
Paul:　　No, she couldn't go to the class party because she was out of town.

1. you enter the exam room
   late
2. Tom give his speech in class yesterday
   very nervous
3. Sarah ski down the mountain
   afraid
4. you study all night
   sleepy
5. Marcia fly to Hawaii last summer
   pregnant

6. your teacher come to school last week
   sick
7. The Nelsons take a trip last summer
   broke
8. you finish the test
   not prepared
9. Ana and Tim go to the movies last Friday
   busy
10. _____

   _____

Non-Count Nouns and Plural Count Nouns:
many, much, a lot of; a few, a little

	PLURAL COUNT NOUNS	NON-COUNT NOUNS
Affirmative	Sue has **a lot of** cups for the party. Sue also has **many** glasses. Sue has **a few** paper plates.	Sue has **a lot of** vanilla ice cream. Sue has **a little** chocolate ice cream.
Negative (**not**)	She doesn't have **many** napkins. She doesn't have **a lot of** napkins.	She doesn't have **much** cake. She doesn't have **a lot of** cake.
Interrogative	Does she have **many** spoons? Does she have **a lot of** spoons? Does she have **a few** knives? How **many** forks does she have?	Does she have **much** coffee? Does she have **a lot of** coffee? Does she have **a little** cream? How **much** sugar does she need?

Notes:
1. *Much, many, a lot of* = a large quantity or a large number of something
2. *A little, a few* = a small quantity or a small number of something
3. In affirmative statements, *a lot of* is more common than *many*.
4. *Much* is rarely used in affirmative statements.

Exercise 24.
PAIRWORK. Ask questions with *how much* or *how many*. Answer the questions with *a little* or *a few*.

STUDENT A

1. How much ice cream do you need?
2. How many bowls do you have?
3. How many spoons do you need?
4. How much coffee do you want?
5. How much cream do you want?
6. How many balloons do you have?
7. How much soda pop do you need?
8. How many sandwiches do you have?
9. How many paper plates do you need?
10. How much cheese do you want?
11. How much _____ ?
12. How many _____

STUDENT B

I need a little ice cream.
I have a few bowls.
I need a few spoons.
I want a little coffee.
I want a little cream.
I have a few balloons.
I need a little soda pop.
I have a few sandwiches.
I need a few paper plates.
I want a little cheese.
_____
_____

Exercise 25.   PAIRWORK. Ask questions with *a lot of*. Answer with *much* or *many*.

STUDENT A		STUDENT B

1. Does Georgia produce a lot of peanuts? 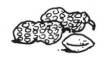 Yes, Georgia produces many peanuts.

2. Does Massachusetts produce a lot of tobacco?  No, Massachusetts doesn't produce much tobacco.

3. Does Iowa produce a lot of peaches?  No, Iowa doesn't produce many peaches.

4. Does Florida produce a lot of cotton?  No, Florida doesn't produce much cotton.

5. Does Washington produce a lot of apples? Yes, Washington produces many apples.

6. Does New Jersey produce a lot of potatoes?  No, New Jersey doesn't produce many potatoes.

7. Does Arizona produce a lot of corn?  No, Arizona doesn't produce much corn.

8. Does California produce a lot of silver? 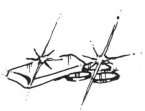 No, California doesn't produce much silver.

Exercise 26.

A. Answer the questions with *a lot of, only a little, only a few,* or *any.*

Examples: Do you drink much coffee?   Yes, I drink *a lot of* coffee.
                                                                         No, I drink *only a little* coffee.
                                                                         No, I don't drink *any* coffee.

                   Do you eat a lot of eggs?   Yes, I eat *a lot of* eggs.
                                                                         No, I eat *only a few* eggs.
                                                                         No, I don't eat *any* eggs.

1. Do you eat a lot of apples?   _____
2. Do you drink much orange juice?   _____
3. Do you eat much candy?   _____
4. Do you drink a lot of tea?   _____
5. Do you eat a lot of hamburgers?   _____
6. Do you eat a lot of lamb?   _____

B.   Write four questions similar to questions 1–6 in part **A**. Ask a classmate your questions.

Exercise 27.

Complete the questions with *much* or *many*. Complete the answers with *many, a lot of, a few,* or *a little*. Add other necessary words.

Examples:

Does Mexico export **many** tomatoes?   Is there **much** oil in Kuwait?
Yes, it exports **many** tomatoes.   Yes, there is **a lot of** oil in Kuwait.

1. Does Thailand export _____ rice?

    Yes, Thailand exports _____ rice.

2. Are there _____ diamonds in South Africa?

    Yes, there are _____ in South Africa.

3. Does the United Kingdom produce _____ corn?

    No, _____ only produces _____ .

4. Does Japan have _____ natural resources?

    No, _____ only _____ .

5. Does the United States import _____ coffee?

    Yes, _____ .

6. Do Spain and Italy grow _____ olives?

    Yes, _____ .

7. Is there _____ gold in Brazil?

    No, _____ only _____ .

8. _____ ?

    _____ .

Exercise 28. Write four *yes/no* questions about countries and their natural resources. Use the questions in Exercise 27 as examples. Ask classmates your questions.

Exercise 29. WRITING. Write about natural resources in your country. Use the answers in Exercise 27 as models.

Can and *May:* Permission

QUESTIONS		ANSWERS	
1. Tatsuo:	**Can** I borrow your dictionary?	Nicolas:	Yes, you **can**.
2. Student:	**May** I leave class early today?	Teacher:	Yes, you **may**.
3. Son:	**Can** I borrow the car tonight?	Father:	No, you **can't**.
4. Students:	**May** we smoke in class?	Professor:	No, you **may not**.

STATEMENTS

1. Parking lot attendant: You **can't** park your car here. You **can** park it over there.
2. Librarian: I'm sorry, but you **may not** eat in the library. You **may** eat in the snack bar.

Notes: 1. The third use of *can* is to express permission. This use of *can* is common in informal English.
2. *May* expresses permission in formal English.
3. *May* is never used with *you* in questions.
4. There is no contraction for *may not.*

Exercise 30. PAIRWORK. Play the roles below with a classmate. Take turns asking and answering questions of permission with *Can I . . . ?* and *May I . . . ?*

Example: student — classmate   "Can I borrow your eraser?"
                                                          "Sure."

1. child — parent
2. student — professor
3. brother — sister

4. student — classmate
5. patient — doctor

Exercise 31. Complete the mini dialogs.

1. Student: May _____ ?
   Teacher: No, _____ .

2. Husband: Can _____ ?
   Wife: Yes, _____ .
   Husband: Thanks.

3. Student: Can _____ ?

   Roommate: No, _____ .

   Student: Why not?

   Roommate: Because _____ .

4. Employee: May _____ ?

   Boss: Yes, _____ .

   Employee: Thank you very much.

5. Son: Can, _____ ?

   Father: Yes, _____ , but _____

   _____ .

   Son: Thanks a lot, Dad!

Exercise 32.

Each of the sentences has at least one grammatical mistake. Look for the errors. Rewrite the sentences correctly with *can* or *can't*.

Incorrect   *Correct*

1. My brother can runs very fast.   _____

2. I can't to speak Portuguese.   _____

3. Does Mary can type?   _____

4. Where I can buy a typewriter?   _____

5. My father doesn't can swim.   _____

6. Now I can playing the piano well.   _____

7. Do I can leave now?   _____

Expressions of Frequency

once a day	every hour
twice a week	every four hours
one day a week	every day
three days a week	every three days
three times a month	every two weeks
four weeks a year	every six months
five times a year	every other day

Examples: I eat **three times a day.**
              He exercises **twice a week.**
              I have vacation **four weeks a year.**
              She goes to the dentist **every six months.**
              I take my vitamins **every morning.**
              Take this medicine **every four hours.**

Exercise 33.
PAIRWORK. Ask questions with "How often do you _____ ?"

1. eat meat
2. watch TV
3. buy clothes
4. catch a cold
5. get a haircut
6. read a book
7. write a letter
8. cry
9. arrive on time for class
10. laugh
11. get angry
12. study
13. brush your teeth
14. go to the dentist
15. exercise
16. eat out
17. have tests in your English class
18. _____

Review of the Present Continuous and the Simple Present

Exercise 34. MINI CONVERSATIONS.

Example: Tom
           bakery
           a birthday cake

Chris: Where is Tom going?
Pat: He's going to the bakery.
Chris: What does he need to get there?
Pat: He needs to buy a birthday cake.

1. Mary
   drugstore
   some aspirin

2. your sisters
   department store
   some perfume

3. your father
   automotive store
   some motor oil

4. you
   sports store
   a pair of tennis shoes

5. you and Lee
   hardware store
   some house paint

6. your roommate
   supermarket
   some eggs and bread

7. Richard
   travel agency
   an airline ticket

8. _____
   _____
   _____

Exercise 35.

Complete the letter below. Use the verbs in parentheses in the present continuous or the simple present.

September 30

Greetings from Madison, Wisconsin.

I _____ outside the student union by Lake Mendota. It _____ a warm day
     (sit)   (be)

and the sun _____ . I _____ the campus of the University of Wisconsin. It
          (shine)   (like)

_____ large and beautiful, and the city of Madison _____ many interesting
     (be)   (have)

places. People from all over the world _____ here to study. At first I was lonely but
                                          (come)

now I _____ a lot of friends. Some of my friends and I _____ soccer in a local
        (have)   (play)

soccer league. My team _____ three times a week.
                          (practice)

My classes _____ interesting. I _____ English this semester.
              (be)   (not / take)

I _____ five difficult courses. All of my professors _____ a lot of homework, so
     (take)   (give)

I _____ much free time. Now I _____ for my first chemistry exam. The exam
     (not / have)   (study)

_____ the first two chapters of my chemistry text.
  (include)

What _____ you _____ this semester? _____ you _____
         (do)   (go)

to school or are you _____ ? _____ you _____ to come visit me in
                       (work)   (plan)

Madison this school year? I _____ you are well. Please write soon.
                              (hope)

Sincerely,

Hugh Brown

Activities

A. INTERVIEW. Work with a classmate.

1. What products does your country export?
2. What products does your country import?
3. Describe the capital of your country.
4. Describe an interesting place in your country.
5. Where do you like to go on vacation in your country?
6. What do you like to do on vacation?
7. What famous person from your country would you like to meet? Why? Describe this person.

B. RIDDLES. What are the answers?

1. What is always in front of you, but you cannot see?
2. How can you divide seven eggs evenly among five people?
3. What has three feet but can't walk?
4. What kind of dress do you have but you never wear?
5. What is always coming but never arrives?

C. PUZZLE.

Antonio is going to visit the United States. He is going to tour the country for six weeks. He is going to visit friends in Dallas, Seattle, Cincinnati, Atlanta, Denver, St. Louis, and Chicago. Antonio is going to fly into New York City, travel around the country, and end his tour in New York City.

Antonio is going to rent a car, and he wants to take the shortest route. Use the map below to find Antonio's shortest route and his total mileage. The numbers by the lines between cities indicate the road mileage. For example, a drive from Chicago to Denver is 996 miles long.

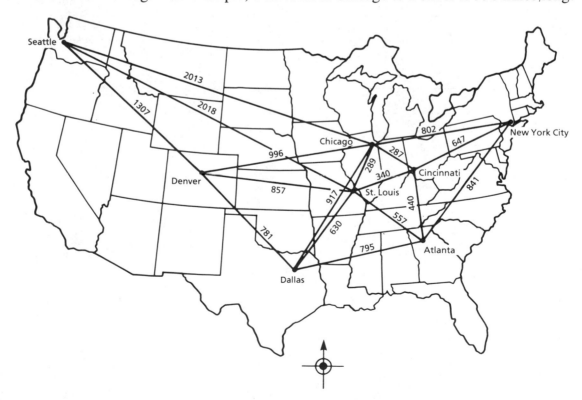

What is Antonio's total mileage?_____

Write Antonio's travel plan. For example: *First Antonio is going to drive from New York City to* _____ . *Next he is going to travel from* _____ *to* _____ . *Then he is going to go* . . . .

D. ROLE PLAYS. Work with a classmate.

1. You want to take a weekend trip. Ask a friend if you may borrow his car for the weekend. Your friend does not want to lend you his car. Discuss the situation and other possibilities with your friend.

2. You and your roommate (or husband or wife) are preparing the grocery list for next week. What groceries are you going to buy? How much are you going to buy of each item? How much money are you going to spend? Discuss the grocery list.

3. A friend from another city is coming to visit you and your cousin for three days. Where are you going to take your friend? What are you going to do during your friend's visit? Plan the visit with your cousin.

E. WRITING. 1. Write about some of the products or natural resources of your country or regions of your country.

2. What are you going to do after this semester? Write about your plans for the future.

F. DICTATION. You will hear each sentence two times. Write exactly what you hear.

1. _____
2. _____
3. _____
4. _____
5. _____
6. _____
7. _____
8. _____

Review Quizzes

A. LISTENING COMPREHENSION: SENTENCES

For each problem, you will hear a short sentence. You will hear each sentence two times. After you hear a sentence, read the four choices. Decide which written sentence is the closest in meaning to the spoken sentence. Circle the letter of the correct answer.

1. (A) She is Japanese.
   (B) She is a Japanese cook.
   (C) She knows how to cook Japanese food.
   (D) She cooks Japanese food from a can.

2. (A) They're going to graduate.
   (B) They're not going to graduate.
   (C) He's going to graduate.
   (D) He isn't going to graduate.

3. (A) It isn't possible to walk there.
   (B) We don't know how to walk to the airport.
   (C) We can walk there.
   (D) We have the ability to walk there.

4. (A) The test is in two days.
   (B) The test isn't in two days.
   (C) The test is today.
   (D) The test isn't today.

5. (A) There aren't any potatoes or rice.
   (B) There are some potatoes and rice.
   (C) There isn't any rice, but there are some potatoes.
   (D) There aren't any potatoes, but there is some rice.

6. (A) She has the ability to speak German.
   (B) She doesn't have the ability to speak German.
   (C) She has permission to speak German.
   (D) It is possible for her to speak German.

7. (A) She goes to school.
   (B) They go to school.
   (C) She's going to school.
   (D) They're going to school.

8. (A) There is a little money.
   (B) There is a lot of money.
   (C) There aren't a few dollars.
   (D) There isn't a little money.

9. (A) I can go.
   (B) I can't go.
   (C) I could go.
   (D) I couldn't go.

10. (A) I'm going to give an example soon.
    (B) I'm going to take an egg sandwich at noon.
    (C) I'm going to give an exam at twelve.
    (D) I'm going to have a test at twelve.

B. STRUCTURE: SENTENCE COMPLETION

Choose the *one* word or phrase that best completes the sentence. Circle the letter of the correct answer.

1. Charles has -------- for you.
   - (A) a food
   - (B) some flower
   - (C) a furniture
   - (D) some mail

2. How many tests -------- this week?
   - (A) does he has
   - (B) does he have
   - (C) he has
   - (D) he have

3. Why -------- ?
   - (A) you are laughing
   - (B) are you laughing
   - (C) are you laugh
   - (D) do you laughing

4. She -------- tomorrow afternoon.
   - (A) going to leave
   - (B) is going leave
   - (C) is going to leave
   - (D) is going to leaves

5. -------- the piano?
   - (A) Can she play
   - (B) Does she can play
   - (C) Is she can play
   - (D) Is she can plays

6. -------- your sister -------- to go bowling?
   - (A) Does ... likes
   - (B) Does ... like
   - (C) Is ... likes
   - (D) Is ... like

7. I have a -------- to do for tomorrow.
   - (A) little homework
   - (B) little homeworks
   - (C) homework
   - (D) few homeworks

8. I would like --------.
   - (A) potato
   - (B) some potato
   - (C) any potato
   - (D) some potatoes

9. -------- of people go to Hawaii in the winter.
   - (A) Much
   - (B) Many
   - (C) A lot
   - (D) A little

10. It -------- a lot in Arizona.
    - (A) not rain
    - (B) not rains
    - (C) rains not
    - (D) does not rain

11. Thomas -------- very fast.
    - (A) can swim
    - (B) can swims
    - (C) can swimming
    - (D) is can swim

12. -------- she nervous?
    - (A) Were
    - (B) Do
    - (C) Does
    - (D) Is

13. I'm going -------- TV tonight.
    - (A) watch
    - (B) watching
    - (C) to watch
    - (D) to watching

14. Who -------- you usually eat lunch with?
    - (A) is
    - (B) are
    - (C) do
    - (D) does

15. I don't drink -------- coffee.
    - (A) much
    - (B) many
    - (C) some
    - (D) little

16. -------- you watching the football game last night at 9:00?
    - (A) Is
    - (B) Are
    - (C) Was
    - (D) Were

C. STRUCTURE: ERROR IDENTIFICATION

Each sentence has four underlined words or phrases. Circle the *one* underlined word or phrase that is not correct. Then correct the sentence.

1. We have a few work to do tonight.
   A   B   C   D

2. What does he making for dinner tonight?
   A   B   C   D

3. Is there many fruit in the refrigerator?
   A   B   C   D

4. Can Michael comes to the party next Saturday night?
   A   B   C   D

5. How many time do we have before the movie begins?
   A   B   C   D

6. Why she is going to the doctor next week?
       A   B   C   D

7. She doesn't have some clean clothes to wear.
       A   B   C   D

8. My sister could playing tennis very well when she was a child.
             A   B   C   D

9. There are some milk in the bottle on the table.
   A   B   C   D

10. What's you going to do tomorrow afternoon?
    A   B   C   D

11. He wants to borrow any money from you.
       A   B   C   D

12. I am doing my English homework every afternoon at 4:00.
        A   B   C   D

13. They are some letters in my notebook on the kitchen table.
    A   B   C   D

14. Does your mother like to listen to a loud music?
    A   B   C   D

CHAPTER 7

The Case of the Bankrupt Businessman   (Part One)

George Mitchell was a rich businessman. He made two million dollars in banking. Four years ago he bought a large house in Southampton, New York. George and his British wife Margaret lived there with their French maid, Mimi Monet.

Recently, Mr. Mitchell lost a lot of his money in a bad business deal. One evening Mr. Mitchell had a conversation with Mimi. "I'm sorry, Mimi," he said. "Mrs. Mitchell and I must move to an apartment. We must sell this house, and you must find a different job." Mr. Mitchell didn't have enough money to pay Mimi's salary.

Mimi was upset. She didn't want to leave New York. She liked her job and she needed a job. She didn't like Mrs. Mitchell, but she secretly loved Mr. Mitchell. She didn't want to lose him or her job.

Early the next afternoon, the Southampton Police Department got a telephone call from a French woman. "Help!" she shouted. "My employer is dead. I found him in his study. His wife murdered him. Come quickly!"

In ten minutes, Detective Hastings, Officer Clemson, and Officer Stamford arrived at the Mitchell home. Detective Hastings questioned the French maid in the living room. Mimi described the murder. "Mrs. Mitchell killed her husband in his study. Then she took a taxi to the airport. She wanted a divorce. She asked him for a divorce last night. He said no. I heard the conversation last night. Early this morning Mrs. Mitchell telephoned a travel agency. She made a reservation on a late afternoon flight to London. Her taxi came forty-five minutes ago. She took six suitcases with her. You have to stop her!"

To Be Continued

Exercise 1.   Answer the questions.

1. Where was Mimi from?
2. What was Mimi's occupation?
3. Where did the Mitchells live?
4. What happened to Mr. Mitchell's money?
5. Did Mimi love Mr. Mitchell?
6. Why was Mimi upset?
7. Why did Mimi call the police?
8. Who investigated Mr. Mitchell's death?
9. What did Mrs. Mitchell want?
10. What did Mrs. Mitchell do in the morning?
11. What did she do in the afternoon?

Simple Past Tense of Regular Verbs: Affirmative Statements

SINGULAR	PLURAL
I **arrived** yesterday. You **arrived** last night. He **arrived** yesterday morning. She **arrived** last Sunday. It **arrived** a week ago.	We **arrived** last month. You **arrived** before Eric. They **arrived** at 2:00 yesterday afternoon.

Note: In the past tense, all singular and plural forms of regular verbs end in **-ed**.

Pronunciation of the Past Tense Ending *-ed*

The past tense ending **-ed** has three different pronunciations.

1. Past tense **-ed** is pronounced /t/ after voiceless sounds except after the sound /t/.

danced	increased	looked	washed
fixed	laughed	stopped	watched
helped	liked	talked	worked

Who worked for the Mitchells?	Mimi worked for them.
Who liked her job?	Mimi liked her job.
Who talked to Mimi one evening?	Mr. Mitchell talked to her.
Who helped Detective Hastings?	Two officers helped him.

2. Past tense **-ed** is pronounced /d/ after voiced sounds except after the sound /d/.

arrived	described	listened	questioned
called	died	lived	telephoned
continued	killed	played	used

Who lived with the Mitchells?	Their maid lived with them.
Who called a travel agency?	Mrs. Mitchell called a travel agency.
Who died in the study?	Mr. Mitchell died there.
Who telephoned the police?	Mimi telephoned them.
Who questioned Mimi?	Detective Hastings questioned her.

3. Past tense **-ed** is pronounced /əd/ after the sounds /t/ and /d/.

loaded	needed	inspected
wanted	shouted	investigated
added	waited	decided

Who wanted a divorce?	Mrs. Mitchell wanted a divorce.
Who shouted, "Help?"	Mimi shouted, "Help!"
Who needed a job?	Mimi needed a job.
Who waited for the police?	Mimi waited for them.
Who investigated Mr. Mitchell's death?	Three police officers investigated his death.

The Simple Past Tense: Negative Statements

FORMULA 7-1	Subject	**did**	**not**	verb [base form]	(complement) .

Note: The contraction of *did not* is *didn't*.

Examples: I **didn't dance** at the party last night.
You **did not arrive** on time.
Laura **didn't like** the music.
The food **did not taste** good.
We **didn't have** a good time.
They **didn't play** many good songs.

Exercise 2.
Make true sentences about what you did and didn't do yesterday. Use the phrases below.

Examples: listen to the radio   *I didn't listen to the radio yesterday.*
telephone my family   *I telephoned my family yesterday.*

1. watch TV
2. cook dinner
3. visit a friend
4. play tennis
5. call a friend
6. work
7. clean my room
8. stay at home
9. talk on the telephone
10. finish my homework
11. wash clothes
12. arrive on time for class

Exercise 3.
Complete the sentences. Use the verbs below or others.

have	speak	read
eat	live	cook
play	drive	smoke
dance	wear	drink
like	know	understand

Example: Six years ago I didn't **speak English**, but now I **speak English**.

1. Last year I didn't _____, but now I _____
2. In 1984 I didn't _____ , but now I _____
3. Last month my classmates didn't _____ , but now they _____
4. Fifteen years ago I didn't _____ , but now I _____
5. Ten years ago my teacher didn't _____ , but now my teacher _____
6. Five years ago I didn't _____ , but now I _____
7. Twenty-five years ago _____ didn't _____ , but now _____
8. _____ didn't _____ , but now _____

Possessive Pronouns:
mine, yours, his, hers, ours, theirs

Possessive adjective + noun			Possessive pronouns	
These are	my your his her our their	photographs.	These are	mine. yours. his. hers. ours. theirs.

A possessive pronoun substitutes for a possessive adjective + noun.
A possessive pronoun also substitutes for a possessive noun + noun.

Examples: This is Joanne's film.
This is **hers**.

That is the teacher's camera.
That is **his**.

That's Mr. and Mrs. Baker's slide projector.
That's **theirs**.

Exercise 4.   Rewrite the sentences. Use possessive pronouns.

1. This is her passport.   *This is hers.* _____

2. Those are our suitcases.   _____

3. That is my backpack.   _____

4. That's your ticket.   _____

5. This is Mr. Simon's.   _____

6. These are his traveler's checks.   _____

7. This is Mrs. Simon's purse.   _____

8. That is the Simons' luggage.   _____

9. This is their black Cadillac.   _____

10. Those are the children's coats.   _____

Exercise 5.
PAIRWORK. Ask and answer the questions. Answer *yes* to 1–5 and *no* to 6–10.

Examples: Are these your keys?   Yes, they're mine.
Is this your book?   No, it isn't mine.

STUDENT A
1. Are those her students?
2. Are these your answers?
3. Is this our classroom?
4. Is that his desk?
5. Is that your teacher's office?
6. Are these your newspapers?
7. Is that Mary's dictionary?
8. Is that Chris and Pat's science project?
9. Are these our grades?
10. Are those Mr. Marino and Mrs. Wilson's students?

STUDENT B
Yes, they're hers.
Yes, they're mine.
Yes, it's ours.
Yes, it's his.
Yes, it's hers.   (or)   Yes, it's his.
No, they aren't mine.
No, it isn't hers.
No, it isn't theirs.
No, they aren't ours.
No, they aren't theirs.

Exercise 6.
Study the picture and the examples. Then complete the sentences.

Examples: *Whose* dog *is that?*   *It's theirs.*
Whose sunglasses *are those?*   *They're hers.*

1. _____ towel _____ ?   _____
2. _____ purse _____ ?   _____
3. _____ backpacks _____ ?   _____
4. _____ sandals _____ ?   _____
5. _____ camera _____ ?   _____
6. _____ ?   _____

Regular Past Tense: Spelling Rules

> **Rule 1:**   consonant + **y** → consonant + **i** + **ed**

carry	carr**ied**
reply	repl**ied**
study	_____
try	_____

> **Rule 2:**   **e** → **e** + **d**

arrive	arrive**d**
continue	continue**d**
die	_____
taste	_____

> **Rule 3:**   consonant + vowel + consonant →
>   (stressed)
>   consonant + vowel + consonant + consonant + **ed**
>   (stressed)   _____/
>   same

admit	admit**ted**
plan	plan**ned**
rob	_____
shop	_____

> **Rule 4:**   all other verb endings → ending + **ed**

happen	happen**ed**
help	help**ed**
listen	_____
rain	_____
stay	_____
want	_____

Note: Do not double final *w, x,* or *y.* Examples: *showed, fixed, played.*

Exercise 7. Write the past tense form of each verb.

1. cry _____
2. enjoy _____
3. stop _____
4. decide _____
5. wait _____
6. hurry _____
7. visit _____
8. permit _____
9. open _____
10. plan _____
11. play _____
12. agree _____

13. marry _____
14. prefer _____
15. enter _____
16. tax _____
17. rub _____
18. drop _____
19. snow _____
20. fry _____
21. clean _____
22. turn _____
23. hope _____
24. hop _____

Exercise 8. Write the base form of each verb.

1. washed *wash* _____
2. begged _____
3. danced _____
4. watched _____
5. dried _____

6. added _____
7. taped _____
8. tapped _____
9. prayed _____
10. smoked _____

The Simple Past Tense:
Yes-No Questions and Short Answers

QUESTIONS	SHORT ANSWERS
Did I fail the exam?	No, you didn't.
Did you get a good grade?	Yes, I did.
Did Patricia pass the test?	Yes, she did.
Did the test take two hours?	No, it didn't.
Did you and Michael finish the exam?	Yes, we did.
Did the students celebrate after the exam?	Yes, they did.

FORMULA 7-2

Did	subject	verb [base form]	(complement) **?**

Note: Long answers are also possible, but they are not as common as short answers.

Examples: Did you past the test?

Yes, I passed it.
Yes, I passed the test.
No, I didn't pass it.
No, I didn't pass the test.

Exercise 9. PAIRWORK.
Student A: Make questions using the words below.
Student B: Answer with *Yes, I did,* or *No, I didn't.*

Examples: Did you do your homework last night?   *Yes, I did.*
Did you eat breakfast this morning?   *No, I didn't.*

| Did you | do your homework
go to a concert
play the piano
eat breakfast
study English
come to class
watch TV
write a letter
see a movie
go shopping
take a trip
read a book
play tennis

_____ | this morning?
last night?
yesterday?
yesterday morning?
last Saturday night?
last weekend?
last Thursday?
last month?
last summer?

_____ ? |

Exercise 10. MINI CONVERSATIONS.

Example: Maggie cook supper last night
              her husband

Chris: Did Maggie cook supper last night?
Jess: No, she didn't. Her husband cooked supper last night.

1. you call a taxi ten minutes ago
   my roommate

2. the President travel to Rome last week
   the Vice-President

3. Mr. and Mrs. Burns visit Caracas last winter
   their son

4. you order a cup of coffee
   my wife

5. you and your brother live in Chicago
   our parents

6. your father work for the telephone company
   my grandfather

7. I receive a package in the mail this morning
   nobody

8. Mr. Mitchell want a divorce
   Mrs. Mitchell

9. Officer Clemson ask Mimi some questions
   Detective Hastings

10. _____

   _____

Exercise 11.   Question review. Write the *yes-no* questions.

Example: __***Does he work hard?***__   Yes, he works hard.

1. _____   Yes, he married his high school sweetheart.
2. _____   Yes, she is my aunt.
3. _____   Yes, they're eating in the cafeteria.
4. _____   Yes, he shaves every day.
5. _____   Yes, the movie was very good.
6. _____   Yes, she can read very fast.
7. _____   No, they didn't buy a new computer.
8. _____   No, those students aren't mine.
9. _____   No, he can't swim.
10. _____   No, they weren't at the meeting.
11. _____   No, she isn't studying at the library now.
12. _____   No, she doesn't like to get up early.

Must: Affirmative Statements

I **must see** a doctor.
You **must get** out of bed.
She **must take** her medicine.

We **must make** an appointment.
They **must go** to the drugstore.

FORMULA 7-3	Subject	**must**	verb [base form]	(complement) .

Must indicates necessity (no choice) in the present or future. There is only one form of *must*. The verb after *must* is always in the base form.

Note: must = have to   See Chapter 5.

Exercise 12. MINI CONVERSATIONS.

Example:　Ted go to the dentist yesterday
　　　　　today

　　　　Jan:　Did Ted go to the dentist yesterday?
　　　　Lee:　No, he didn't. He must go today.

1. you complete your homework last night
　 this morning before class

2. Scott and Paul telephone their parents last night
　 tonight after supper

3. your roommate shop for groceries yesterday
　 this evening before supper

4. you and your husband open an account at the bank last Friday
　 today by 2 p.m.

5. you close the windows
　 before it rains

6. you get gas for the car
　 soon

7. your students send in their applications for the next TOEFL
　 before the deadline

8. Mrs. Freeman see a doctor last week
　 this week

9. David fix his car
　 before his trip to Colorado

10. the Kellys sell their house
　　before they move to Canada

11. _____

　　_____

Exercise 13. WRITING. Write about the things that you must do in the morning before class. Use paragraph form. Use *must*.

Every morning before class I must _____

_____

_____

_____

_____

_____

_____

Exercise 14.

WRITING. Write about the things that you must do before you take a trip. Use paragraph form. Use *must*.

_____
_____
_____
_____
_____
_____
_____

Must: Question Formation

Must I pay the tuition before classes begin?   Yes, you must.
What must she do to take the TOEFL?   She must send in an application and pay a fee.

FORMULA 7-4	(Question word)	**must**	subject	verb [base form]	(complement) **?**

Note: Questions with *must* are more formal than questions with *have to*

Exercise 15.

Read the answers below. For each answer write the question that corresponds to the underlined section of the answer.

1. *Must I answer all of the questions?*   Yes, you must answer all of the questions.
2. *Where must Jeff go tomorrow?*   Jeff must go to the hospital tomorrow.
3. _____   Amy must leave at three.
4. _____   The Henseys must see a lawyer.
5. _____   Joan must go to work by bus tomorrow.
6. _____   Yes, she must take the final exam.
7. _____   I must go to the post office for stamps.
8. _____   We must get passports before our trip.
9. _____   Tom must go to the dentist because he has a cavity.
10. _____   _____

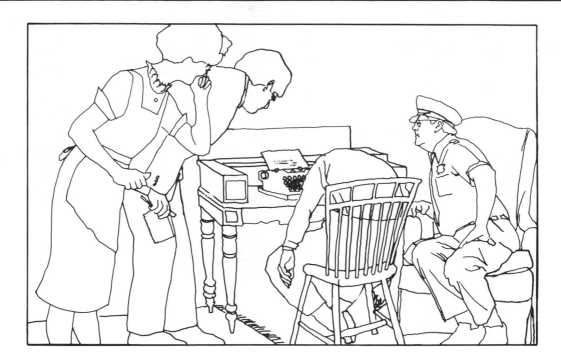

Mimi and the three police officers entered the study. Mr. Mitchell was at his desk. His head was on the desk, and a gun was on the floor. Detective Hastings went directly to Mr. Mitchell's body. Officer Clemson looked around the room, picked up the gun, and inspected it. Officer Stamford investigated the area around Mr. Mitchell's desk.

"Detective Hastings, you must to stop Mrs. Mitchell before her flight leaves for England," Mimi begged. "She didn't love Mr. Mitchell. She never loved him. She only wanted his money. About an hour ago Mrs. Mitchell went into her husband's study. They began to fight. I listened for a few minutes. Then the telephone rang in my bedroom upstairs. I talked on the phone with a friend for about fifteen minutes. The front door slammed shut, and I looked out my bedroom window. I saw a taxi. The driver loaded the luggage, and Mrs. Mitchell got in the taxi. Detective Hastings, she did it! She killed him, and then she . . ."

Officer Stamford stopped Mimi in the middle of her sentence. "Come here, Detective Hastings. Mrs. Mitchell didn't kill him. He killed himself. He wrote this note before he died. I found it in his typewriter." Detective Stamford read it out loud.

I am very depressed. I am bankrupt. I lost my house, and now I am losing my wife. I must to die. I don't want to live any more.

"There you are, Detective Hastings. Mrs. Mitchell didn't murder him. He killed himself," said Officer Stamford.

"No, he didn't kill himself," replied Detective Hastings. "Read the note again. Now I know what happened to Mr. Mitchell."

Exercise 16. Answer the questions.

1. What happened to Mr. Mitchell? How did Detective Hastings know?
2. Where was the gun?
3. What did Officer Clemson do?
4. Did Mr. Mitchell kill himself?
5. Did Mrs. Mitchell kill her husband?
6. Who typed the note? How do you know?
7. Who killed George Mitchell?

Simple Past Tense: Irregular Verbs

BASE FORM	PAST FORM	BASE FORM	PAST FORM
begin	began	lose	lost
buy	bought	make	made
come	came	read	read
find	found	ring	rang
get	got	say	said
go	went	see	saw
have	had	take	took
hear	heard	write	wrote

Exercise 17. PAIRWORK.

Student A: Read the negative sentence about last week.
Student B: Respond with your book closed. Change the negative sentence to an affirmative sentence about yesterday.
Student A: Check Student B's answer.

STUDENT A	STUDENT B
1. Susan didn't lose her purse last week.	Susan lost her purse yesterday.
2. Pat didn't find Susan's purse last week.	Pat found Susan's purse yesterday.
3. We didn't take the TOEFL last week.	We took the TOEFL yesterday.
4. I didn't get a telegram last week.	I got a telegram yesterday.
5. They didn't have a party last week.	They had a party yesterday.
6. We didn't begin Chapter 7 last week.	We began Chapter 7 yesterday.
7. My parents didn't make their reservation last week.	My parents made their reservation yesterday.
8. She didn't hear the story last week.	She heard the story yesterday.
9. He didn't say "yes" last week.	He said "yes" yesterday.
10. The fire alarm didn't ring last week.	The fire alarm rang yesterday.
11. They didn't come _____ .	They came_____ .

12. I didn't read _____ . I read _____ .
13. He didn't see_____ . He saw_____ .
14. The teacher didn't write _____ . The teacher wrote _____ .
15. Mr. Mitchell didn't buy _____ . He bought _____ .
16. Mrs. Mitchell didn't go _____ . She went _____ .

Exercise 18. PAIRWORK.

Student A: Ask the question.
Student B: Answer the question. Use the first choice in your answer. Respond with your book closed.
Student A: Check Student B's answer.

STUDENT A	STUDENT B
1. Did she say yes or no?	She said yes.
2. Did he take a bus or a train?	He took a bus.
3. Did she lose her house keys or car keys?	She lost her house keys.
4. Did he write a letter or a postcard?	He wrote a letter.
5. Did they get a letter or a package?	They got a letter.
6. Did she have a baby girl or a baby boy?	She had a baby girl.
7. Did the telephone ring once or twice?	It rang once.
8. Did they buy a _____ ?	They bought _____ .
9. Did the class begin at _____ ?	It began at _____ .
10. Did she come _____ ?	She came _____ .
11. Did he find _____ ?	He found _____ .
12. Did they go to _____ ?	They went to _____ .
13. Did he read _____ ?	He read _____ .
14. Did she make a_____ ?	She made _____ .
15. Did they see _____ ?	They saw _____ .

Exercise 19. Complete the sentences. Look at the example.

Example: (invent) A: _**Did**__ Alfred Nobel _*invent*__ the typewriter?

B: No, he _*didn't invent*___ the typewriter.

He _*invented*___ dynamite.

1. (die) A: _____ Alexander the Great _____ in 332 BC?

B: No, he _____ in 332 BC.

He _____ in 323 BC.

2. (buy) A: _____ the United States _____ Alaska from Canada?

B: No, the United States _____ Alaska from Canada.

The United States _____ Alaska from Russia.

3. (try) A: _____ Carry Nation _____ to ban tobacco in the United States?

B: No, she _____ to ban tobacco in the United States.

She _____ to ban alcohol.

4. (write) A: _____Agatha Christie _____ romance novels?

B: No, she _____ romance novels.

She _____ mystery stories.

5. (occur) A: _____ the assassination of John F. Kennedy _____ in Houston, Texas?

B: No, it _____in Houston.

It _____in Dallas, Texas.

6. (defeat) A: _____ Napoleon's army _____ the British army at Waterloo?

B: No, Napoleon's army _____ the British army at Waterloo.

The British army _____ Napoleon's army.

7. (begin) A: _____ World War I _____ in 1915?

B: No, it _____ in 1915.

It _____ in 1914.

8. (play) A: _____ Frank Robinson _____ football?

B: No, he _____ football.

He _____ baseball.

9. (get) A; _____ Elizabeth Taylor _____ an Oscar for the movie *Cleopatra?*

B: No, she _____ an Oscar for *Cleopatra.*

She _____ an Oscar for *Who's Afraid of Virginia Woolf.*

10. (rob) A: _____Bonnie and Clyde _____ trains?

B: No, they _____ trains.

They _____ banks.

11. (study) A: _____ ?

B: No, _____ .

_____ .

12. (plan) A: _____ ?

B: No, _____ .

_____ .

The Simple Past Tense: *Wh*-Questions

Answer the questions.

1. When did you begin to study English?
2. Why did you decide to study English?
3. What did you learn in your last class?
4. How did you get to class today?
5. Who did you talk to last night?
6. Where did you live last year?

Study the questions above. All of these questions follow the formula given below.

FORMULA 7-5

(Wh-word)	**did**	subject	verb [base form]	(complement) **?**

Exercise 20. Combine the *Wh*-words below with the verbs below to make questions in the past tense. Ask a classmate your questions.

who	where
what	why
when	how

go	read	cook	listen
buy	eat	work	watch
see	live	play	travel
ask	learn	study	decide

Examples: What did you eat last night?
Where did you travel on your last vacation?

Exercise 21. Complete the questions in the past tense. Write an answer for each question.

1. When _____ go _____ ?
   _____

2. Where _____ buy _____ ?
   _____

3. Who _____ see _____ ?
   _____

4. What _____ do _____ ?
   _____

Exercise 22.

Change the statements into questions. Use question words (*who, what, when, where*) that correspond to the underlined parts of the statements.

1. *When did Kathy work?*   Kathy worked <u>yesterday</u>.
2. _____ Charles was <u>at home</u>.
3. _____ Jennifer went to <u>Dallas</u>.
4. _____ She went to Dallas <u>last weekend</u>.
5. _____ She went to Dallas with <u>her mother</u>.
6. _____ Lee saw Lynn <u>at school</u>.
7. _____ Chris was talking to <u>Pat</u>.
8. _____ Rick can play <u>the guitar</u>.
9. _____ Michael loves <u>Barbara</u>.
10. _____ They bought <u>a new boat</u>.
11. _____ Kim usually studies <u>at the library</u>.
12. _____ Judy must get <u>a new passport</u>.
13. _____ Pat had <u>steak</u>.
14. _____ Pat usually has <u>steak</u> for dinner.

Possessive Pronouns: Subject Position

Lee: Which blanket is yours, and which is Linda's?

Pat: **Mine** is the brown blanket, and **hers** is the green one.

Possessive pronouns in the subject position have the same form as the possessive pronouns studied earlier. They also substitute for a possessive adjective + noun or a possessive noun + noun.

Notes: 1. *Which is a Wh-question word. It requires the selection of one thing or one group of things from two or more things or groups.*

         2. *One* and *ones* are pronouns. *One* substitutes for a singular noun. *Ones* substitutes for plural nouns.

Exercise 23. Complete each sentence with an appropriate possessive pronoun.

1. Which tablecloth is Mom's?

2. Which picnic table is yours and Barbara's?

3. Which picnic basket is Aunt Linda's?

4. Which grill is Uncle Glenn's?

5. Which hamburgers are yours?

6. Which dessert is Cousin Sarah's?

7. Which chairs are Grandma's and Grandpa's?

*Hers*_____ is the big square one.

_____ is the round table.

_____ is the one under the round table.

_____ is the small one near the tree.

_____ are the ones on the large grill.

_____ is the cake.

_____ are the rocking chairs.

Write questions and answers.

8. _____ sandwiches _____ ?   _____

9. _____ salad _____ ?   _____

10. _____ plates _____ ?   _____

Exercise 24. Complete the sentences with possessive adjectives or possessive pronouns that correspond to the underlined word(s).

1. I didn't finish _*my*_ homework, but she finished _*hers*_ .

2. Susan's English dictionary is small, but _____ Spanish dictionary is large.

3. We don't own these books. They're not _____ .

4. They got _____ grades, but I didn't get _____ .

5. This briefcase is Mrs. Mitchell's. It's _____ .

6. We did_____ homework, but they didn't do _____ .

7. That calculator belongs to Bob. It's _____ .

8. I have _____ student ID. Do you have _____ ?

9. Which classroom is Mrs. Gilman's? _____ is the one on the left.

10. Did you find _____ glasses?

11. They didn't write _____ lab reports, but we wrote _____ .

Past Necessity

Bobby: You left work early yesterday. Where did you go?
Chris: I had to go to the telephone company.
Bobby: What did you have to do there?
Chris: I had to pay my phone bill by 5 p.m.

Employee: I'm sorry I'm late. My wife and I had to go to the bank.
Boss: Why did you have to go today?
Employee: We had to open an account.

The past tense of *have* followed by an infinitive (*to* + verb) expresses necessity in the past.

Exercise 25. Write about five things that you had to do last month. Use *I had to*.

___*Last month I*_____

_____

_____

_____

_____

Exercise 26. Complete the three questions below. Make questions expressing past necessity.

1. Did you _____

2. When did you _____

3. What _____

Exercise 27. Complete the dialogs below using *must, have,* or *had*.

1. Lee: What _____ you do tomorrow?

   Les: I _____ to go to the dentist.

2. Pat: Did your parents _____ to get visas for their trip to China?

   Sandy: Yes, they _____ to get visas.

3. Tom: Did your brother _____ to take the SAT exam?

   Joe: No, he didn't _____ to take the SAT. He's a graduate student. He _____ to take the GRE.

4. Carmen: What do you _____ to do before your vacation abroad?

   Chris: I _____ apply for a passport.

Exercise 28.   Complete the questions. Select words from the two lists.

Who What When Where	is are was were do does did

Example: QUESTIONS

___**Where does**___ Susan live?

___**Who is**___ that man?

ANSWERS

She lives on State Street.

He's my teacher.

1. _____ he go to the movie?   Last week.
2. _____ the next train leave?   At 2:30.
3. _____ your books?   They're at home.
4. _____ the first President?   George Washington was.
5. _____ she going now?   To school.
6. _____ this?   It's a microchip.
7. _____ you last night?   I was at home.
8. _____ she study?   She studies computer science.
9. _____ he telephone you?   Yesterday.
10. _____ she marry?   She married Tom.
11. _____ you have for dinner last   Fish and a salad.
night?
12. _____ Mimi and Scott usually do   They usually go out to eat.
on Friday night?
13. _____ you doing?   I'm making some yogurt.
14. _____ the party yesterday?   At Mark and Jane's house.

Exercise 29.   Fill in the blanks with *isn't, aren't, wasn't, weren't, doesn't, don't,* or *didn't.*

1. Napoleon Bonaparte _____ a king. His title was emperor.

2. We _____ have a car. We need to buy one.

3. Marie Curie _____ discover vitamin C. She discovered radium.

4. Arizona is a dry state. It _____ rain very much there.

5. It _____ rain very much in Arizona last year.

6. They _____ do their laundry last week.

7. Marie and Pierre Curie _____ brother and sister. They were husband and wife.

8. It _____ very hot in Texas at this time of year.

9. They had a big lunch. They _____ very hungry now.

10. The President of the United States _____ live in the state of Washington.

Exercise 30.

Complete the dialog below. Use the words in parentheses. Use correct verb forms: base form, present continuous, simple present, or simple past. Use auxiliaries when necessary.

Lee: Didn't your sister (go) _____ to France three months ago?

Pat: No, she (go) _____ last month. I (receive) _____ a letter from her yesterday.

Lee: (she, go) _____ by ship?

Pat: No, she (take) _____ a plane. She (want) _____ to take a ship, but she (not, have) _____ enough money.

Lee: (she, travel) _____ directly to France?

Pat: No, she (stop) _____ in London first.

Lee: Which hotel (she, stay) _____ in?

Pat: She (not, stay) _____ in a hotel. She (stay) _____ with friends. She (have) _____ a good time in London, and she (want) _____ to return there on her trip back home.

Lee: Where (she, be) _____ now?

Pat: She (be) _____ in Paris. She (live) _____ with a French family. The family members (not, speak) _____ English.

Lee: (she, take) _____ any courses now?

Pat: Yes, she (find) _____ a good French language school. She (study) _____ there five hours a day.

Lee: (she, have) _____ a lot of time to explore Paris?

Pat: No, she (not, have) _____ much free time. She (need) _____ money for her trip home. She (see) _____ an ad for a baby-sitting job. She (apply) _____ for the job and (get) _____ it. She (work) _____ twenty hours a week.

Lee: (she, enjoy) _____ her stay in Paris?

Pat: Yes, she is, but she (must, return) _____ home in August. Her university classes (begin) _____ in early September.

Activities

A. INTERVIEW/WRITING. Write past tense questions to ask a classmate. Begin each question with *Did you . . . ?* or a *Wh*-question word. Include time expressions in your questions (this morning, yesterday, last Saturday, two months ago, etc.). Note your classmate's answers. Write the questions and answers in the form of a dialog or a composition.

B. SENTENCE COMPLETION. Complete the story below using the past tense form of all of the verbs in the box below. Use each verb only once.

be	find	hear	say
begin	go	lose	see
buy	get	make	take
come	have	ring	write

George Mitchell _____ a rich businessman. He _____ a big house. He _____ bad luck and _____ his money. One day the police _____ a call from Mr. Mitchell's maid, Mimi Monet. She _____ , "My boss is dead!" Mimi explained the murder of Mr. Mitchell. "His wife didn't love him. I _____ her conversation with him. She wanted a divorce. She _____ an airplane reservation to fly to England at 4:00. She _____ into Mr. Mitchell's study. They _____ to fight. The telephone _____ , and I was on the phone for fifteen minutes. Then I _____ a taxi from my bedroom window. It _____ at about 4:45. I think the taxi _____ Mrs. Mitchell to the airport."

The police arrived at the Mitchell home. The police and Mimi entered the study. There they _____ a note on the floor. Who _____ the note?

C. WRITING. The police discovered the murderer of George Mitchell. What happened during the week after Mr. Mitchell's murder? Write an ending to the story in the past tense. Include both Mrs. Mitchell and Mimi Monet in your ending.

D. GUESSING GAME. Think of a famous person of the past. Other students ask you questions to identify the person. Their questions are only *yes-no* questions. The questions begin *Was he (she) ...?* or *Did he (she) ...?*

Example:	Was the person a man?	Yes, he was.
	Was he from this century?	No, he wasn't.
	Was he from the nineteenth century?	Yes, he was.
	Did he live in Europe?	No, he didn't.
	Was he American?	Yes, he was.
	Was he an author?	No, he wasn't.
	Did he play an instrument?	No, he didn't.
	Was he an artist?	No, he wasn't.
	Was he a politician?	Yes, he was.
	Did he live in Washington, D.C.?	Yes, he did.
	Was he a president?	Yes, he was.
	Was he tall?	Yes, he was.
	Did he have a beard?	Yes, he did.
	Was he Abraham Lincoln?	Yes.

E. MEMORY GAME. Student A: Tell something you did in the past, and include a time expression. Include a verb from the box below in its past forms.

Student B: Tell what Student A did, and then tell what you did.

Other students: Continue the game by repeating previous sentences and adding a sentence about what you did. ·

Example: Student A (Gary): I went to a party last Saturday night.
Student B (Mary): Gary went to a party last Saturday night, and I played tennis yesterday.
Student C (Kim): Gary went to a party last Saturday night. Mary played tennis yesterday, and I bought a pair of shoes last night.

(etc.)

/t/	/d/	/əd/	irregular
cook	arrive	attend	buy
dance	call	paint	find
finish	listen	plant	get
help	study	wait	go
talk	play	want	make
watch			see
work			write

Idea: When you finish the chain, write the sentences.

F. PUZZLE. Below are thirteen verbs in their base forms. Fit the past tense forms of the verbs into the spaces below. One letter is given for each verb. Discover a surprise message in the vertical column of circles.

stay	1. (h) e a r d
✔ hear	2. ___ ○ ___ t ___ ___
pray	3. ___ ___ ___ ○ p ___ ___
want	4. ___ ○ ___ ___ i ___ ___ ___
say	5. ___ ___ a ○ ___ ___
see	6. ___ ○ ___ ___ a ___ ___
fry	7. ___ a ○ ___
buy	8. ___ ○ i ___ ___
add	9. ___ ___ ○ ___ ___ ___ ___ e ___
shop	10. ___ o ○ ___ ___ ___
begin	11. ___ ___ ○ ___ d
apply	12. ___ ○ w ___
continue	13. ___ ___ a ○ ___ ___

G. RIDDLES. What are the answers?

1. What did Baby Corn ask Momma Corn?
2. I dropped a full glass and didn't spill a drop of water. Why?
3. Three men were in a boat that capsized. Why did only two of them come out of the water with wet hair?
4. Why did my grandfather put roller skates on his rocking chair?

H. PRONUNCIATION. Listen to the story about the murder of Mr. Mitchell. When you hear each regular past tense verb below, put a check (✔) in the column that corresponds to the pronunciation of the past tense ending.

	/t/	/d/	/əd/
1. lived		✔	
2. liked			
3. needed			
4. shouted			
5. murdered			
6. arrived			
7. entered			
8. inspected			
9. looked			
10. investigated			
11. picked			
12. killed			
13. asked			
14. replied			
15. begged			

I. DICTATION. You will hear each sentence two times. Write exactly what you hear.

1. _____
2. _____
3. _____
4. _____
5. _____
6. _____
7. _____

Review Quizzes

A. LISTENING COMPREHENSION: SENTENCES
For each problem, you will hear a short sentence. You will hear each sentence two times. After you hear a sentence, read the four choices. Decide which written sentence is the closest in meaning to the spoken sentence. Circle the letter of the correct answer.

1. (A) I have an international driver's license.
   (B) I must get an international driver's license.
   (C) It's not necessary to get a license.
   (D) I got an international driver's license.

2. (A) The car is ours.
   (B) The car is yours.
   (C) The car is mine.
   (D) The car is theirs.

3. (A) He can't find his job.
   (B) He doesn't have a job.
   (C) He didn't have a job.
   (D) He has a job.

4. (A) He didn't go there.
   (B) He went there last summer.
   (C) She didn't travel there.
   (D) She went there last summer.

5. (A) You came at six.
   (B) You come at six.
   (C) You are coming at six.
   (D) You were coming at six.

6. (A) They took the plane.
   (B) They didn't take the plane.
   (C) They didn't miss the plane.
   (D) They lost the plane.

7. (A) The money is yours.
   (B) The money is theirs.
   (C) The money is hers.
   (D) The money is his.

8. (A) He may go to the hospital.
   (B) He can go to the hospital.
   (C) He wants to go to the hospital.
   (D) He needs to go to the hospital.

9. (A) She cleaned her child.
   (B) She looked at her child.
   (C) She bought a watch for her child.
   (D) She saw her child.

10. (A) She waited for the food.
    (B) She left before the food came.
    (C) She didn't work in a restaurant.
    (D) She didn't leave before the food arrived.

B. STRUCTURE: SENTENCE COMPLETION

Choose the *one* word or phrase that best completes the sentence. Circle the letter of the correct answer.

1. She -------- it yesterday.   (spelling)
   - (A) returnned
   - (B) listenned to
   - (C) plaied
   - (D) cleaned

2. Did he -------- a new camera for his trip?
   - (A) buy
   - (B) buys
   - (C) bought
   - (D) buying

3. He -------- his mother tomorrow.
   - (A) must help
   - (B) must helps
   - (C) must helping
   - (D) must to help

4. Is this pen -------- ?
   - (A) her
   - (B) hers
   - (C) of she
   - (D) of her

5. In the word *watched*, final -ed is pronounced -------- .
   - (A) /t/
   - (B) /d/
   - (C) /ət/
   - (D) /əd/

6. She didn't -------- TV yesterday.
   - (A) watch
   - (B) watche
   - (C) watches
   - (D) watched

7. -------- you in her class last semester?
   - (A) Do
   - (B) Did
   - (C) Was
   - (D) Were

8. That boat is -------- .
   - (A) my
   - (B) her
   - (C) they
   - (D) theirs

9. She -------- to the doctor yesterday.
   - (A) must go
   - (B) must went
   - (C) must going
   - (D) had to go

10. I -------- my birthday presents last night.
    - (A) doesn't open
    - (B) didn't opened
    - (C) wasn't open
    - (D) opened

11. In the word *changed*, final -ed is pronounced -------- ,
    - (A) /t/
    - (B) /d/
    - (C) /ət/
    - (D) /əd/

12. Did she -------- her umbrella with her when it started to rain?
    - (A) had
    - (B) has
    - (C) have
    - (D) having

13. -------- the tuition before classes begin?
    - (A) Is he must pay
    - (B) Is he must pays
    - (C) Must he pay
    - (D) Does he must pay

14. It -------- very windy yesterday.
    - (A) weren't
    - (B) wasn't
    - (C) didn't
    - (D) didn't was

15. Her parents are old, but -------- are young.
    - (A) my
    - (B) mine
    - (C) them
    - (D) their

C. STRUCTURE: ERROR IDENTIFICATION

Each sentence has four underlined words or phrases. Circle the *one* underlined word or phrase that is not correct. Then correct the sentence.

1. <u>Did</u> she <u>arrived</u> <u>on time</u> <u>for the</u> test yesterday morning?
      A   B   C   D

2. It <u>didn't</u> very cold <u>in</u> New York City <u>last winter</u>.
   A B   C   D

3. They have <u>some</u> <u>new cups</u> but <u>theirs</u> glasses are very <u>old</u>.
             A   B   C   D

4. My father <u>didn't</u> <u>worked</u> last week because he <u>was</u> <u>in</u> the hospital.
            A   B   C D

5. He <u>can't</u> <u>go swimming</u> this afternoon because he <u>must</u> <u>to cut</u> the grass.
      A   B   C   D

6. <u>Those</u> <u>brown</u> shoes over there are <u>his</u> not <u>my</u>.
     A   B   C   D

7. I had <u>stay</u> <u>home</u> last night and <u>babysit</u> <u>my little</u> brother.
        A   B   C   D

8. I <u>wasn't</u> eat <u>a lot</u> <u>for dinner</u> <u>last night</u>.
     A   B   C   D

9. We have <u>our</u> passports, but she <u>doesn't</u> <u>have</u> <u>her</u>.
         A   B   C D

10. She <u>didn't have</u> <u>hers</u> house <u>keys</u> with <u>her</u>.
         A   B   C   D

11. He <u>didn't</u> very hungry when I <u>talked to</u> <u>him</u> <u>this</u> morning.
       A   B   C D

12. She <u>must</u> <u>gets</u> a job because she <u>doesn't have</u> <u>any</u> money.
       A   B   C   D

13. He says he <u>didn't</u> his homework <u>yesterday afternoon</u> because he <u>was</u> <u>too</u> busy.
            A   B   C D

14. I wanted <u>to see</u> John last night, but when <u>I called him</u> he <u>didn't be</u> <u>at home</u>.
           A   B   C   D

15. I <u>had not</u> <u>a good</u> time <u>at</u> <u>Mary's</u> party last Saturday night.
      A   B   C   D

CHAPTER **8**

Dialog

Two university students meet on campus outside the student union.

Paul: Hi Bob. How's it going?
Bob: Fine. Hey, let's go to the cafeteria and get a cup of coffee.
Paul: Okay. When are you going to register for classes?
Bob: I don't know. Soon, I hope.
Paul: You need to hurry, or you won't get the classes you want. Do you want to go to registration with me this morning?
Bob: No, I can't go this morning.
Paul: Well, this semester I'm going to register early, because last semester I waited until the last day. I was waiting in line to register for Computer Science 302 when they closed the last section of 302.
Bob: Let's play a quick game of pool. Okay?
Paul: I don't have time now. Maybe tomorrow. Why can't you register this morning?
Bob: I don't have enough money to pay the tuition. I'm waiting for a check from my parents. Maybe it'll come this afternoon or tomorrow.

Exercise 1.
Questions 1–11 are about the dialog. If an answer is not in the dialog, respond with *I don't know*. Questions 12–16 are about you.

1. Where do Paul and Bob meet?
2. What are Paul and Bob going to get at the cafeteria?
3. Are Paul and Bob freshmen at the university?
4. When is Paul going to register?
5. What happened to him last semester?
6. When is Bob going to register?
7. What does Bob want to play?
8. What is Bob's major?
9. Why can't Bob register this morning?
10. What is Bob waiting for?
11. What is the name of the university?
12. When did you register for your current English course?
13. Where did you register?
14. How much was the registration fee?
15. What English course are you taking?
16. Are you going to register for a course next semester?

Pronunciation of [ō], [ɔ], and [ä]

Exercise 2.

A. Listen to the pronunciation of [ō], [ɔ], and [ä]. Then repeat the words.

[ō]	[ɔ]	[ä]
won't	**Pau**l	**Bob**
don't	coffee	want
told	**bought**	lot
grow	fall	shop
hope	cost	stop
only	talk	possible
go	**awful**	not

B. Listen to the sentences. Repeat the sentences. Then circle the [ō] sounds, underline the [ɔ] sounds, and put a box around the [ä] sounds.

1. Paul and Bob want to drink some coffee.
2. Bob won't register with Paul.
3. It costs a lot to go to a university.
4. It's not possible for Bob to pay all of the cost.
5. Call the Geology Office now. It's not open after five o'clock.

Irregular Past Tense Verbs

BASE FORM	PAST FORM	BASE FORM	PAST FORM
break	broke	hit	hit
bring	brought	leave	left
do	did	meet	met
drink	drank	put	put
drive	drove	run	ran
eat	ate	sleep	slept
fall	fell	tell	told
give	gave	wear	wore

Exercise 3. PAIRWORK.

Student A: Cover the questions. Look at the answers. Make *Wh*-questions.

Student B: Check Student A's questions. Answer the questions.

QUESTIONS	ANSWERS
1a. Where did Mark and Sally eat?	Mark and Sally ate *at home*.
1b. What did they drink?	They drank *lemonade*.
2a. Where did Mrs. White put her money?	Mrs. White put her money *under the mattress*.
2b. How did she sleep?	She slept *well*.

3a. Where did Mr. Ramos fall?   Mr. Ramos fell *on the steps.*

3b. What did he break?   He broke *his arm.*

4a. Where did Hassan run?   Hassan ran *in the park.*

4b. What did he wear?   He wore *a jogging suit.*

5a. Who did Yumi bring to the party?   Yumi brought *her brother* to the party.

5b. Why did he leave early?   He left early *because he was tired.*

6a. Who did Dr. Cruz meet?   Dr. Cruz met *the president.*

6b. What did the president give her?   The president gave her *an award.*

7a. What did Jeff drive?   Jeff drove *a motorcycle.*

7b. What did he hit?   He hit *a tree.*

8a. What did Susan tell Fatima?   Susan told Fatima *the homework assignment.*

8b. When did Fatima do the homework?   She did the homework *last night.*

Exercise 4. Complete the passage. Use the past tense form of verbs in the box. Use each verb only once.

break	go	put
do	give	run
drink	hear	sleep
drive	hit	take
eat	leave	tell
fall	meet	

A Camping Trip

Last Saturday Tom and Betty Clark _____ their van to Jackson State Park. They

_____ home at 10 a.m. and _____ a tent with them. They _____ the tent near

Lake Jackson. At the park the Clarks _____ some other people. That night Tom and Betty

_____ hamburgers and _____ iced tea by a campfire. They _____ the dishes and

_____ stories about camping trips when they were young. They _____ to bed at

midnight. They _____ until 4 a.m. At that time, they _____ thunder, and they looked

out of their tent. At that moment, two trees _____ onto their van. One tree _____ the

roof, and the other tree _____ a window of the van. The Clarks _____ to their new

friends' tent. Their friends _____ them a ride to the guardhouse.

Finish the story. Write at least two sentences.

_____

_____

Enough + (Noun) + (Infinitive)

Dialog

Bob: Do you want to go to a movie tonight?
Paul: I'd like to go, but I don't have **enough time to go** to a movie tonight. I have to study for a physics exam.
Bob: How about you, Brad? Do you want to go?
Brad: I don't have **enough money**.
Bob: I have **enough to pay** for both of our tickets.
Brad: Are you sure you have **enough**?
Bob: Yes, I just got a paycheck today.
Brad: Okay, I'll go.

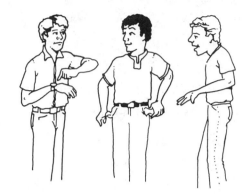

FORMULA 8-1

Subject	verb	**enough**	(noun)	(infinitive)	(complement) .
He	has	enough	money	to go	to a movie.
He	has	enough	money.		
He	has	enough		to go	to a movie.
He	has	enough		to go.	
He	has	enough.			

Examples:

Enough means a sufficient amount.

Exercise 5. MINI CONVERSATIONS.

Example: time / go shopping
 go out for lunch

Pat: Do you have enough <u>time</u> to <u>go shopping</u>?
Lee: No, I don't have enough <u>time</u> to <u>go shopping</u>, but I have enough <u>time</u> to <u>go out for lunch</u>.

1. energy / play racquetball
 play golf

2. food / feed twenty people
 feed ten people

3. money / buy a stereo
 buy a cassette player

4. flour / make two loaves of bread
 make one loaf

5. gas / drive to Washington, D.C.
 drive to Boston

6. _____ / _____
 _____

Exercise 6. Answer the questions. Use *enough* in all answers.

1. Are there enough people in your English class to form a soccer team?
2. Is there enough space in your classroom for twenty people?
3. Did you have enough time to do all of your homework last night?
4. Can you buy a new car this year?
5. Do you have enough patience to babysit children?
6. Can you make an omelette today?

Exercise 7. Complete the sentences. Use *enough* + noun, and complete the infinitive.

1. I don't have _____ to _____ .
2. There isn't _____ to _____ .
3. I would like to have _____ to _____ .
4. There aren't _____ to _____ .
5. _____ doesn't have _____ to _____ .

Future Time: *will*

Dialog

Jean: Will you take the next English course here?
Saleh: Yes, I will.
Jean: What will you do after that?
Saleh: I'll study for my Bachelor's degree.
Jean: Where will you study?
Saleh: At the University of Colorado.
Jean: Why there?
Saleh: My brother studies there. He'll be there for
         two more years.
Jean: Will you live with your brother?
Saleh: No, I won't. I'll live in a dormitory. I hope
         to have an American roommate.

In the sentences in the dialog, *will* expresses future time.
Going to (Chapter 6) also expresses future time.

Write two examples from the dialog for each formula.

FORMULA 8-2	Subject	**will**	**(not)**	verb [base]	(complement) .

1. _____
2. _____

FORMULA 8-3	(Wh-word)	**will**	subject	verb [base]	(complement) ?

1. _____
2. _____

1. Affirmative contractions. Complete the list.

I will = ___*I'll*___   we will = ___*we'll*___

he will = _____   you will = _____

she will = _____   they will = _____

it will = _____

2. Affirmative contractions are usually formed with pronouns, not nouns. For example, the following forms are not usually used in written English:

   the dog'll   and   *Pat'll*

3. Negative contractions. Complete the list.

I will not = ___*I won't*___   we will not = _____

he will not = _____   you will not = _____

she will not = _____   they will not = _____

it will not = _____   Pat and Bob will not = _____

4. Examples of short answers with *will:*   Yes, I will.   No, I won't.
                                                    Yes, she will.   No, she won't.

5. Contractions are not used in affirmative short answers.

   Examples: *Correct*   *Incorrect*
               Yes, I will.   Yes, I'll.
               Yes, he will.   Yes, he'll.

 ## Exercise 8. MINI CONVERSATIONS.

Example: you spend the weekend at the beach
             Where / spend the weekend
             in the mountains

Jamila: Will you spend the weekend at the beach?
Olga: No, I won't.
Jamila: Where will you spend the weekend?
Olga: I'll spend the weekend in the mountains.

1. you play tennis tomorrow
   What / play tomorrow
   play golf

2. your parents travel to London next summer
   Where / travel next summer
   to Dublin

3. you and your girlfriend go out to dinner Friday night
   When / go out to dinner
   Saturday night

4. you see your brother in Detroit
   Who / see in Detroit
   my sister

5. your mother buy a Volkswagen
   What kind of car / buy
   a Ford

6. the plane from Tokyo arrive soon
   When / arrive
   in about two hours

Exercise 9.   INTERVIEW. Interview a classmate.

1. Will you study English next semester?
2. Why or why not?
3. What will you do when you finish studying English?
4. Where will you be a year from now?
5. What will your occupation be?
6. Where will you work?
7. When will you retire?
8. What will you do when you retire?
9. _____ ?

Exercise 10.   Complete the sentences. Use *will* in the questions and answers.

1. A: Will you _____ next year?
   B: Yes, _____ .

2. A: Where _____ your next vacation?
   B: _____ .

3. A: Will you and your _____ ?
   B: No, _____ .

4. A: When _____ your _____ ?
   B: _____ .

5. A: Will _____ soon?
   B: No, _____ .

6. A: How many _____ ?
   B: _____ .

7. A: _____ ?
   B: _____ .

Let's

Dialog

Mark: Let's go to Los Angeles next weekend.
Terry: Let's not go there. Let's go to San Francisco instead.
Mark: Okay.
Terry: Let's leave on Friday after work.
Mark: No, let's wait until Saturday morning.
Terry: That's fine with me. I'll reserve a room at the Gregory Hotel.

Let's (common) = *Let us* (formal). *Let's* introduces an idea or a suggestion of something for two or more people to do, including the speaker.

FORMULA 8-4

Let's	(not)	verb [base]	(complement) .

Exercise 11.   Complete the conversations.

1. *In a classroom*

   Student 1:   Let's _____

   Student 2:   Let's not _____

                Let's _____

   Student 1:   _____

2. *At a party*

   Person 1:   Let's _____

   Person 2:   No, let's not _____

   Person 3:   Let's _____

   Person 1:   _____

3. *At home*

   Wife: Let's _____

   Husband: Let's not _____

   Wife: _____

   Husband: _____

   Wife: _____

4. _____

   _____ :_____

   _____ :_____

   _____ :_____

   _____ :_____

Past Continuous: With *when*

Examples:

Tom and Betty **were driving** to the lake **when** they had a flat tire.
They **were putting** up the tent **when** they met their neighbors.
Betty **was cooking** supper **when** the other people arrived.
Tom **was telling** a story **when** they heard thunder.
Their friends **were leaving when** it started to rain.
Tom and Betty **were sleeping when** the trees fell on their car.

FORMULA 8-5

Subject	was were	(not)	verb + **ing**	(complement)	**when**	subject	verb [simple past]	(complement) .

This formula indicates that an activity was in progress when something else happened. It describes a complex sentence. The sentence has two subjects and two verbs. The sentence has two parts (or clauses). One part has the past continuous statement. This part can be written independently. The second part of the formula has a simple past tense verb. This part begins with *when* and is dependent. It can not be used alone. The two parts can change order.

Example: Their friends were leaving when it started to rain.
            When it started to rain, their friends were leaving.

Notice the comma between the two parts of the second sentence.

Exercise 12.   Answer the questions below. Refer to the example sentences at the top of the page.

Where were Tom and Betty driving when they had a flat tire?
What were Tom and Betty doing when they met their neighbors?
Who was cooking supper when the other people arrived?
Was Betty telling a story when they heard the thunder?
What happened when Betty and Tom were sleeping?

 ## Exercise 13.   MINI CONVERSATIONS.

Example: you do / break your foot
            ski

Jamal: What <u>were you doing</u> when <u>you broke your foot</u>?
Mike: <u>I was skiing</u>.

1. you do / fall off the ladder
   paint the ceiling

2. your brother eat / break his tooth
   eat a piece of candy

3. Miss West do / it start to snow
   drive to the theater

4. Tom and Betty do / meet their neighbors
   put up their tent

5. you talk about / the teacher tell you to be quiet
   talk about the party last Saturday

6. Sonia do / you leave the party
   dance with Roger

7. you and Maria do / I call last night
   watch a movie on TV

8. _____

   _____

Exercise 14.

Complete the sentences. In the blank after *when*, use a verb in the simple past tense from the box. In the other blank use any appropriate verb in the past continuous.

break	come	give	hear	ring	start
bring	fall	have	hit	see	tell

1. I _*was taking a shower*_ when _*the doorbell rang*_ .

2. My teacher _____ when _____

3. When _____ , my classmates _____

4. My friend and I _____ when _____

5. When _____ , some people _____

6. The president _____ when _____

7. When _____ , _____

8. _____ when _____

Exercise 15. Answer the questions.

1. What were you doing before the semester started?
2. What were we studying when class ended yesterday?
3. What were you doing at nine o'clock last night?
4. When class began today, what were you doing?
5. What was the teacher doing when the bell rang today?
6. _____ ?

Exercise 16.

Complete the sentences with the correct forms of the verbs in parentheses. Use the simple past or the past progressive.

1. She _____ (leave) five minutes ago.

   She _____ (walk) out the door when I _____ (arrive).

2. They _____ (watch) TV at 8:30 last night.

   They _____ (watch) TV when I _____ (get) home.

   They _____ (watch) TV for two hours last night.

3. I _____ (have) a bad experience yesterday. I _____ (walk) across the street when a car almost _____ (hit) me. The driver _____ (not/pay) attention. He _____ (eat) a hamburger.

4. I _____ (be) at the library yesterday afternoon. A strange thing _____ (happen). An old man _____ (come) into the library. He _____ (wear) dirty clothes, and he _____ (carry) a big box. Hc _____ (put) the box on a table. He _____ (sit) at the table when three kittens _____ (jump) out of the box. They _____ (play) on the table when a librarian _____ (see) them. The librarian _____ (run) to the table and _____ (tell) the man to take his kittens out of the library. He _____ (walk) out the door with his kittens when he suddenly _____ (give) one of the kittens to the librarian.

Write one or two sentences to complete the story. Use the simple past and/or past progressive.

_____

_____

Go + Verb + ing

Dialog

Talal: Would you like to go <u>running</u> now?
Fran: No, I went <u>running</u> this morning.
Talal: Then, let's go <u>swimming</u>.
Fran: It's too cold to go <u>swimming</u>.
Talal: Well, do you want to go <u>bowling</u> instead?
Fran: Sure, let's go.

A few verbs, particularly verbs related to sports and recreation, are used with a form of *go* + the verb in its *-ing* form.

Exercise 17. PAIRWORK. Practice the dialog above once. Then do it two or three more times. Each time substitute any three different verbs from the box for the underlined words.

bowl	fish	jog	skate
canoe	hike	run	(water) ski
dance	hunt	shop	swim

Exercise 18.
INTERVIEW. Complete the questions with verbs from the box above. Use the *-ing* form. Ask a classmate your questions.

1. Do you ever go _____?
2. How often do you go _____?
3. Where do you go _____?
4. Do you like to go _____?
5. Did you go _____ last weekend?
6. Are you going to go _____ next weekend?

Exercise 19.
QUESTION REVIEW. Write the questions.

A.
1. _____ Yes, Bob was here an hour ago.
2. _____ Yes, he brought his two children.
3. _____ Yes, Bob's mother called me.
4. _____ No, I wasn't sleeping when she called.

B.
1. _____ No, Kathy won't be late.
2. _____ No, she can't drive.
3. _____ Yes, she usually takes a taxi.
4. _____ Yes, Pat and Cher are going to come soon.
5. _____ Yes, they have a car.
6. _____ Yes, they are arriving now.

Exercise 20.
Complete the sentences. Use *not* in all of the sentences. Use the same verb from the first part of each sentence.

1. Toshio drove to New York, but he _____ to Boston.
2. He could stay with relatives in Brooklyn, but he _____ with friends in Manhattan.
3. He saw the Empire State Building, but he _____ the Statue of Liberty.
4. He likes to drive, but he _____ to drive at night.
5. He will visit Montreal, but he _____ Quebec City.
6. He's going to leave today, but he _____ to leave until noon.

Exercise 21.

Use the verbs in parentheses to complete the following passage. Add auxiliaries when necessary.

My brother _____ (study) English for six years in our country. Five years ago when he _____ (be) eighteen, he _____ (decide) to _____ (go) to the United States to study English. He _____ (want) to _____ (improve) his English quickly. He _____ (plan) to study computer science at the University of Washington.

One day he _____ (study) at the library when he _____ (meet) a young woman. They _____ (get) married the following summer. They _____ (not / have) a big wedding. My brother _____ (begin) his freshman year at the University of Washington in the fall.

My brother and his wife _____ (live) in an apartment in Seattle, Washington now. They _____ (have) a baby boy. He _____ (be) almost one year old. He _____ (learn) to walk. He _____ (can / not / talk) yet, but he _____ (make) a lot of noise. My brother _____ (go) to classes in the morning and _____ (study) at home in the afternoon. Now he _____ (prepare) for his final exams.

In three weeks my brother _____ (graduate) from the University of Washington. Two months ago he _____ (receive) a scholarship from our government to study for a Master's degree at Ohio State University. At the end of the summer my brother and his family _____ (move) to Columbus, Ohio.

Complete the passage below with two or three sentences.

Now my brother _____ (be) very homesick. This summer he and his wife and son _____ (travel) _____

_____

_____

_____

_____

Will: Offering Help or Making a Promise

Dialog

Jane: Are you going to the party tomorrow night?
Jess: I don't know. I want to go, but my car's not working.
Jane: I'll give you a ride to the party.
Jess: Thanks. What time do you want to go?
Jane: How about seven o'clock?
Jess: Fine, I'll wait for you outside of my apartment building. I won't be late.

You can use *will* to offer help, and you can use *will* or *won't (will not)* to make a promise.

In the dialog, find the three sentences with these uses of *will*. Write them below.

Offering help: _____

Making a promise: _____

_____

Exercise 22.   Complete the short dialogs. Use *will* or *won't* and other appropriate words.

1. Karen: The movie begins at 5:30. When do you want to meet me?

   Cindy: _____ in the lobby at 5:20.

2. Carl: I need some help with my algebra homework.

   Bill: I _____ after class if I have time then.

3. Robert: It's raining. Drive carefully.

   Marcia: I will. I _____ fast.

4. Pat: Do we need anything from the store?
   Lee: Yes, we need a loaf of bread.

   Pat: Okay, _____ a loaf of bread after work.

5. Jenny: Do you want to go out for lunch?
   Lilly: I don't have enough money to go out for lunch.

   Jenny: That's okay. _____ lunch today.

6. Phil: I'm cooking. I can't answer the phone.

   Judy: _____ it.

7. Teacher: You got a low grade on your last quiz. The next quiz will be on Monday.

   Student: I _____ _____

8. _____: _____

   _____: I _____

Activities

A. RIDDLES. What are the answers?

 1. You can take off my skin. I won't cry, but you will. What am I?
 2. What yesterday was, and what tomorrow will be.
 3. How many eggs can you eat on an empty stomach?

B. INTERVIEW. Work with a classmate.

Student A: Ask a classmate questions about your future related to money, work, family, and life in general.

Student B: Answer Student A's questions. Make predictions about his or her future.

Example questions:

Where will I be in _____ years?

Will I have _____ ?

Will I have enough _____ ?

How many _____ ?

How long will I _____ ?

C. ROLE PLAY. A group of citizens are meeting with a political candidate. They ask questions about what the candidate will do if he or she wins the election.

Example questions: What will you do about _____ ?

How much money will you spend on _____ ?

Who/When/Where will you _____ ?

D. WRITING.

 1. Write about a classmate's future.

 2. You are a political candidate. Write a political statement. Begin with *If I win the election, I will . . .*

 E. LISTENING. Listen to the following passage. Complete the passage with the words you hear.

Life in the Twenty-First Century

Life in the twenty-first century _____ _____ very different from life today. In the year 2000 _____ will work an average of thirty hours per week _____ _____ United States. The number of engineers in North America will increase _____-_____ percent. Factories will operate with _____ people.

Robots _____ _____ most of the work. Cars _____ have metal engines or bodies. They _____ _____ ceramic engines and plastic bodies. _____ percent of all jobs _____ involve the use of computers. Before 2010 computers will _____ instant translations of languages.

At _____ beginning of the 21st century, Russian cosmonauts will make _____ _____ flight to the planet Mars. American astronauts will establish a base _____ _____ moon by the year 2007. In 2020 jet airplanes will travel _____ _____ miles per hour. A flight between Asia and North America _____ _____ one hour.

The world will be more crowded in the _____ century. In 1986 _____ _____ five billion people on earth. _____ the year 2000 there will be 6.2 billion people. One and _____ _____ million babies will be born each week. People born in the next century _____ _____ an average of one hundred years. Will there be enough water for all of _____ people? Will _____ _____ enough houses? The world will grow and change in _____ ways in the next century. Some changes in the 21st century will improve _____ , but other changes will _____ new problems.

F. LISTENING / DISCUSSION. *Part 1:* Listen to the passage in Part E again. Answer the following questions about the passage.

1. Will life in the 21st century be very different from life today?
2. How many hours per week will people work in the United States?
3. What occupation will increase thirty-six percent in North America?
4. Will people do most of the work in factories?
5. What type of bodies will cars of the future have?
6. What will computers do by the year 2010?
7. Where will Russian cosmonauts travel to at the beginning of the 21st century?
8. Where will American astronauts establish a base by the year 2007?
9. How long will a flight between Los Angeles and Toyko take in the year 2020?
10. How many people were there on Earth in 1986?
11. How many babies will be born each week in the year 2000?
12. How long will the average person live?

Part 2: Answer the related questions about ideas from the passage in E. (The answers are not in the passage. Your opinions form the answers.)

1. In your opinion, will there be enough food for everyone in the world in the next century?

2. What changes will occur in your country before the year 2000?

3. What language(s) will be the international language(s) of business and science in the year 2050?

4. What changes will occur in your life between now and the year 2000?

G. PUZZLE.

Tom is a new college student. He has a job on campus in a university cafeteria. He works every weekday from 11:00 a.m. until 1:45 p.m. He has a piano lesson every Monday, Wednesday, and Friday from 3:30 p.m. until 4:30 p.m.

Study the listing from a university course schedule. The listing includes six different courses and the sections available for each course. Tom must register for one section (Sec.) of each of the courses below. Plan Tom's weekly schedule. Include his job, piano lessons, and six courses. Write Tom's weekly schedule in the chart.

COURSE SCHEDULE

All classes on Mondays (M), Wednesdays (W), and Fridays (F) meet for fifty minutes. All classes on Tuesdays (Tu) and Thursdays (Th) meet for ninety minutes.

ENGLISH 301	MATH 316	HISTORY 314	FRENCH 103	BIOLOGY 101	BIOLOGY 101 (Lab)
M, W, F	*M, W, F*	*Tu, Th*	*M, TU, W, TH, F*	*Tu, Th*	*W (only)*
Sec. 1 8 a.m.	Sec. 1 10 a.m.	Sec. 1 8 a.m.	Sec. 1 8 a.m.	Sec. 1 10 a.m.	Sec. 1 8 a.m.
Sec. 2 9 a.m.	Sec. 2 11 a.m.	Sec. 2 10 a.m.	Sec. 2 9 a.m.	Sec. 2 1 p.m.	Sec. 2 9 a.m.
Sec. 3 10 a.m.	Sec. 3 1 p.m.	Sec. 3 1 p.m.	Sec. 3 10 a.m.	Sec. 3 3 p.m.	Sec. 3 10 a.m.
Sec. 4 11 a.m.	Sec. 4 2 p.m.	Sec. 4 4 p.m.	Sec. 4 2 p.m.		Sec. 4 2 p.m.
Sec. 5 1 p.m.	Sec. 5 3 p.m.		Sec. 5 3 p.m.		Sec. 5 3 p.m.
Sec. 6 2 p.m.			Sec. 6 4 p.m.		Sec. 6 4 p.m.
Sec. 7 3 p.m.					Sec. 7 5 p.m.
Sec. 8 4 p.m.					

WEEKLY SCHEDULE

	Monday	Tuesday	Wednesday	Thursday	Friday
8 a.m.					
9 a.m.					
10 a.m.					
11 a.m.					
12 noon					
1 p.m.					
2 p.m.					
3 p.m.					
4 p.m.					
5 p.m.					

H. PREDICTIONS. What are your predictions for next year? Make five predictions about world events, world leaders, famous people, classmates, and sports.

Examples: _____ will $\begin{bmatrix} \text{win} \\ \text{lose} \end{bmatrix}$ _____

An earthquake will occur in _____

_____ will get married to _____

_____ will have a baby in the month of _____

_____ will win the next World Cup.

I. DICTATION. You will hear each sentence two times. Write exactly what you hear.

1. _____
2. _____
3. _____
4. _____
5. _____
6. _____
7. _____
8. _____
9. _____
10. _____

Review Quizzes

 A. LISTENING COMPREHENSION: SENTENCES

For each problem, you will hear a short sentence. You will hear each sentence two times. After you hear a sentence, read the four choices. Decide which written sentence is the closest in meaning to the spoken sentence. Circle the letter of the correct answer.

1. (A) They don't have any money.
   (B) They have enough money.
   (C) They don't have a sufficient amount of money.
   (D) They have a lot of money.

2. (A) I'll spend some money.
   (B) I will not save any money.
   (C) I won't send any money.
   (D) I will save money.

3. (A) When you called, we were reading.
   (B) We were reading when you came.
   (C) We were riding when you called.
   (D) When you called, we were writing.

4. (A) Jean broke her ankle last fall.
   (B) Jean has a broken ankle.
   (C) Jean felt sad about her broke uncle.
   (D) Jean's uncle broke her fall.

5. (A) I like shopping.
   (B) I like to go shopping.
   (C) I want to shop.
   (D) Let's go shopping.

6. (A) Well, fix the dress tomorrow.
   (B) We're going to repair the dress tomorrow.
   (C) We'll finish the dress tomorrow.
   (D) We'll fit the dress tomorrow.

7. (A) She will be here soon.
   (B) She won't be here soon.
   (C) They will be here soon.
   (D) They won't be here soon.

8. (A) There's time to write letters.
   (B) There are enough letters to write.
   (C) There aren't enough letters to write.
   (D) I have enough letters.

9. (A) They lift here.
   (B) They live here.
   (C) They left here.
   (D) They were living here.

10. (A) It's a lettuce salad.
    (B) Let's eat some salad.
    (C) The salad has lettuce.
    (D) Let's save some salad.

B. STRUCTURE: SENTENCE COMPLETION

Choose the *one* word or phrase that best completes the sentence. Circle the letter of the correct answer.

1. -------- when I called?
   - (A) Was you sleeping
   - (B) Were you sleeping
   - (C) Did you sleep
   - (D) Did you sleeping

2. She -------- tomorrow morning.
   - (A) will to arrive
   - (B) will arriving
   - (C) will arrives
   - (D) is going to arrive

3. I have five dollars. I have -------- go to a movie.
   - (A) money enough
   - (B) enough money
   - (C) very money
   - (D) enough money to

4. What -------- about?
   - (A) did the movie
   - (B) was the movie
   - (C) did the movie is
   - (D) the movie did

5. He -------- his bedroom today.
   - (A) has clean
   - (B) is have to clean
   - (C) has to clean
   - (D) has to cleaning

6. -------- you with your homework?
   - (A) Is he will help
   - (B) Will he help
   - (C) Is he will helps
   - (D) Does he will help

7. -------- when you left?
   - (A) Was it rained
   - (B) Did it rained
   - (C) Was it rain
   - (D) Was it raining

8. My sister is very busy this summer. She doesn't have -------- take a vacation.
   - (A) time enough
   - (B) enough time
   - (C) enough time to
   - (D) enough of time to

9. I -------- hungry this morning.
   - (A) wasn't
   - (B) didn't
   - (C) didn't was
   - (D) am didn't

10. My friend is -------- .
   - (A) hungry
   - (B) pilot
   - (C) a strong
   - (D) wait

11. I'm ready. Let's -------- now.
   - (A) go
   - (B) going
   - (C) to go
   - (D) to going

12. It -------- rain much here last year.
   - (A) isn't
   - (B) doesn't
   - (C) wasn't
   - (D) didn't

13. The weather -------- very cold yesterday.
   - (A) wasn't
   - (B) weren't
   - (C) didn't
   - (D) didn't was

14. He -------- for an hour last night.
   - (A) studies
   - (B) didn't study
   - (C) was studying
   - (D) didn't studying

C. STRUCTURE: ERROR IDENTIFICATION

Each sentence has four underlined words or phrases. Circle the *one* underlined word or phrase that is not correct. Then correct the sentence.

1. She <u>usually goes</u> to <u>a movie</u> <u>on Saturdays,</u> but she <u>didn't goes</u> last Saturday.
          A   B   C   D

2. He <u>didn't can't</u> go <u>to school</u> yesterday because he <u>was</u> <u>sick</u>.
        A   B   C D

3. We <u>were</u> <u>walked</u> to <u>work</u> when we <u>saw</u> the car accident.
        A   B   C   D

4. My roommate and I <u>am</u> going <u>to</u> <u>take</u> <u>a trip next</u> week.
                    A   B C   D

5. <u>Does he will</u> <u>have</u> to <u>get</u> a <u>new visa</u> for next semester?
        A   B   C   D

6. <u>He's</u> <u>going</u> to <u>washing</u> <u>the dishes</u> after dinner.
     A   B   C   D

7. He <u>must go</u> <u>to the</u> supermarket last night because he <u>didn't have</u> <u>any food</u>.
        A   B   C   D

8. <u>Let's</u> <u>studying</u> <u>until</u> they <u>come</u>.
     A   B   C   D

9. I <u>studying</u> <u>at</u> home <u>yesterday afternoon</u> when the fire <u>began</u>.
      A   B   C   D

10. Did you <u>have</u> <u>to go</u> <u>to</u> work <u>last</u> evening?
            A   B   C   D

CHAPTER 9

Dialog

Donna: Hello.
Bob: Hi, Donna. This is Bob Thompson. Would you like to go to a movie with me tonight?
Donna: I'm sorry, Bob. I'm too tired to go out tonight.
Bob: How about going to a movie tomorrow night?
Donna: I'll be studying for a chemistry test all evening.
Bob: Would you like to go out to eat on Friday?
Donna: I'm on a diet, and I have to wash my hair on Friday night.
Bob: Let's go to a baseball game this Saturday.
Donna: It's too hot to sit outside at a baseball game. I hate the heat and I don't like baseball.
Bob: Why don't we go to a concert next weekend?
Donna: I'll be very busy next weekend, but I have an idea.
Bob: What's that?
Donna: I have a friend. Her name is Holly. She's energetic and she loves baseball. She might not be busy tonight or this weekend. Give her a call. Her number is 453-7803. Say "hi" to Holly for me. Bye, Bob.

(*Click.*)

Exercise 1.   Answer the questions. If the answer is not in the dialog, respond, *I don't know*.

1. Does Donna want to go to a movie with Bob tonight? Why or why not?
2. What will she be doing tomorrow night?
3. Where will she be studying tomorrow night?
4. Why doesn't Donna want to go out to eat?
5. What concert is next weekend?
6. Does Bob want to go to a baseball game this weekend?
7. Why doesn't Donna want to go to a baseball game on Saturday?
8. Does Donna want to see Bob?
9. What's Donna's idea?
10. Why does Donna recommend her friend Holly?
11. Will Bob call Holly?
12. Will Holly want to go out with Bob?

Exercise 2.   Complete each of the short dialogs with excuses.

1. Teacher: You were late for class.
    Student: *I missed the bus.*
    (or)   _____

2. Teacher: You weren't in class yesterday.
    Student: *I had to go to the doctor's office.*
    (or)   _____

3. Teacher: You didn't do your homework.
    Student: _____
    (or)   _____

4. Teacher: You got a bad grade on the test.

   Student: _____

   (or)   _____

Pronunciation of [ə] and [ä]

Exercise 3.   **A.** Listen to the difference between the pronunciation of [ə] and [ä].
Then repeat the word.

[ə]	[ä]
luck	lock
study	on
young	hot
month	Bob
a	not
what	want

B. Listen to the sentences. Repeat the sentences. Then circle the [ə] sounds and underline the
[ä] sounds.

1. Bob Thompson wants to see Donna on Monday.
2. Donna wants to study, but she does not want to go to the library.
3. It's too hot to go to a baseball game.
4. What's Holly Johnson's phone number?

May and *might:* Possibility

Examples: What **might** Bob Thompson do now?
              He **might** call Holly.
              She **might** not be at home.
              She **might** be at the library.
              Bob **may** invite her to go to a movie.
              Holly **may** not want to go.

Both *may* and *might* express an uncertain possibility either at the present time or in the future.
There are no contractions with *may*. The contraction of *might* and *not* (mightn't) is rarely used.
Might occurs infrequently in questions. *May* does not occur in questions that express possibility.

FORMULA 9-1	Subject	**may** **might**	(not)	verb [base]	(complement) .

Exercise 4. MINI CONVERSATIONS.

Examples:

you
stay home
go shopping

Ed: What <u>are you</u> going to do tonight?
Sue: I don't know. <u>I</u> might <u>stay home</u>.
Ed: What <u>are you</u> going to do tomorrow night?
Sue: I'm not sure. <u>I</u> may <u>go shopping</u>.

Tom
go to the library
go to a party

Ali: What <u>is Tom</u> going to do tonight?
Jim: I don't know. <u>He</u> might <u>go to the library</u>.
Ali: What <u>is he</u> going to do tomorrow night?
Jim: I'm not sure. <u>He</u> may <u>go to a party</u>.

1. Patricia
study for an exam
go bowling

2. you
go to bed early
go out to eat

3. your parents
watch TV
go to a movie

4. you and your wife
stay home and relax
go dancing

5. Holly and Donna
listen to records
go to a concert

6. Bob
clean his apartment
visit his girlfriend

7. you
do my laundry
play cards with some friends

8. _____
_____
_____

Exercise 5. Complete the sentences. Write what you might do in the future. Use *may* or *might* in each sentence.

Example: This weekend ***I might go to a play*** .

1. Tomorrow _____
2. This weekend _____
3. Next week _____
4. Next month _____
5. During my next vacation _____
6. Next year _____

Exercise 6. What might be wrong? Read the situation. For each situation give two possible explanations. Use *may* or *might* in each explanation.

1. The baby is crying. ***It might be hungry.***
   (or) ***It*** _____

2. Our teacher is absent. ***She may have a problem with her car.***
   (or) ***She*** _____

3. There's smoke in the next room. _____

   (or) _____

4. There's a police car across the street. _____

   (or) _____

5. The car won't start. _____

   (or) _____

6. My friend is very quiet today. _____

   (or) _____

Exercise 7. MINI CONVERSATIONS.

Example: you / play tennis

Lee: Are you going to play tennis today?

Kim: I ⎡ may ⎤ not play tennis today, but I will play tennis tomorrow.
      ⎣ might ⎦

1. you / exercise
2. Elizabeth / go downtown
3. Mom and Dad / go shopping
4. Patrick / write letters
5. you and your cousin / go to the beach

6. _____ / _____

Irregular Past Tense Verbs

BASE FORM	PAST FORM	BASE FORM	PAST FORM
build	built	lend	lent
catch	caught	pay	paid
cost	cost	ride	rode
cut	cut	send	sent
feel	felt	speak	spoke
fly	flew	spend	spent
hurt	hurt	teach	taught
know	knew	win	won

Exercise 8. PAIRWORK. Student A: Read the questions.

Student B: Cover the answers. Look at the pictures. Answer the questions.

Student A: Check Student B's answers.

QUESTIONS		ANSWERS

1a. Did you ride the subway?

No, I rode the bus.

b. Did it cost fifty cents?

No, it cost a dollar.

2a. Did you hurt your leg?

No, I hurt my arm.

b. Did the door cut your wrist?

No, it cut my elbow.

3a. Did you pay five dollars for the lottery tickets?

No, I paid ten dollars.

b. Did you win a hundred dollars in the lottery?

No, I won three hundred dollars.

4a. Did you build a house in the city?

No, I built a house in the country.

b. Did your parents lend you the money?

No, a bank lent me the money.

FIRST NATIONAL BANK

Exercise 9. MINI CONVERSATIONS.

Example: a. Mike lend you his bicycle for the weekend
me his motorcycle

Ann: Did Mike lend you his bicycle for the weekend?
Bob: No, he didn't lend me his bicycle. He lent me his motorcycle.

Example: b. you ride his motorcycle to the lake
it to the beach

Ann: Did you ride his motorcycle to the lake?
Bob: No, I didn't ride his motorcycle to the lake. I rode it to the beach.

1a. the boss catch the 10 o'clock flight from Kennedy Airport
the nine o'clock flight

1b. fly to San Francisco
to Oakland

2a. you send your mother flowers for her birthday
her a plant

2b. spend twenty dollars
thirty dollars

3a. you teach your sister how to ice skate in Switzerland
her how to ski

3b. she feel nervous at the top of the mountain
very excited

4a. you and your sister speak French to the old Swiss man
German

4b. he know your father many years ago
our grandfather

Too + **Adjective (+ Infinitive)**

Dialog

Customer: Excuse me.
Waitress: Yes?
Customer: I can't eat this meal. The steak is **too raw to eat.** The French fries are **too greasy,** and the coffee is **too bitter to drink.**
Waitress: I'm very sorry. I'll bring you another meal.
Customer: I don't have time to wait for another meal. It's **too late.** I have to go back to work soon.

In the sentences above, *too* expresses an excessive amount, a negative result, something wrong.

Examples: I can't drink this coffee. It's **too hot.** It's **too hot to drink.**
I can't eat this food. It's **too spicy.** It's **too spicy to eat.**

Exercise 10. MINI CONVERSATIONS.

Example: you move these desks
    They / heavy

A: Can you move these desks?
B: No, I can't. They're too heavy (to move).

1. you play basketball
 I / short

2. Tom lift one hundred pounds
 He / weak

3. John and Charles play on the football team
 They / thin

4. your grandmother ride a bike
 She / old

5. you help me now
 I / busy

6. Elizabeth drive a car
 She / young

7. you do the homework
 It / difficult

8. you fall asleep here
 It / noisy

9. we go swimming
 It / cold

10. your nephews walk
 They / young

11. you buy that house
 It / expensive

12. _____

   _____ / _____

Exercise 11. Complete the sentences with *too* or *very*. Use *very* for emphasis. Use *too* for an excessive amount.

1. The food is _____ good.

2. I'm _____ tired to go out tonight.

3. I'm _____ sorry.

4. This shirt doesn't fit. It's _____ big for me.

5. She is _____ beautiful.

6. This is a _____ easy exercise.

7. I can't wear these shoes. They're _____ tight.

8. It's _____ hot to go jogging.

9. The store isn't far away. It's _____ near.

10. That apartment is _____ small. It's _____ small for four people.

11. Let's take the car. It's _____ hot to walk.

12. The movie was _____ funny.

13. We can't swim in this lake. The water is _____ dirty.

14. I'm _____happy to be here.

15. I'm _____ pleased to meet you.

16. It's _____ nice to see you.

Reading

Study the chart on page 219 before reading the passage. The chart describes the primary and secondary educational systems of the United States.

Education in the United States
(Primary and Secondary Education)

Many children in the United States begin school by the age of four or five. They go to kindergarten classes for half a day. Some children start school at an earlier age in a nursery school or pre-school.

At about age six, children in the United States begin first grade. Elementary school is usually six years long, from the first grade to the sixth grade. Children study about seven hours a day Monday through Friday for approximately thirty-six weeks each year. The school year begins in August or September and usually ends in June. Students have several weeks of vacation in December and January, and one or two weeks of vacation in the spring. Summer vacation usually begins in June.

After elementary school, students enter secondary school. Generally, the first two years are junior high school. The last four years, called freshman, sophomore, junior and senior years, are senior high school. In most states education is compulsory until the age of sixteen. About eighty percent of high school students continue through the twelfth grade (the senior year) and graduate from high school. They receive a high school diploma. One third study in an institution of higher education after high school graduation.

Some students attend private elementary and secondary schools. Private schools are often expensive. Public schools are free. Most students attend public schools. Local school districts in each state control public education. For this reason school programs differ from one school district to another. About fifty million students attend primary and secondary schools in the United States each year.

Exercise 12.   Answer the questions based on the reading about education.

1. At what age do children begin school in the United States?
2. How long do children in the United States study each day?
3. How many weeks do children in the United States study each school year?
4. When does the school year in the United States begin?
5. When does the school year in the United States end?
6. How long is elementary school in the United States?
7. Until what age is education compulsory in the United States?
8. What percentage of students finish high school?
9. Who controls public education in the United States?
10. Are public school programs the same in each school district in the United States?

Exercise 13.
Complete the chart (below, right) to describe the primary and secondary educational systems in your country (or in another country).

Educational Systems: Primary and Secondary Levels

The United States

_____
(country)

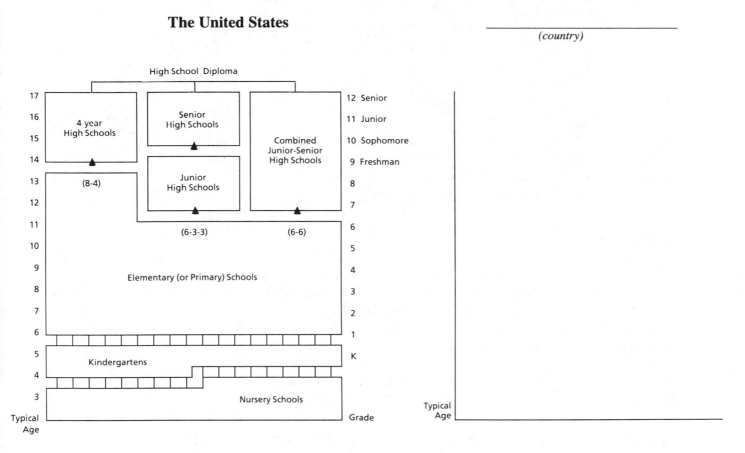

Exercise 14.
Answer the questions about education in your country.

1. At what age do children begin school?
2. How many hours do children study each day?
3. When does the school year begin?
4. When does the school year end?
5. How long is elementary school?
6. Until what age is education compulsory?
7. Who controls public education?
8. Are public school programs the same in each part of the country?
9. Where did you study?

Future Continuous

Dialog

Rick: Bye, Dad. I'll be home at noon.
Father: Rick, can you clean up your room this afternoon?
Rick   I'm sorry. I'll be studying all afternoon.
Father: Can you clean it up this evening?
Rick: No, I can't. I'll be working from seven until eleven.
Father: How about tomorrow morning?
Rick: I can't. I'll be helping Jeff with his car.
Father: What will you be doing at one p.m.?
Rick: Uh, well Jeff and I will be shopping.
Father: That's too bad. I have two tickets to the football
            game. I'll have to invite someone else.

Exercise 15.   Answer the questions.

1. What will Rick be doing this afternoon?
2. When will Rick be working?
3. Who will Rick be helping tomorrow morning?
4. What will Rick be doing tomorrow at one p.m.?
5. What will Rick's father be watching tomorrow afternoon?

FORMULA 9-2

Subject	**will**	**(not)**	**be**	verb + **ing**	(complement) .

The future continuous expresses an action that will be in progress at some time in the future.

Write two example sentences of this formula from the dialog above.

1. _____
2. _____

FORMULA 9-3

(*Wh*-word)	**will**	subject	**be**	verb + **ing**	(complement) **?**

Write an example sentence of this formula from the dialog above.

1. _____

Exercise 16.   MINI CONVERSATIONS.

Example: Susan / ski tomorrow morning at 9 o'clock
              ice skate

Sid: Will Susan be <u>skiing</u> <u>tomorrow morning at 9 o'clock</u>?
Beth: No, <u>she</u> won't. <u>She'll</u> be <u>ice skating</u>.

1. Kiyomi / study this afternoon at 3 o'clock
   shop

2. you / fix your car tomorrow at noon
   fix my motorcycle

3. your grandparents /
   drive home this afternoon about 4 o'clock
   fly home

4. you and your friends /
   play basketball tomorrow evening at seven
   play football

5. Fatima / write letters tonight after supper
   do homework

6. David / jog this evening around 7 o'clock
   swim

7. James and Patrick / travel next week
   work

8. _____ / _____
   _____

Exercise 17. MINI CONVERSATIONS.

Example: you / 4:00
            work
            6:00
            watch TV

Ali: What will you be doing at 4:00?
Jose: I'll be working.
Ali: Will you still be working at 6:00?
Jose: No, I won't. I'll be watching TV then.

1. Margie and Ted / 10:00 a.m.
   paint the living room
   noon
   paint the kitchen

2. Carmen / 6:00
   cook
   7:30
   eat

3. you and Yoshi / 1:00
   exercise
   2:00
   relax

4. Nabil / 3:00
   fix his car
   5:00
   drive it

5. you / 2:00
   do the laundry
   4:00
   take a nap

6. _____ / _____
   _____
   _____
   _____

Exercise 18. Complete the sentences. Write predictions about what some of your class-mates will be doing in the future.

1. _____ will be _____ this evening at 8:00.

2. _____ tonight at ten.

3. _____ not _____ tonight at midnight.

4. _____ tomorrow morning at 5:00.

5. _____ tomorrow at 8 a.m.

6. _____ not _____ tomorrow afternoon at two.

7. _____ next Saturday evening.

8. _____ not _____ next Sunday afternoon.
9. _____ studying _____ next year.
10. _____
11. _____

Exercise 19. Ask and answer the questions.

1. What will you be doing tomorrow at this time?
2. How will you be practicing English this weekend?
3. Where will you be spending the weekend?
4. Will you be studying English next year?
5. Where will you be living next year?
6. _____ ?

$$\text{Too} + \begin{bmatrix} \textbf{\textit{much}} \\ \textbf{\textit{many}} \end{bmatrix} + \text{(Noun)} + \text{(Infinitive)}$$

Dialog

Nicky: Do you want to play cards this afternoon?
Chris: I can't. I have **too much** work to do. I'm moving to a small apartment on Wilson Street.
Nicky: Why are you moving?
Chris: I pay **too much** rent for my old apartment. However, I have **too many** things for my new apartment. I have **too much** furniture and **too many** books. What can I do?

Too much indicates an excessive amount of a non-count item.
Too many indicates an excessive amount of a count item.

Exercise 20. Complete the dialogs with *too much* or *too many*.

1. Terry: Did you buy that brown suit we saw at Macy's?

   Lee: No, it cost _____ . I already have _____ bills to pay this month.

2. Jeff: Would you like to go sailing this weekend?

   Dan: I'd love to, but I have _____ homework to do.

3. Mark: Do you like living in New York City?

   Ann: I like my job there, but there are _____ people in New York, _____ traffic, and _____ crime.

4. Barb: There isn't any more room in the refrigerator.

   Liz: I know. We bought _____ food. We have _____ meat and _____ vegetables.

5. Kate: Did you like Martha's new recipe for spaghetti and meatballs?

   Ted: Not really. There was _____ salt and _____ grease, and she used _____ tomatoes in the sauce.

6. Mary: Are you ready for the trip?

   Ray: No, I'm still packing.

   Mary: You're taking _____ luggage. You're packing _____ clothes and _____ books for one week at the beach.

Indefinites

Affirmative (+)	**Someone** wants to see you. There is **someone** at the door.
Negative (−)	**No one** wants to see you. There isn't **anyone** at the door.
Interrogative (?)	Does **someone** want to see me? Does **anyone** want to see me? Is there **someone** at the door? Is there **anyone** at the door?

Notes: 1. *Any* is used in negative sentences after *not*.
2. Indefinite pronouns: *someone = somebody*
   anyone = anybody
   no one = nobody.
3. Other indefinite pronouns: *something, anything, nothing.*
4. Indefinite adverbs: *somewhere, anywhere, nowhere.*
5. Indefinite pronouns and adverbs are singular. Third person singular verb forms follow these terms.

Exercise 21. Complete the short dialogs with *something, somebody, anything,* or *anybody.*

1. A: Are you going to take _____ to eat to the party?

   B: No, I'm not going to take _____ .

2. A: Are you going with _____ to the party on Sunday?

   B: Yes, I am going with _____ from my hometown.

3. A: Do you know _____ about French history?

   B: No, I don't know _____ about French history, but I know _____ about British history.

4. A: _____ is bothering Tom. Did he say _____ to you?

   B: Yes, he told me _____ about his problems yesterday.

   A: Is there _____ we can do to help him?

   B: No, there isn't _____ we can do.

5. A: Did you eat _____ before you left for work?

   B: No, I didn't eat _____ at home, but I ate _____ on the way to work.

6. A: _____ is wrong with my stomach.

   B: Is there _____ you can take for it?

   A: There isn't _____ here.

   B: I can get you _____ at the drugstore.

   A: Thanks.

7. A: Did Angela see _____ from her English class at the library?

   B: No, she didn't see _____ from her English class there, but she saw _____ from her history class.

Exercise 22.   Complete the short dialogs with *anything, anybody, nothing,* or *nobody*.

1. A: Did _____ call me this morning?

   B: No, _____ called you all morning.

2. A: Did _____ come in the mail for me?

   B: I didn't see _____ for you.

3. A: _____ sent Paula a birthday card last week. She was very sad.

   B: Well, did _____ have her new address?

   A: I don't know.

4. A: Is _____ going to drive you to the airport tomorrow morning?

   B: No, _____ can take me in the morning. I'm going to call a taxi.

5. A: What are you going to watch on TV tonight?

   B: _____ . I'm going to study tonight.

6. A: There's _____ wrong with your computer, and there isn't _____ wrong with your printer.

   B: Is there _____ wrong with my disk?

   A: I don't know. Maybe that's the problem.

Exercise 23.

PAIRWORK. Student A: Ask the questions.

Student B: Cover the questions and answers. Look at the cues. Answer the questions.

Student A: Check Student B's answers.

STUDENT A (Questions and Answers)	STUDENT B (Cues)

1a. Do you want anything to eat now?
(No, I don't want anything to eat.)

No

1b. Would you like anything to drink?
(Yes, I'd like something to drink.)

Yes

2a. Is there anyone at the door?
(No, there isn't anyone at the door.)

No

2b. Is there anything in the mailbox?
(Yes, there's something in the mailbox.)

Yes

3a. Do you have anything to do this weekend?
(No, I don't have anything to do this weekend.)

No

3b. Do you want to go anywhere?
(No, I don't want to go anywhere.)

No

4a. Do you know anyone to play tennis with?
(Yes, I know someone to play tennis with.)

Yes

4b. Is there anywhere to play tennis near here?
(No, there isn't anywhere to play tennis near here.)

No

5a. Do you have anything to read?
(No, I don't have anything to read.)

No

5b. Do you have anything to do now?
(Yes, I have something to do now.)

Yes

Exercise 24. Read the passage.

Mayville, U.S.A.

Mayville is a small town near Metropolis. About three hundred people live in Mayville. The people in Mayville speak only English. There are two restaurants in Mayville. There aren't any factories, movie theaters, or discotheques in Mayville. Weekends can be very boring in Mayville. Many people go to Metropolis on weekends.

A. Answer the questions with *no one, nothing, nowhere,* or *somewhere.*

1. Is there anywhere to dance in Mayville?
2. Does anyone work in a factory in Mayville?
3. Is there anything to do on weekends in Mayville?
4. Is there anywhere to eat in Mayville?
5. Does anyone speak Spanish in Mayville?

B. Answer the questions about your hometown.

1. Is there anywhere to eat Chinese food in your hometown?
2. Is there anything to do on weekends in your hometown?
3. Does anyone speak English in your hometown?
4. Is there anywhere to dance in your hometown?
5. Does anyone work in a factory in your hometown?

C. Complete the questions. Then ask a classmate your questions.

1. Is there anywhere to _____ in your hometown?
2. Is there anywhere to _____ near your hometown?
3. Does anyone _____ in your hometown?
4. Is there anything _____ in your hometown?

Exercise 25.

Complete the sentences with *someone, something, somewhere, anyone, anything, anywhere, no one, nothing,* or *nowhere.* (Some sentences have more than one answer.)

1. _____ brought food to the party. Everyone brought drinks.
2. I didn't go _____ during vacation.
3. I can't believe it. I don't have _____ to do today.
4. I need _____ to drive me to the airport this afternoon.
5. Can _____ here fix my typewriter?
6. _____ answered the phone.
7. Is there _____ to swim in your hometown?
8. _____ is wrong with my car. It won't start.
9. Would you like _____ for dessert?
10. I don't know _____ about Australia.
11. Elizabeth knows _____ about computers, but her husband doesn't.
12. _____ in this office speaks French. Everyone speaks English or Spanish.
13. There's _____ to park on campus.
14. She told _____ in the office about her new job.
15. I don't want to stay in town next weekend. I want to go _____ to relax.
16. I felt sick all day yesterday. I didn't eat _____ .
17. _____ can help him. He has to do it alone.

Exercise 26.

Verb tense review. Use the verbs in parentheses to complete the following passage.

Events in Aviation History

Charles Lindbergh _____ (be) the first person to fly alone across the Atlantic Ocean. He _____ (leave) from New York at 7:52 a.m. on May 20, 1927 and _____ (reach) Paris thirty-three hours later. Because of his flight, Lindbergh _____ (win) $25,000.

Today jumbo jets _____ (transport) passengers between cities around the world every day. The Boeing 747 Jumbo Jet _____ (have) a capacity of 400–500 passengers. The Boeing 747 _____ (begin) service in 1970. It _____ (be) still a popular aircraft.

Air France and British Air _____ (introduce) the Concorde in 1976. On January 1, 1983 a supersonic jet _____ (carry) travelers between New York and London in two hours and fifty-six minutes. In the twenty-first century hypersonic jets _____ (make) transatlantic flights in under half an hour.

Exercise 27. Verb tense review. Use the verbs in parentheses to complete the following letter.

Dear Mom and Dad,

Greetings from TWA Flight 804. I _am flying_ (fly) between New York and Paris.

I _____ (enjoy) my flight over the Atlantic.

I _didn't enjoy_ (not, enjoy) my flight from Miami to New York. It _____ (be) very unpleasant. We _____ (fly) over Washington when the plane _____ (begin) to shake. A bad storm _____ (cause) the turbulence in the air. When we _____ (arrive) in New York, it _____ (rain) very hard. We _____ (have) to wait an hour before we _____ (can / land).

At Kennedy Airport I _____ (hurry) to the TWA terminal to catch my flight to London, but I _____ (miss) it. When I _____ (get) to the terminal, the plane to London _____ (take) off. It _____ (be) the last flight to London.

The ticket agent _____ (put) me on this flight to Paris. From Paris I _____ (fly) to London. I _____ (arrive) in London at 10 a.m. At home in Miami it _____ (be) 5 a.m.

The flight attendants _____ (serve) dinner now. I _____ (mail) this letter from Paris, and I _____ (send) you a postcard from London soon.

Love,

Activities

A. RIDDLES. What are the answers?

   1. What has two hands but no fingers?
   2. What has four legs, a back, and two arms, but no body?
   3. Why do birds fly south for the winter?
   4. What kind of dog doesn't have a tail?
   5. Who always goes to bed with his shoes on?

B. CHAIN STORIES. (Whole class or class divided into groups of four students or more)

Student A: Read the first sentence of the story. Add a sentence to continue the story.
Student B: Add another sentence. Student C: Continue with another sentence.
Other students: Add additional sentences.

Story 1: "An Unusual Person"

   Yesterday I met a very unusual person.

Story 2: "An Awful Day"

   Last Monday was a terrible day!

Story 3 "Vacation Plans"

   My vacation next month will be wonderful.

C. WRITING.

Select one of the stories from Part B. Write 8–10 sentences to complete it.

D. ROLE PLAY / INTERVIEW. One student is a reporter. Another student is a famous
entertainer (actor, singer, or musician). The reporter asks the entertainer the questions.

   1. Where did you study acting / singing / music?
   2. Who taught you to act / sing / play the_____ ?
   3. Were you a good student?
   4. Do you still take lessons?
   5. Did you win any awards last year?
   6. Who are your favorite entertainers?
   7. Where will you be performing next week?
   8. Who might you perform with next year?
   9. What do you do during a typical day?
  10. Where will you spend your next vacation?
  11. Do you _____ ?
  12. Can you _____ ?
  13. Did you _____ ?
  14. Will you _____ ?
  15. _____ ?
  16. _____ ?

E. PUZZLE. Unscramble the words below to form dialog sentences.

Last Day of the Semester

Lou: _____
going / this / do / you / to / are / what / summer / ?

Ben: _____
this / am / to / to / school / planning / I / go / summer / . ‖

_____
classes / take / might / I / three / . ‖ you / how / about / ?

Lou: _____
take / I / to / want / any / don't / summer / classes / this / . ‖

_____
all / I / summer / going / relax / am / to / .

Ben: _____
learning / you / be / nothing / I / be / will / but / doing / something / will / . ‖

_____
to / summer / very / take / good / a / is / time / classes / .

Lou: _____
school / really / go / why / to / do / to / you / want / summer / ?

Ben: _____

_____
didn't / classes / two / this / of / pass / I / semester , / my / and / again / must / take / I / them / .

F. DICTATION. You will hear each sentence two times. Write exactly what you hear.

1. _____
2. _____
3. _____
4. _____
5. _____
6. _____
7. _____
8. _____
9. _____

Review Quizzes

A. LISTENING COMPREHENSION: SENTENCES

For each problem you will hear a short sentence once. After you hear the sentence, read the four choices. Decide which written sentence is the closest in meaning to the spoken sentence. Circle the letter of the correct answer.

1. (A) He may stay there next year.
   (B) He won't be studying there next year.
   (C) He might study there next year.
   (D) He will study there next year.

2. (A) She won't want to go.
   (B) She might want to go.
   (C) She may not want to go.
   (D) She can't go.

3. (A) The Tigers won one game.
   (B) The Tigers lost one game.
   (C) The Lions lost two games.
   (D) Both the Tigers and the Lions won one game.

4. (A) He was late, but he caught a train to London.
   (B) He flew to London.
   (C) He took a train to London.
   (D) He was late and missed a flight to London.

5. (A) She couldn't drive.
   (B) She drove an old car.
   (C) She wasn't too young to drive.
   (D) Her car was too old to drive.

B. LISTENING COMPREHENSION: CONVERSATIONS

You will hear short conversations between two people. At the end of each conversation, a third person will ask a question about the conversation. You will hear the question only once. After you hear the conversation and the related question, read the four possible answers. Decide which answer is the best response to the question. Circle the letter of the best answer.

Example: You hear:

    You read: (A) The name of the post office.
                  (B) The directions to the post office.
                  (C) The street that the post office is on.
                  (D) The address of the post office.

    The best answer is (B).

1. (A) He doesn't want to buy it.
   (B) He may want to buy it.
   (C) He wants to buy it next week.
   (D) He can buy it next week.

2. (A) They liked the movie.
   (B) The movie was good.
   (C) They didn't like the movie.
   (D) The movie was funny.

3. (A) She can meet him at 6:30.
   (B) She will order meat at the Italian restaurant.
   (C) She will meet him at work at six.
   (D) She doesn't want to meet him at the Italian restaurant.

4. (A) She'll register in an hour.
   (B) She'll be here late to register.
   (C) She'll register tomorrow.
   (D) She registered an hour ago.

5. (A) It won't be warm enough this afternoon.
   (B) It's not too cold now.
   (C) It might be warm enough now.
   (D) It's not warm enough now.

C. STRUCTURE: SENTENCE COMPLETION

Choose the *one* word or phrase that best completes the sentence. If none of the choices correctly completes the problem, choose (D) *None of the above*. Circle the letter of the correct answer.

1. My sister might -------- to Japan next summer.
   (A) go
   (B) goes
   (C) going
   (D) is going

2. Pat -------- leave early today.
   (A) maybe
   (B) may be
   (C) may
   (D) may to

3. I only have five dollars. I don't have -------- money to buy this record.
   (A) a lot
   (B) very
   (C) enough
   (D) *None of the above*

4. We can't play tennis now. It's -------- to play tennis.
   (A) very hot
   (B) too hot
   (C) enough hot
   (D) hot enough

5. I didn't ride a horse. I -------- a camel.
   (A) ride
   (B) read
   (C) rode
   (D) rided

6. At 9:00 tomorrow morning she -------- an English test.
   (A) will be taking
   (B) will be take
   (C) going to take
   (D) is going be taking

7. He doesn't eat -------- fruit.
   (A) very
   (B) enough
   (C) many
   (D) *None of the above*

8. -------- your uncle rich?
   (A) Do
   (B) Does
   (C) Are
   (D) *None of the above*

9. Did your brother -------- a good time at the party last night?
   (A) has
   (B) had
   (C) have
   (D) having

10. He can play on the basketball team. He is -------- .
    (A) too tall
    (B) enough tall
    (C) very tall
    (D) *None of the above*

D. STRUCTURE: ERROR IDENTIFICATION

Each sentence has four underlined words or phrases. Circle the *one* underlined word or phrase that is not correct. Then correct the sentence.

1. It <u>wasn't</u> snow <u>very much</u> <u>in</u> Montreal <u>last</u> winter.
       A   B   C   D

2. <u>Who</u> <u>does</u> you <u>usually talk</u> to <u>about</u> your problems?
     A   B   C   D

3. I <u>will</u> be <u>study</u> <u>for</u> a test <u>all night</u> tonight.
      A   B   C   D

4. He <u>is</u> <u>very</u> <u>short</u> <u>to play</u> on a college basketball team.
       A   B   C   D

5. Sarah <u>may</u> <u>gets</u> a scholarship <u>to study</u> <u>at</u> Oxford University.
          A   B   C   D

6. <u>These</u> watches are <u>too much</u> <u>expensive</u> for <u>us</u> to buy.
     A   B   C   D

7. He <u>smoked</u> <u>too</u> <u>much</u> cigarettes <u>at work</u> today.
      A   B   C   D

8. When <u>he is</u> <u>going</u> <u>to</u> <u>come</u> back?
         A   B   C D

9. We <u>don't have</u> <u>eggs enough</u> <u>to make</u> <u>a</u> cake.
       A   B   C   D

10. He <u>did</u> not <u>caught</u> <u>any</u> fish <u>at</u> the lake yesterday.
       A   B   C   D

11. How <u>many</u> <u>children</u> <u>does</u> she <u>has</u>?
         A   B   C   D

12. <u>Were</u> you <u>have to</u> <u>work</u> <u>every day</u> last week?
      A   B   C   D

13. His sister <u>might</u> <u>is</u> a doctor, but <u>I'm</u> not <u>sure</u>.
            A   B   C   D

CHAPTER 10

Dialog

Two people meet by the mailboxes of an apartment building.

Lee Chandler: Pardon me. You're Dr. Jensen, aren't you?

Dr. Jensen: Yes, I am. How did you know?

Lee Chandler: I saw your name on the mailbox. I'm Lee Chandler. It's nice to meet you. I live in apartment 201. You live in apartment 204, don't you?

Dr. Jensen: Yes, I do.

Lee Chandler: Welcome to Continental Apartments. How do you like it here?

Dr. Jensen: Fine. My apartment is very nice. It's larger and more comfortable than my old apartment.

Lee Chandler: You moved in yesterday, didn't you?

Dr. Jensen: Yes, I did and I feel very tired today.

Lee Chandler: I do too. This morning I had a bad headache and I felt dizzy all afternoon. Now I feel a little sick. What should I do?

Dr. Jensen: I don't know. Maybe you should make yourself some chicken soup and go to bed early tonight.

Lee Chandler: What medicine should I take?

Dr. Jensen: I really don't know. Maybe you should see a doctor.

Lee Chandler: Aren't you a doctor?

Dr. Jensen: I'm not a medical doctor. I have a Ph.D. in education.

Exercise 1. Answer the questions. If the answer is *not* in the dialog, respond, *I don't know*.

1. Where do the two people meet?
2. What street is Dr. Jensen's new apartment on?
3. Do Lee Chandler and Dr. Jensen live in a two-story apartment building?
4. Which apartment is smaller, Dr. Jensen's new apartment or Dr. Jensen's old apartment?
5. Is Dr. Jensen's apartment more comfortable than Lee Chandler's apartment?
6. How does Lee Chandler feel today?
7. How did Lee Chandler feel this morning?
8. According to Dr. Jensen, what should Lee Chandler do?
9. Is Dr. Jensen a medical doctor?

Pronunciation of [sh], [ch], and [j]

 ## Exercise 2. A. Listen to the pronunciation of [sh], [ch], and [j]. Then repeat the words.

[sh]	[ch]	[j]
should	**Ch**andler	**J**ensen
shop	**ch**eap	**j**oin
sugar	**ch**ance	**g**ymnasium
special	future	ob**j**ect
na**t**ion	ques**t**ion	sub**j**ect
fre**sh**	rea**ch**	lar**g**er
fini**sh**	whi**ch**	pa**g**e

B. Listen to the sentences. Repeat the sentences. Then circle the [sh] sounds, underline the [ch] sounds, and put a box around the [j] sounds.

1. Dr. Jensen just moved into a much larger apartment.
2. The large apartment has a special view of the river and a lot of natural light.
3. Maybe Lee Chandler should see a doctor.
4. Which medicine should Lee Chandler take?

Comparative Forms of Adjectives

Ottawa and London: Two Capital Cities

Ottawa

London

Ottawa, the capital city of Canada, is almost two hundred years old, but it is younger than London, the capital of the United Kingdom. These two capital cities are very different. Ottawa is smaller than London. Ottawa's climate is colder than London's climate, but it is wetter and foggier in London than in Ottawa. London is more crowded and more polluted than Canada's capital. It's also noisier and dirtier. Life in London is faster and more expensive than life in Ottawa.

Which city is more pleasant? Which city is more interesting? Is life better in Ottawa than in London? What's your opinion?

Exercise 3. Answer the questions about the previous passage.

1. Which city is newer, Ottawa or London?
2. Is London larger than Ottawa?
3. Is Ottawa noisier and more crowded than London?
4. Which city is warmer?
5. Is Ottawa wetter and foggier than London?
6. In which city is life calmer?
7. In your opinion, which city is more pleasant?
8. In your opinion, which city is more interesting?
9. In your opinion, is life better in London than in Ottawa?

Comparative Forms of Adjectives: Using -er

With the comparative, we compare *two* people, places, or things.

	ADJECTIVE	COMPARATIVE
1. Add **-er** to one-syllable adjectives.	slow young cheap	slower younger cheaper
2. If a one-syllable adjective ends in a single consonant preceded by a single vowel, double the final consonant and then add **-er**. [Exceptions: adjectives ending in *w* (slower) or *y* (grayer).]	hot big thin	hotter bigger thinner
3. If a one-syllable adjective ends in *e*, add only **-r**.	large nice free	larger nicer freer
4. If a one-syllable adjective or a two-syllable adjective ends in a consonant +y, change the **y** to **i** and add **-er**.	dry noisy dirty	drier noisier dirtier
5. Exceptions	good bad far	better worse farther

Exercise 4.   Write the comparative forms of the following adjectives.

1. easy _____
2. fat _____
3. late _____
4. lazy _____
5. bad _____
6. low _____

7. funny _____
8. clean _____
9. wet _____
10. dry _____
11. sad _____
12. good _____

13. early _____
14. deep _____
15. heavy _____
16. fair _____
17. big _____
18. happy _____

Exercise 5.   MINI CONVERSATIONS.

Example: London
            Ottawa / small

Sue: Let's visit <u>London</u>.
Ted: I'd rather visit <u>Ottawa</u> because it is <u>smaller</u> than <u>London</u>.

1. San Francisco
   Los Angeles / warm

2. Chicago
   Denver / clean

3. Miami
   Orlando / safe

4. Hartford
   Boston / big

5. Toronto
   Montreal / old

6. Honolulu
   San Diego / cheap

7. Disneyland
   Disney World / new

8. _____
   _____ / close

9. _____
   _____ / pretty

10. _____
    _____ / nice

Exercise 6. Write sentences to compare vehicles. For each sentence use two vehicles from the box with the adjective in parentheses. Write about different vehicles in each sentence.

car	boat	motorcycle	moped
bus	ship	helicopter	airplane
jet	train	moving van	bicycle
jeep	truck	spaceship	_____

Examples: (small) *A moped is smaller than a motorcycle.*
                    Mopeds are smaller than motorcycles.

(cheap)   1. _____

(good)   2. _____

(big)   3. _____

(safe)   4. _____

(noisy)   5. _____

(slow)   6. _____

(long)   7. _____

(large)   8. _____

(heavy)   9. _____

(bad)   10. _____

(fast)   11. _____

Comparative Forms of Adjectives: Using *more*

Use *more* with adjectives that have two syllables (but do not end in *y*) and with adjectives that have more than two syllables.

Examples: | Adjective | Comparative |
|---|---|
| pleasant | more pleasant |
| famous | more famous |
| beautiful | more beautiful |

Exercise 7. MINI CONVERSATIONS.

Example: secretary
efficient

A: My <u>secretary</u> resigned two weeks ago.
B: That's too bad. Your <u>secretary</u> was very <u>efficient</u>.
A: I know, but my new <u>secretary</u> is <u>more efficient</u> than my old one.

1. boss
   generous

2. receptionist
   cheerful

3. supervisor
   energetic

4. assistant
   intelligent

5. maid
   helpful

6. gardener
   pleasant

7. driver
   careful

8. piano teacher
   patient

9. _____

   _____

Exercise 8. Complete the sentences. Use the words in parentheses in the comparative form with *than*.

Examples: (comfortable) A Jaguar is <u>*more comfortable than*</u> a Volkswagen.
        (cheap) A Volkswagen is <u>*cheaper than*</u> a Jaguar.

1. (modern) Is Dublin _____ Glasgow?
2. (hot) Madrid is _____ London in the summer.
3. (important) Is the Queen of England _____ the Prime Minister?
4. (handsome) Is Prince Charles _____ Prince Andrew?
5. (famous) The Beatles are _____ the Rolling Stones.
6. (deep) The Irish Sea is _____ the English Channel.
7. (foggy) Is Dover _____ London?
8. (big) Buckingham Palace is _____ Windsor Castle.
9. (elegant) The Ritz Hotel is _____ the Britannia Hotel.
10. (noisy) Is Manchester _____ Liverpool?
11. (far) From London, Scotland is _____ Wales.
12. (interesting) Is the British Museum _____ the Tate Gallery?
13. (old) Oxford University is _____ Cambridge University.
14. (busy) London Heathrow Airport is _____ London Gatwick Airport.
15. (wide) King's Road is _____ Sloane Street.
16. (beautiful) Is Hyde Park _____ Regent's Park?
17. (expensive) Harrods Department Store is _____ Selfridges.
18. (long) Is Tower Bridge _____ London Bridge?
19. (large) Is Victoria Station _____ Waterloo Station?
20. (popular) In England, cricket is _____ baseball.

Exercise 9.

Compare the following pairs of nouns. Use the comparative forms of adjectives and *than*.

Example: Porsche
Volkswagen

A Porsche is faster than a Volkswagen.
A Porsche is more expensive than a Volkswagen.

1. dog
   cat

2. boxing
   tennis

3. skiing
   swimming

4. a trumpet
   a piano

5. TV
   radio

6. The President of the U.S.A.
   The Premier of the U.S.S.R.

7. English
   my language

8. a steak
   a cake

9. January
   July

10. Japan
    Australia

11. _____
    _____

12. _____
    _____

Exercise 10. WRITING.

A. Compare two people. Write 8–10 sentences.

B. Compare two places. Write 8–10 sentences.

Tag Questions

A tag question has two parts. The first part is a statement; the second part is a question. The second part has an auxiliary and a pronoun. The pronoun refers to the subject. There is a comma between the two parts and a question mark at the end. When the first part is affirmative, the second part is negative.

Examples:

QUESTION	EXPECTED ANSWER
I have enough food for the party, **don't I?**	Yes, you do.
You drink coffee, **don't you?**	Yes, I do. / Yes, we do.
The children like hamburgers, **don't they?**	Yes, they do.
Tom eats meat, **doesn't he?**	Yes, he does.
You bought ketchup, **didn't you?**	Yes, I did. / Yes, we did.
Judy baked a cake, **didn't she?**	Yes, she did.

When the first part is negative, the second part is affirmative.

Examples:

QUESTION	EXPECTED ANSWER
I don't have enough beverages for everybody, **do I?**	No, you don't.
You don't put sugar in your coffee, **do you?**	No, I don't. / No, we don't.
Tom doesn't eat sweets, **does he?**	No, he doesn't.
The children didn't eat all of the hamburgers, **did they?**	No, they didn't.
Judy didn't bring any ice cream for dessert, **did she?**	No, she didn't.
We didn't forget anything, **did we?**	No, we didn't. / No, you didn't.

Tag questions are often used in speaking. They are seldom used in writing. With tag questions the speaker is asking for confirmation of the statement. When the speaker is *not* sure of the answer, the tag question ends with rising intonation (↗). When the speaker *is* sure of the answer, the tag question has falling intonation (↘).

Exercise 11. Write the correct tag endings and the expected answers.

1. You speak Spanish, *don't you* ?   *Yes, I do.*
2. You don't speak French, *do you* ?   *No, I don't.*
3. Carlos didn't lose his book, _____ ?   _____
4. Mary lives in an apartment, _____ ?   _____
5. You have your keys, _____ ?   _____
6. John doesn't smoke, _____ ?   _____
7. Mr. and Mrs. Harris don't have any children, _____ ?   _____
8. You had a good time, _____ ?   _____
9. Barbara went to a concert, _____ ?   _____
10. They like to play tennis, _____ ?   _____
11. Your parents didn't call last night, _____ ?   _____
12. You don't know my friend Charles, _____ ?   _____
13. The class ends at 11:00, _____ ?   _____
14. You have my telephone number, _____ ?   _____
15. Linda doesn't know how to type, _____ ?   _____
16. You didn't speak English two years ago, _____ ?   _____
17. It rained last night, _____ ?   _____
18. David plays the piano, _____ ?   _____
19. _____ , _____ ?   _____
20. _____ , _____ ?   _____

Exercise 12. MINI CONVERSATIONS.

Example: The United States has fifty states.   Morocco doesn't have a president.

A: The United States has fifty states, doesn't it?   A: Morocco doesn't have a president, does it?
B: Yes, it does.   B: No, it doesn't.

1. Mexico doesn't import oil.
2. Australia exports a lot of wool.
3. Spain and Portugal produce a lot of grapes.
4. Canada has two official languages.
5. A lot of Americans don't speak a foreign language.
6. Japan doesn't have a tropical climate.
7. The Rocky Mountains extend from Alaska to New Mexico.
8. Puerto Rico and Cuba don't have volcanoes.

9. Sir Isaac Newton taught at Cambridge University.
10. Indira Ghandi didn't study in France.
11. Sir Alexander Fleming discovered penicillin.
12. Pablo Picasso and his family didn't live in Italy.
13. _____
14. _____

Exercise 13.　PAIRWORK. One student completes the tag questions. Another student gives appropriate answers.

1. You want _____ , _____ ?
2. You didn't _____ , _____ ?
3. Your country has _____ , _____ ?
4. Your country doesn't _____ , _____ ?
5. You like _____ , _____ ?
6. You don't _____ , _____ ?
7. Your family _____ , _____ ?
8. Your family doesn't _____ , _____ ?

Reading

Study the chart on page 243 before reading the passage. The chart describes the system of higher education in the United States.

Education in the United States
(Higher Education)

High school graduates in the United States have several options. They can look for a job, go to a vocational or technical school, enter a two-year junior or community college, or enroll in a four-year college or university. After two years of study in a junior college or community college, students receive an A.A. (Associate of Arts) or an A.S. (Associate of Science) degree.

After high school many students enter an undergraduate program in a four-year college or university. There are more than 3000 four-year schools in the United States. Undergraduate education at a college or university in the United States usually consists of four years—freshman, sophomore, junior and senior years. By the junior year, university students must select a major.

Full-time students attend classes for approximately fifteen hours each week. They should also study independently for at least twenty hours per week. Some American students have a job and study at a university at the same time. A full-time student must take a minimum of twelve credits per semester. To graduate from a university, a student must complete at least 120 credit hours. The most common undergraduate degrees are the B.A. (Bachelor of Arts) and the B.S. (Bachelor of Science) degrees. Approximately one million students receive a Bachelor's degree each year.

After a Bachelor's degree, some students study for about two years for a graduate or advanced degree, such as an M.A. (Master of Arts) or an M.S. (Master of Science) degree. After a Master's degree, a few students continue in a Ph.D. (Doctor of Philosophy) degree program or in another doctoral program for several more years. After a Bachelor's degree, some students do not enter an M.A. program, but attend a professional school, such as law school or medical school for an advanced degree.

　　More than twelve million students study in institutions of higher education in the United States each year. This number includes about 360,000 international students.

Exercise 14. Answer the questions based on the reading about education.

1. What are four options of high school graduates in the United States?
2. What degree do community colleges and junior colleges give?
3. How many four-year colleges and universities are there in the United States?
4. How long are undergraduate programs?
5. What must an undergraduate student do by the junior year?
6. How many hours each week do full-time undergraduate students attend class?
7. How many credit hours must a student complete to graduate?
8. What graduate degree programs follow a Bachelor's degree?
9. What are two professional schools?
10. What degree do students receive before entering professional schools?
11. How many students study in institutions of higher education in the United States each year?

Exercise 15. Complete the chart (below, right) to describe the system(s) of higher education in your country (or in another country).

Educational Systems: Higher Education

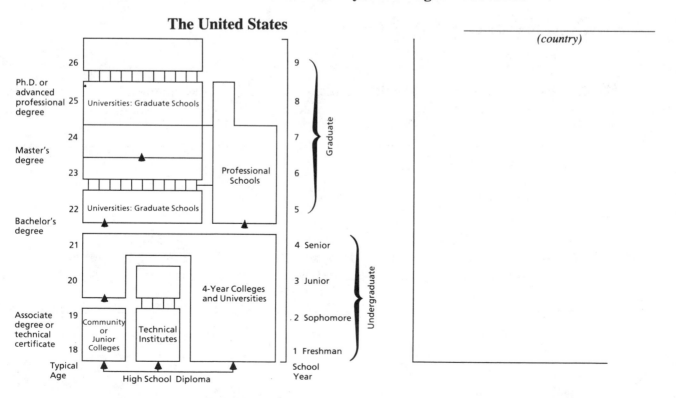

Exercise 16.
Answer the questions about education in your country.

1. What are two options of high school graduates in your country?
2. What degrees do universities give?
3. How long are academic programs?
4. Approximately how many hours each week do students attend class?
5. Do many students have jobs and study at the same time?

Should: Advice

Dialog

Courtney:	Hello.
Terry:	Hello, Courtney. This is Terry.
Courtney:	Hi, how are you?
Terry:	Oh, I feel terrible. Yesterday I got a headache, and I still have it.
Courtney:	You should take some aspirin.
Terry:	I did, but it didn't help. Last night I had a nightmare. I woke up at 3 a.m. and I couldn't fall asleep again.
Courtney:	Maybe you should take a nap.
Terry:	And today I have a backache. It's killing me. I also have a stomachache.
Courtney:	Terry, you should see a doctor.
Terry:	What kind of doctor should I see?
Courtney:	You should see a psychiatrist! These illnesses are in your head!

Should expresses advice (a recommendation or a good idea).

Write examples from the dialog for each formula.

FORMULA 10-1

Subject	**should**	(not)	verb [base]	(complement) .

1. _____
2. _____

Note: should not = shouldn't

FORMULA 10-2

(*Wh-*word)	**should**	subject	verb [base]	(complement) ?

1. _____
2. _____

Exercise 17. MINI CONVERSATIONS.

Example: My tooth hurts.
go to a dentist

Tim: My tooth hurts. What should I do?
Lou: You should go to a dentist.

1. My sister lost her passport.
   call the consulate

2. Elizabeth and Rick saw a car accident.
   report it to the police

3. I'm very tired.
   take a nap

4. Our car won't start.
   call a mechanic

5. I can't see the blackboard.
   sit in the front of the room

6. I am bored today.
   call a friend

7. I didn't understand the last lesson.
   talk to your professor

8. I can't find the key to my apartment.
   go to the manager's office

9. _____
   _____

10. _____
    _____

Exercise 18.
Respond to the situations. Include *should* or *shouldn't* in your recommendations.

Example: I have the flu.
You should get a lot of rest. or *You shouldn't go to class.*

1. I want to lose some weight.
2. My back hurts.
3. I have trouble falling asleep at night.
4. I have a cold.
5. I'm cold.
6. I want to quit smoking.
7. My mother's birthday is tomorrow.

8. I'm homesick.
9. My neighbor is very noisy.
10. I want to get a good grade in this class.
11. My brother needs to learn English.
12. I want to make a lot of money.

13. _____

14. _____

Exercise 19.
Some people write letters to newspaper columnists to ask for personal advice. Complete the letters below to Alice, a columnist. Then play the role of Alice. Write letters in response with advice. Use *should* and *shouldn't* in your letters from Alice.

A. *Dear Alice,*

I have some problems with my two roommates. One of my roommates _____

_____ *. My other roommate* _____

and _____ *. Also, my roommates* _____

_____ *. What should I do?*

Cordially,

Getting Angry

Dear Getting Angry,

_____

_____

_____

_____

Your friend,

Alice

B. *Dear Alice,*

I need your advice. My job is very _____

I work in a _____

My boss _____ *and* _____

Every day I _____

I have to _____

One of my co-workers _____

_____ . *What do you recommend?*

Sincerely,

Problems at Work

- - - - - - - - - - -

Dear Problems,

_____

_____

_____

_____

_____

Your friend,

Alice

Irregular Past Tense Verbs

BASE FORM	PAST FORM	BASE FORM	PAST FORM
feed	fed	sit	sat
fight	fought	stand	stood
forget	forgot	steal	stole
grow	grew	swim	swam
hold	held	think	thought
sell	sold	throw	threw
shake	shook	understand	understood
sing	sang	wake up	woke up

 Exercise 20. MINI CONVERSATIONS.

Examples:

Pat: Mary didn't fight with her sister, <u>did she</u>?
Chris: No, <u>she didn't</u>.
Pat: Who <u>did she fight with</u>?
Chris: <u>She fought with</u> her brother.

Lee: The robbers stole your TV, <u>didn't they</u>?
Fran: Yes, <u>they did</u>.
Lee: When <u>did they steal it</u>?
Fran: <u>They stole it</u> last weekend.

1. A: You fed the baby, _____ ?
   B: Yes, _____ .
   A: What _____ ?
   B: _____ some cereal.

2. A: Frank didn't hold your baby, _____ ?
   B: No, _____ .
   A: Whose _____ ?
   B: _____ my sister's baby.

3. A: Mr. and Mrs. Wilson didn't grow carrots, _____ ?
   B: No, _____ .
   A: What _____ ?
   B: _____ tomatoes.

4. A: The Wilsons sold their tomatoes, _____ ?
   B: Yes, _____ .
   A: Where _____ ?
   B: _____ at the farmers' market.

5. A: Carl forgot to set his alarm clock, _____ ?

   B: Yes, _____ .

   A: Why _____ ?

   B: _____ because he was very sleepy last night.

6. A: Carl woke up late, _____ ?

   B: Yes, _____ .

   A: What time _____ ?

   B: _____ at ten o'clock.

7. A: Nancy sat in the front of the bus, _____ ?

   B: Yes, _____ .

   A: Who _____ with?

   B: She _____ Marsha.

8. A: Your father shook hands with the President, _____ ?

   B: Yes, _____ .

   A: Where _____ ?

   B: _____ at the airport.

9. A: He understood the lecture, _____ ?

   B: Yes, _____ .

   A: How much of the lecture _____ ?

   B: _____ everything.

10. A: Olga swam across the English Channel, _____ ?

    B: Yes, _____ .

    A: When _____ ?

    B: _____ last summer.

11. A: Tommy threw a piece of cake at his sister, _____ ?

    B: Yes, _____ .

    A: Why _____ ?

    B: _____ because she was bothering him.

12. A: You bought a new car, _____ ?

    B: Yes, _____ .

    A: What kind of car _____ ?

    B: _____ a sports car.

13. A: Barbara didn't sing with Tony, _____ ?

    B: No, _____ .

    A: Who _____ with?

    B: _____ with Neil.

Exercise 21.

Select verbs from the boxes to complete the sentences in the passages. Fill in the blanks with past tense verb forms. Use each verb *only once*. Then write one or two sentences in the past tense to complete the passages.

A.

feed	hold	sing	think
forget	ring	tell	wake

Nora's baby Laura _____ up at eight a.m. Nora _____ Laura in her arms and _____ a song to Laura. Then she _____ Laura breakfast. Laura was eating when the telephone _____ . It was Dr. West's receptionist. She called about Laura's nine a.m. appointment with Dr. West. Nora _____ the appointment was at ten a.m. "I'm sorry. I _____ to write the time of the appointment on my calendar," Nora _____ the receptionist. _____

_____

_____

_____

B.

be	go	say	sit	swim
come	grow	sell	stand	throw
drive	run	shake	steal	understand

Two years ago a neighbor _____ me a small puppy for fifteen dollars. I named the puppy Max. Max _____ very fast, and soon he weighed fifty pounds.

Yesterday after lunch Max _____ by the door. He wanted to go outside. We went out to the car, and I _____ to a small lake. There Max and I played with a small rubber ball. I _____ the ball into the lake several times, and said, "Get it, Max." Each time Max _____ my order, jumped into the water, and _____ to get the ball. When he _____ out of the water with the ball in his mouth, he _____ to dry off. Then we _____ down under a tree and relaxed for a while.

On the way home I stopped at a supermarket. I _____ into the supermarket to buy some groceries. Max waited for me in the car. When I returned to the car, Max _____

not in the car. I _____ to a pay phone and called the police. "Help," I _____.
"Someone just _____ my dog!" _____

_____

_____

_____

Tag Questions

Examples:

QUESTION	EXPECTED ANSWER
You're a senior, **aren't you**?	Yes, I am.
Mary's studying nursing, **isn't she**?	Yes, she is.
They're going to study at Georgetown University, **aren't they**?	Yes, they are.
There's a student from China in your English class, **isn't there?**	Yes, there is.
Phil can take Calculus 381 next semester, **can't he**?	Yes, he can.
You will graduate next May, **won't you**?	Yes, I will. / Yes, we will.
I should take the SAT in January, **shouldn't I?**	Yes, you should.
Susan was absent yesterday, **wasn't she**?	Yes, she was.
You were in class on Monday, **weren't you**?	Yes, I was. / Yes, we were.
This is Professor Simon's class, **isn't it**?	Yes, it is.
These are your books **aren't they**?	Yes, they are.

When the verb phrase in the first part of the sentence is a form of *be* or a modal auxiliary (*can, will, should*), use the same form of *be* or the same modal in the second part of the sentence.

Notes: 1. When a sentence begins with *this* or *that*, use *it* in the tag (second part of the sentence).
2. When a sentence begins with *these* or *those*, use *they* in the tag.
3. When a sentence begins with *there*, use *there* in the tag.

Examples:

QUESTION	EXPECTED ANSWER
I shouldn't take six classes, **should I**?	No, you shouldn't.
You won't be late again tomorrow, **will you**?	No, I won't. / No, we won't.
Paul can't read German, **can he**?	No, he can't.
Elsa isn't going to go to summer school, **is she**?	No, she isn't.
They aren't taking chemistry this semester, **are they**?	No, they aren't.
Our final exam isn't on Friday, **is it**?	No, it isn't.
There isn't a copy machine in this building, **is there**?	No, there isn't.

Exercise 22. Write the correct tag questions and the expected answers.

1. You weren't sleeping, _were you_ ?   _No, I wasn't._

2. Charles isn't sick, _____ ?   _____

3. Charles is coming to the party, _____ ?   _____

4. I wasn't wrong, _____ ?   _____

5. We should always speak English in class, _____ ?   _____

6. That isn't your notebook, _____ ?   _____

7. I'm not late, _____ ?   _____

8. Mr. and Mrs. Hawkins are going to Europe soon, _____ ?   _____

9. You can speak French, _____ ?   _____

10. The party was nice, _____ ?   _____

11. These are your gloves, _____ ?   _____

12. You're going to do your homework today, _____ ?   _____

13. Patricia will be in the library, _____ ?   _____

14. This television is on sale, _____ ?   _____

15. You couldn't speak English two years ago, _____ ?   _____

16. You won't be late, _____ ?   _____

17. There isn't a test tomorrow, _____ ?   _____

Exercise 23. PAIRWORK. Student A: Complete the tag questions.
                                      Student B: Give appropriate answers (expected or
                                      unexpected).

Examples: A: **You weren't sick yesterday**, were you?
                B: Yes, I was.
                A: You didn't **go to school yesterday, did you?**
                B: No, I didn't.

1. You're not _____ , _____ ?

2. _____ , isn't she ?

3. _____ going to _____ , _____ ?

4. _____ , should you?

5. There's _____ , _____ ?

6. Those _____ aren't _____ , _____ ?

7. _____ , can't you?

8. _____ were _____ , _____ ?

9. _____ , won't _____ ?

10. _____ , _____ ?

Exercise 24.

Below is a commercial about an exercise center. Complete the commercial. Use the verbs and modals in parentheses. Use *will* to express future time. Add auxiliaries where necessary.

_____ you _____ (feel) tired after a day at work? _____ you _____ (gain) weight? _____ (not / go) directly home from work. You _____ (should / come) to Jim's Gym on Fortieth Street. After several visits to Jim's Gym you _____ (feel) much better.

Six months ago Matthew Wilson _____ (feel) tired all of the time. He _____ (be) very weak. He _____ (weigh) 263 pounds. He never _____ (exercise). Every day after work he _____ (go) home and _____ (sleep) for an hour or two. When he _____ (wake up) he _____ (make) a big meal. Every night after supper he _____ (sit) in front of the TV and _____ (eat) potato chips and _____ (drink) soft drinks. He _____ (not / sleep) well at night. He _____ (not / enjoy) life. He _____ (decide) to change his lifestyle.

Today Matthew Wilson _____ (be) stronger and thinner than before. He _____ (go) to Jim's Gym three times a week. He _____ (weigh) 170 pounds. He _____ (not / eat) junk food any more.

The instructors at Jim's Gym _____ (be) ready to help you. They _____ (tell) you how to exercise correctly and how to eat well. You _____ (want) to feel better, _____ you? At Jim's Gym we _____ (wait) to help you!

Activities

A. RIDDLES. What are the answers?

1. Where should you go when you're dying?
2. Who is bigger, Mr. Bigger or his baby?
3. What's worse than a worm in your apple?
4. Why are Saturday and Sunday stronger than the other days of the week?

B. INTERVIEW ABOUT PAST EVENTS. One student makes a one-sentence statement about a past event. The student should be very familiar with the situation. Other students ask 5–10 questions about the event.

Examples of situations: Last Saturday I went out to dinner.
When I was twelve years old I broke my arm.
My brother won a prize two years ago.
Recently my family and I went on vacation.

Question starters:

Where did _____ ? When _____ ? Why _____ ?

How _____ ? Who _____ ? How much / many _____ ?

Were you _____ ? Did you _____ ? What time _____ ?

C. ROLE PLAYS. Work with a classmate.

1. A friend plans to get married, but you think it's a bad idea. Discuss with your friend why he or she shouldn't get married.

2. You're a doctor. A patient has a serious problem. Discuss the problem with your patient and discuss what he or she should and shouldn't do.

3. A friend is asking to borrow some money from you again. Your friend frequently asks to borrow money and other things. You don't want to lend your friend any more money. Discuss the problem with your friend. Tell him or her why you don't want to lend the money. Tell your friend what he or she should do.

D. CROSSWORD PUZZLE. To do the crossword puzzle, complete the sentences with forms of the verbs in the boxes. The numbers in parentheses after the sentences refer to the numbers on the crossword puzzle. Most of the forms are past tense verb forms, but other forms are in the puzzle. Add the auxiliaries *did* and *didn't* where necessary. Use the verbs in each box only once.

Across

break	ring	✔ stand	wake
build	rob	teach	win
fall	say	think	
feed	shake	throw	
forget	sleep	understand	

1. When his new client entered the room, Bob _**stood**_ (18) up. They _____ (2) hands, and Bob _____ (26), "How do you do?

2. After Alice Jones _____ (28) a lot of money in a lottery, she _____ (3) a new house.

3. Nina was very tired. She was still _____ (6) at ten o'clock this morning. The telephone _____ (11). It _____ (27) her up.

4. Martin's history instructor _____ (22) ten lessons before he gave his students an exam. Martin _____ (17) all of the lessons very well. The night before the exam Martin couldn't sleep. He _____ (8) about the exam until three a.m. He _____ (30) to set his alarm clock, and he woke up late the next morning.

5. Mrs. Conway was _____ (13) some peas to her baby boy when he took some of the peas from his bowl and _____ (10) them at his mother.

6. _____ (16) that man _____ (20) the First National Bank?

7. Yesterday Jack _____ (29) down the stairs. As a result, he _____ (23) his leg.

Down

begin	hear	lose	sing
✔fight	hold	put	steal
get	hurt	ride	swim
grow	know	sell	wear

1. Muhammad Ali _**fought**_ (1) many boxers during his boxing career. His professional career _____ (21) after the 1960 Olympics. In 1978 Muhammad Ali _____ (4) to Leon Spinks. During the fight he _____ (19) his back.

2. Mr. Ramirez _____ (5) his baby daughter in his arms last night. He _____ (2) a song to her.

3. Last Saturday I was _____ (6) at the lake. Before I went into the water, I _____ (7) my wallet under my beach towel. Someone _____ (18) my wallet while I was in the water.

4. I _____ (9) about the party at the Plaza Hotel last week from Stella. I _____ (15) a new suit for the party. I _____ (28) it with a white shirt and a red tie. I _____ (24) the subway to the Plaza Hotel. I _____ (25) many of the people at the party, but I met a few new people there.

5. Mr. Minski _____ (12) a lot of vegetables in his garden last summer. He _____ (14) _____ (26) any of them. He gave them to friends.

E. WRITING.

1. Complete the letter below to Alice, the newspaper columnist. Then write Alice's response, using *should* or *shouldn't*.

Dear Alice,

Help! I am engaged to be married, but _____

_____

_____

_____

_____

Sincerely,

_____

Dear _____ ,

_____

_____

_____

_____

_____

_____

Sincerely,

Alice

2. Write your own letter to Alice. Ask another student to play the role of Alice and to write an answer to your letter.

3. a. Compare two members of your family. Use some of the adjectives in the box below.
   b. Compare two famous people. Use some of the adjectives in the box.
   c. Compare yourself to a famous person. Use some of the adjectives in the box.

artistic	funny	old	shy
athletic	generous	pretty	strong
beautiful	handsome	quiet	talkative
creative	healthy	relaxed	tall
emotional	intelligent	rich	thin
energetic	lazy	serious	weak
friendly	nervous	short	young

Examples: I am _____ than _____ .

My sister is _____ than _____ .

F. DICTATION. You will hear each sentence two times. Write exactly what you hear.

1. _____

2. _____

3. _____

4. _____

5. _____

6. _____

7. _____

Review Quizzes

A. LISTENING COMPREHENSION: SENTENCES

For each problem you will hear a short sentence once. After you hear the sentence, read the four choices. Decide which written sentence is the closest in meaning to the spoken sentence. Circle the letter of the correct answer.

1. (A) You should go somewhere.
   (B) You should stay here.
   (C) You shouldn't stay here.
   (D) You shouldn't grow anything.

2. (A) Houston is longer than Miami.
   (B) Houston is shorter than Miami.
   (C) Miami is bigger than Houston.
   (D) Miami is smaller than Houston.

3. (A) We remembered her last name.
   (B) We didn't remember her last name.
   (C) She remembered her last name.
   (D) She didn't remember her last name.

4. (A) You won't help him, will you?
   (B) You're going to help him, aren't you?
   (C) He's going to help you, isn't he?
   (D) He's not going to help you, is he?

5. (A) The river is prettier than the lake.
   (B) The lake is more beautiful than the river.
   (C) The river isn't more beautiful than the lake.
   (D) The lake isn't uglier than the river.

B. LISTENING COMPREHENSION: CONVERSATIONS

You will hear short conversations between two people. At the end of each conversation, a third person will ask a question about the conversation. You will hear the question only once. After you hear the conversation and the related question, read the four possible answers. Decide which answer is the best response to the question. Circle the letter of the best answer.

1. (A) read four chapters after 8 a.m.
   (B) sleep during the test
   (C) study all night
   (D) take the test at night

2. (A) not to go into the water
   (B) not to stay on the beach
   (C) not to sit in the sun
   (D) to go swimming

3. (A) be bored on the flight
   (B) look for Gate 6
   (C) buy a ticket for Flight 471
   (D) miss Flight 471

4. (A) skis
   (B) sunglasses
   (C) shoes
   (D) jeans

5. (A) at a fair
   (B) on a plane
   (C) in a taxi
   (D) on a bus

C. STRUCTURE: SENTENCE COMPLETION

Choose the *one* word or phrase that best completes the sentence. If none of the choices correctly completes the problem, choose (D) *None of the above*. Circle the letter of the correct answer.

1. My father is -------- than your father.
   - (A) more old
   - (B) more older
   - (C) older
   - (D) *None of the above*

2. Mrs. Fredericks -------- go to New York next week.
   - (A) maybe to
   - (B) may to
   - (C) won't to
   - (D) might

3. There aren't any more flights to Chicago tonight, --------?
   - (A) are there
   - (B) are they
   - (C) aren't there
   - (D) aren't they

4. Maria should -------- more fruit.
   - (A) eat
   - (B) to eat
   - (C) eating
   - (D) eats

5. The people in Mayville are -------- the people in Metropolis.
   - (A) the friendlier
   - (B) friendlier than
   - (C) friendly that
   - (D) friendly than

6. You don't have an extra pencil, --------?
   - (A) don't you
   - (B) do you
   - (C) has it
   - (D) does it

7. Did you like this movie -------- than the last one?
   - (A) gooder
   - (B) the better
   - (C) a lot
   - (D) *None of the above*

8. She -------- to leave soon.
   - (A) can
   - (B) likes
   - (C) wants
   - (D) *None of the above*

9. There is homework for tomorrow, --------?
   - (A) is there
   - (B) is it
   - (C) isn't there
   - (D) isn't it

10. -------- to a doctor?
    - (A) Does he should go
    - (B) Does he should goes
    - (C) Should he go
    - (D) Should he goes

11. Did you -------- the ball through the window?
    - (A) throw
    - (B) throwed
    - (C) throwing
    - (D) threw

12. My chemistry grade was -------- than my math grade.
    - (A) badder
    - (B) more bad
    - (C) more badder
    - (D) *None of the above*

D. STRUCTURE: ERROR IDENTIFICATION

Each sentence has four underlined words or phrases. Circle the *one* underlined word or phrase that is not correct. Then correct the sentence.

1. Everyone <u>should</u> <u>to bring</u> some <u>food</u> <u>to the</u> picnic.
           A   B   C   D

2. <u>There</u> weren't <u>many people</u> at the party, <u>were</u> <u>they</u>?
   A   B   C   D

3. <u>The</u> Sears Tower <u>in</u> Chicago <u>is</u> <u>taller</u> the Empire State Building.
   A   B   C   D

4. <u>Is</u> anyone here <u>more younger</u> <u>than</u> eighteen <u>years old</u>?
   A   B   C   D

5. The next test <u>will</u> <u>be</u> <u>easy</u> <u>than</u> the test last week.
              A   B   C   D

6. <u>Her brother</u> always <u>arrive</u> on time for his English class, <u>doesn't</u> <u>he</u>?
      A   B   C   D

7. I <u>was talked</u> <u>to</u> my mother <u>on the phone</u> at 9:30 <u>yesterday morning</u>.
       A   B   C   D

8. I <u>was</u> <u>hungry</u> <u>than</u> you <u>were</u>.
     A   B   C   D

9. There is <u>enough food</u> for <u>everyone</u> , <u>isn't</u> <u>it</u>?
            A   B   C D

10. Mrs. Seng <u>should</u> <u>gets</u> <u>a new</u> car, <u>shouldn't she</u>?
             A   B   C   D

11. Your brother didn't <u>forgot</u> to <u>mail</u> the check, <u>did</u> <u>he</u>?
                 A   B   C   D

12. Yesterday the weather <u>was</u> <u>worser</u> <u>than</u> the weather <u>on</u> January 20.
                      A   B   C   D

CHAPTER 11

An Ancestor

My great-grandfather, Arnoldus Blix, was born north of the Arctic Circle in Norway in 1858. His father was a fisherman. Arnoldus was sixteen when his father died at sea. Two years later his mother died. At the age of eighteen, Arnoldus decided to leave his homeland with two of his younger sisters. Arnoldus's sister, Olea, was sixteen years old, and his sister, Harda, was four years old. They took a ship from Norway to the United States in 1876.

In New York City, the three young immigrants boarded a train to the state of Wisconsin. Relatives were waiting for them in northern Wisconsin. During his first summer in Wisconsin, my great-grandfather worked in a lumber camp. In the winter he went to school to learn English. Because he knew only a little English, he had to study in a primary school. He felt uncomfortable in school because most of his classmates already spoke English, and they were ten years younger than he was. In the spring Arnoldus left school and got a job. He studied English by himself, and a few years later he attended college.

In 1889 Arnoldus married Louise Langum, one of his classmates. For several years, he worked in various shops. In 1904 he opened his own store in the town of Turtle Lake, Wisconsin. In his store he sold groceries, clothes, and household goods. All five of his children worked in the store over the years. He worked in the store almost every day for the next fifty-six years. My great-grandfather, Arnoldus Blix, died in 1960 at the age of one hundred one.

Exercise 1.   Answer the questions based on the reading.

1. When and where was Arnoldus born?
2. What was his father's occupation?
3. What happened to Arnoldus's parents when he was young?
4. What did Arnoldus decide to do?
5. How did Arnoldus and his sisters travel to the United States?
6. How did they travel to Wisconsin?
7. What did Arnoldus do during his first year in Wisconsin?
8. What did Arnoldus do in 1904?
9. How old was Arnoldus when he died?

Exercise 2.   Answer the questions.

1. Where were you born?
2. Did any of your ancestors come from another country?
   If yes, what country did they come from?
   Why did they move to another country?
3. What is a good way for an adult to learn another language?
4. Is a primary school a good place for an adult to study a foreign language?

Pronunciation of [p], [b], [f], and [v]

Exercise 3.

A. Listen to the pronunciation of [*p*], [*b*], [*f*], and [*v*]. Then repeat the words.

[p]	[b]	[f]	[v]
parents	**b**orn	**f**ather	**v**ery
cou**p**le	**b**oat	**f**rom	o**v**er
shi**p**	lum**b**er	**f**i**f**ty	se**v**eral
Euro**p**e	jo**b**	him**s**el**f**	o**f**

B. Listen to the sentences. Repeat the sentences.

1. Arnoldus Blix was born in eighteen fifty-eight.
2. His father was a fisherman on a very big boat.
3. His mother passed away in the spring of 1876.
4. He decided to leave Europe with a couple of his sisters.
5. They traveled by ship from Norway to the United States.

Indirect Objects with *to*

Some verbs can have two objects—a direct object and an indirect object. A *direct object* refers to a thing or a person (or an animal). An *indirect object* refers to a person (or an animal).

The verbs in the box can have direct objects and indirect objects.

describe	introduce
explain	recommend

With these verbs the word *to* goes before the indirect object. These verbs must have a direct object. The direct object goes before the indirect object.

FORMULA 11-1

Subject	verb	direct object	**to**	indirect object .

> *Examples:* Olea introduced <u>her little sister</u> to <u>her aunt</u>.
>
> Arnoldus described <u>the trip</u> to <u>his brother</u> in a letter.
>
> Arnoldus's uncle recommended <u>Milton College</u> to <u>him</u>.
>
> The professor explained <u>the lesson</u> to <u>Arnoldus</u> in English.

Exercise 4.
Read the sentences about a business meeting. Put a line under each direct object. Circle each indirect object. Then answer the questions.

Three business people, Mr. Chen from Singapore, Mr. Dato from Malaysia, and Ms. Baker from the United States, were meeting in Singapore.

The host, Mr. Chen, introduced <u>Mr. Dato</u> to (Ms. Baker.)

Mr. Chen described <u>a new Asian computer</u> to the visitors.

He explained the benefits of the new computer to them.

Ms. Baker recommended a visit to her company in Chicago to the Asian businessmen.

1. Who introduced Mr. Dato to Ms. Baker?
2. What did Mr. Chen describe to the guests?
3. Who explained the benefits of the new computer to the visitors?
4. What did Ms. Baker recommend to the Asians?

Exercise 5. MINI CONVERSATIONS.

Example: introduced the new manager to you
      my boss / him / me

Ken: Who <u>introduced the new manager to you</u>?
Pat: <u>My boss introduced him</u> to <u>me</u>.
Ken: When did <u>your boss introduce him</u> to <u>you</u>?
Pat: <u>He introduced him</u> to <u>me</u> yesterday.

1. explained the homework to Tom
   his sister / it / him

2. recommended the movie to your sister
   her teacher / it / her

3. described the computers to you and your father
   a salesman / them / us

4. introduced you to your new neighbors
   my grandmother / them / me

5. explained the lesson to you
   a classmate / it / me

6. _____

   _____

Exercise 6. Complete the sentences with a direct object from the first box, *to*, and an indirect object from the second box.

me	the problem
anything	the Sands Hotel
the answer	the accident
her illness	a good doctor
the teacher	_____

me	her husband
us	the students
you	the audience
anyone	her new friend
his dad	the employees
everyone	_____

Example: He explained **the problem to me** .

1. My mother introduced _____.
2. The newspaper article described _____.
3. Our teacher explained _____.
4. My sister recommended _____.

5. A classmate introduced _____.

6. My boss explained _____.

7. My father described _____.

Exercise 7.

Four of the six sentences are incorrect. Draw a line through each incorrect sentence. Then write the correct sentence.

1. He explained me the lesson.   _____

2. He explained to me the lesson.   _____

3. I introduced her to my father.   _____

4. She described to him the movie.   _____

5. She described him the movie.   _____

6. My mom recommended the book to me.   _____

Comparisons: *be* + (*not*) + *as* + Adjective + *as*

My father is fifty years old. My mother is fifty years old.	My mother is **as old as** my father.
My father is six feet tall. My mother is five feet tall.	My mother isn't **as tall as** my father.

Exercise 8.

Use a form of the verb *be* and the words below to make comparisons. Substitute *as … as* for the symbol =. Write *not as … as* for the symbol <.

Examples: (young)   my sister = you
My sister is as young as you.

(big)   England < the United States
England isn't as big as the United States.

1. (sweet)   sugar < honey   _____

2. (deep)   a lake < an ocean   _____

3. (humid)   Houston = New Orleans   _____

4. (expensive)   chicken < beef   _____

5. (dangerous)   guns = rifles   _____

6. (high)   Mt. Fuji < Mt. Everest   _____

7. (intelligent)   cats < dolphins   _____

8. (interesting)   London = Paris   _____

9. (fast)   a Ferrari = a Porsche   _____

10. (beautiful)   sunrises = sunsets   _____

11. (_____)   _____ < _____   _____

12. (_____)   _____ = _____   _____

Exercise 9. Complete the comparative sentences.

1. I am as _____
2. _____ as strong _____
3. _____ difficult as _____ .
4. _____ as his brother.
5. _____ not as delicious _____
6. _____ enjoyable as _____
7. _____ important as _____
8. _____ isn't _____ as _____
9. _____ are as _____
10. _____ as _____ as _____

Exercise 10. English has many expressions to compare people or things to animals or to other things. Some of these expressions are in the box. Use five different expressions from the box to describe people. Use two expressions to describe things. Write complete sentences.

as clever as a fox	as hard as a rock
as sick as a dog	as cold as ice
as stubborn as a mule	as light as a feather
as strong as an ox	as sweet as honey
as quiet as a mouse	as pretty as a picture
as gentle as a lamb	as good as gold
as soft as a kitten	as thin as a rail
as busy as a bee	as big as a barn
as hungry as a bear	as old as the hills

Examples: **My baby niece is as pretty as a picture.**
She is as good as gold.
Her skin is as soft as a kitten.

1. _____
2. _____
3. _____
4. _____
5. _____
6. _____
7. _____

Must: Logical Conclusion

Tina: Dorothy and Frank returned from their trip around the world last night, didn't they?

Roger: Yes, they did. They **must not** be very tired, because they went golfing early this morning.

Tina: They **must** be glad to be home.

Roger: They are, but they plan to take another trip in two weeks.

Tina: They **must** have a lot of free time.

Roger: They both retired a few months ago.

Tina: They **must** love to travel.

Roger: Yes, they do, but Dorothy says that there's no place like home.

Exercise 11.

Complete the short dialogs with a logical conclusion. Use *must (not)*, a verb, and additional words.

Example: A: Courtney got a scholarship to study at Yale, didn't he?
B: Yes, he did. He ___*must be very happy.*___ (or)
He ___*must have good grades.*___ (or)
He *must be intelligent.*

1. A: Dan worked late last night, didn't he?

   B: Yes, he did. He _____ today.

2. A: Sarah isn't in class today, is she?

   B: No, she isn't. She _____ today.

3. A: Mark's ordering a large pizza for himself, isn't he?

   B: Yes, he is. He _____ .

4. A: Are Mr. and Mrs. Hunt really going to buy a jet?
   B: Yes, they are.

   A: They _____ .

5. A: That's your fourth or fifth glass of water, isn't it?
   B: Yes, it is.

   A: You _____ .

6. A: The Wilsons lost their dog, didn't they?

   B: Yes, they did. They _____ now.

7. A: Mr. Villa won some money in the lottery two times last year, didn't he?
   B: Yes, he did.

   A: He _____ .

8. A: Bob and Paul studied all day today, didn't they?

   B: Yes, they did. They _____ tomorrow.

9. A: _____

   B: _____

Reflexive Pronouns

SINGULAR	PLURAL
I burned **myself** with a frying pan.	**We** enjoyed **ourselves** at the party.
Did **you** buy **yourself** anything?	**You** didn't hurt **yourselves,** did you?
Grandpa shaved **himself.**	**The children** fed **themselves.**
Sue went swimming by **herself.**	

A reflexive pronoun refers back to the subject of the sentence.

Note: by + reflexive pronoun = *alone*

Examples: **I** don't like to go to movies **by myself.**
You should do your homework **by yourself.**
We ate dinner **by ourselves.**
Jim and Bill fixed the car **by themselves.**

Exercise 12.   Complete each sentence with the correct reflexive pronoun.

1. I burned __*myself*__ at work today.

2. My little niece fed _____ this morning.

3. My parents like to go to restaurants by _____ .

4. Did you hurt _____ ?

5. My dog cut _____ on a piece of glass.

6. Elizabeth and her husband painted their house by _____ .

7. We wrote the book by _____ .

8. I saw _____ in the mirror.

9. Their children always behave _____ at parties.

10. We told him to do it by _____ .

11. Did you and your wife enjoy _____ on your vacation?

12. The young boy bathed _____ this morning.

Exercise 13.   PAIRWORK. Student A: Ask the question. Student B: Answer the question. Include a reflexive pronoun in your answer.

Examples: A: Who fed Tommy?
B: *He fed himself.*
        (he / feed)

A.   Did your mother prepare the meal?
B.   No, *I prepared it by myself* .
        (I / prepare / it / by)

1. A.   Did the Satos have a good time in Hawaii?

    B.   Yes, _____
            (they / enjoy)

2. A.   What happened to Barbara?

    B.   _____
        (She / burn / in the kitchen)

3. A. Did you study with Hamid?

 B. No, _____
         (I / study / by)

4. A. Did you buy yourselves anything?

 B. Yes, _____
         (we / buy / some clothes)

5. A. What happened to you?

 B. _____
         (I / hurt / in the gymnasium)

6. A. Does Kiyomi walk to school alone?

 B. Yes, _____
         (she / walk / by)

7. A. What's wrong with those carpenters?

 B. _____
         (They / cut / in the workshop)

8. A. Who did you eat with?

 B. No one, _____
         (I / eat / by)

9. A. Do Mom and Dad like the photographs?

 B. Yes, _____
         (they / love to see / in pictures)

10. A. Did anyone help Sam fix his bicycle?

 B. No, _____
         (he / fix / it / by)

11. A. Was Joey a good boy at the party?

 B. Yes, _____
         (he / behave)

12. A. Are Marta and Elena going to call a taxi?

 B. Yes, _____
         (they / not want to walk home / by)

13. A. Did you give Tommy a bath?

 B. No, _____
         (he / bathe)

Exercise 14. Complete each sentence with a reflexive pronoun and other necessary words.

1. Mrs. Moreno hurt _____ at _____ .

2. _____ went _____ by _____ .

3. The boys fed _____ some _____ .

4. I usually _____ by _____ .

5. Did you and Paul _____ ?

6. We enjoyed _____ in _____ .

7. She cleaned _____ by _____ , didn't she?

8. Be careful or you will cut _____ with that _____ .

9. _____ by _____ .

10. _____ self _____ .

Indirect Objects with *to*

Dialog

Jamal: Did you write **Bill a letter**?

Lupe: No, I didn't write **Bill a letter,** but I wrote **a letter to Tom.**

Jamal: Did you send **any postcards to your sisters**?

Lupe: I sent **Ann a postcard**, but I didn't send **a postcard to Joan**.

Notes: 1. With some verbs the indirect object can go before or after the direct object.

2. When the direct object is a pronoun, the direct object must go before the indirect object.

Example: I sent it to Nancy.

FORMULA 11-1

Subject	verb	direct object	to	indirect object .

Example: I sent a letter to Tom.

FORMULA 11-2

Subject	verb	indirect object	direct object .

Example: I sent Tom a letter.

With the verbs in the box the indirect object can go before or after the direct object.

give	read	show
lend	sell	tell
mail	send	write

Exercise 15. MINI CONVERSATIONS.

Example: give the key / the manager
her assistant

Pat: Did you <u>give the key</u> to <u>the manager</u>?
Lee: No, I <u>gave the key</u> to <u>her assistant</u>.

1. sell your car / Barbara
Susan

2. send a card / your brother
my sister

3. lend your textbook / Hector
Ali

4. show the photographs / grandma
grandpa

5. tell the news / your boss
my secretary

6. give the message / Mr. Gilman
Mrs. Gilman

7. write _____ / _____
_____

8. mail _____ / _____
_____

Exercise 16. MINI CONVERSATIONS.

Example: send her mother candy
a plant

Terry: Did Maria <u>send her mother candy</u>?
Chris: No, she <u>sent her mother a plant</u>.

1. give you a check
cash

2. lend you her car
her bicycle

3. sell you her computer
typewriter

4. read her boss the letter
the telegram

5. tell you the truth
a lie

6. write her parents a postcard
a long note

7. give you dishes for your wedding
silverware

8. sell _____
_____

9. send _____
_____

Exercise 17. Rewrite each sentence using the other formula.

FORMULA 11-1

Example: Aunt Nora mailed an invitation to me.

1. _____

2. Maria sent flowers to Mom.

3. _____

4. _____

5. Susan offered some cake to everyone.

6. _____

FORMULA 11-2

Aunt Nora mailed me an invitation.

I gave my mother a birthday present.

_____

Tony wrote Mom a letter.

Nora read Mom the letter.

_____

Uncle Ed told us a joke.

Comparisons: *The same* + (Noun) + *(as)*; *similar (to)*; *different (from)*

The Seng Family

The Mason Family

Mr. Seng is **the same height as** Mr. Mason.
Mrs. Seng isn't **the same weight as** Mrs. Mason.
Mr. and Mrs. Seng have **the same number of children as** Mr. and Mrs. Mason.
The Sengs' house and the Masons' house are not **similar** .
The Sengs' house is **different from** the Masons' house.
Their garages are also **different.**
The Sengs' car is **similar to** the Masons' car.
It is **the same size as** the Masons' car.

Exercise 18.

Complete the sentences about the picture. Use *(not) the same (as)*, *similar (to)*, and *different (from)*. Include a form of *be* or *have* and other necessary words.

1. Mike and Mary Mason are both ten years old. Mike __*is the same*__ age __*as*__ Mary.

2. They __*are the same*__ age __*as*__ Steve and David Seng.

3. The Sengs' trees and the Masons' trees _____ .

4. The Sengs _____ number of trees _____ the Masons.

5. The Sengs' driveway _____ the Masons' driveway.

6. The Sengs' driveway _____ length _____ .

7. The Sengs' driveway _____ width _____ .

8. _____ similar to _____ .

9. _____ height _____
10. _____ different _____
11. _____ size _____
12. _____ similar.
13. _____ different from _____
14. _____

Exercise 19. INTERVIEW. Choose a classmate to interview. Then complete the questions. Ask your classmate the questions.

1. Are you the same age as _____ ?

2. Are your eyes the same color as _____ ?

3. Do you have the same number of brothers and sisters _____ ?

4. How are you and _____ similar?

5. How are _____ and _____ different?

6. Is _____ the same height as _____ ?

7. Are _____ and _____ similar?

8. Is the weather here similar to the weather in _____ ?

9. Is the food in _____ different from the food in _____ ?

10. _____ similar?

11. _____ different from _____ ?

12. _____ as _____ as _____ ?

13. _____ similar to _____ ?

14. _____ have the same number of _____ as _____ ?

15. _____ different?

Could: **Polite Requests**

Dialog

Lynn: **Could** you please give me a ride to the university now?
Lee: Of course.
Lynn: And **could** you pick me up after my last class at 3:30?
Lee: Sure.
Lynn: **Could** I borrow your car tonight?
Lee: No, I'm sorry. I need to use it, and I won't be home until midnight.

Could is used for polite requests. These requests can refer to the present or future. *Could* is more polite than *can*.

Exercise 20. MINI CONVERSATIONS.

Example: bring me a cup of coffee
I also have some cream

A: Could you please <u>bring me a cup of coffee</u>?
B: Sure.
A: Could I <u>also have some cream</u>?
B: Certainly.

1. lend me your camera
I also borrow your flash attachment

2. pass me the rolls
I also have the butter

3. give me Mary's address
you also tell me her phone number

4. take this computer to room 301
you also connect it to the printer

5. lend me your accounting textbook
I also borrow your calculator

6. mention the meeting to your boss
you also tell your boss about the dinner
after the meeting

7. lend me some paper
I use your typewriter for a few minutes

8. wash the windshield
you also check the oil

9. get me some popcorn
you also save me a seat

10. wait a minute
I ask you a few questions

11. cash this check
you also give me change for a dollar

12. _____

_____

Exercise 21. PAIRWORK. Read the situations. Student A: Make a polite request with *could*. Student B: Respond to the request. Some possible responses are in the box.

Sure.	Certainly.	Of course.
I'd be glad to.	I'd be happy to.	I'm sorry.
No, you / I can't (because _____).		

Example: You need to make a phone call.

A: *Could you lend me a quarter?*
(or) A: *Could I use your phone?*
(or) A: *Could you excuse me for a minute? I need to make a call.*
(or) A: *Could I borrow your telephone directory?*
B: *Certainly.*

1. You would like some bread.
2. You have to go to the airport.
3. You need to borrow ten dollars.
4. You're hungry.
5. You need some medicine from the pharmacy.
6. You can't find your textbook.
7. You need help with your homework.
8. You want to watch a program on television.
9. _____

Using *more, less,* and *fewer* with Nouns

Brian

Mickey

Brian and Mickey are brothers. Brian drinks **more juice** than Mickey. Mickey drinks **more soft drinks** than Brian. Brian eats **less candy** than Mickey. Mickey eats **fewer vegetables** than Brian. Brian takes **more vitamins** than Mickey. Brian gets **more exercise**. He spends **more time** at the gym than Mickey. Mickey gets **less sleep** than Brian. Brian is healthier than Mickey.

Less and *fewer* are the opposite of *more*.
Less is used with non-count nouns.
Fewer is used with count nouns.

Exercise 22. Complete the sentences with *more, less,* or *fewer*. Use the previous information to make statements about Brian and Mickey.

1. Brian eats _____ sugar than Mickey.

2. Mickey eats _____ cookies than Brian.

3. Brian eats _____ candy bars than Mickey.

4. Mickey eats _____ fruit than Brian.

5. Brian drinks _____ soft drinks than Mickey.

6. Brian drinks _____ coffee than Mickey.

7. Mickey uses _____ salt on his food than Brian.

8. Mickey takes _____ vitamins than Brian.

9. Every week Brian walks _____ miles than Mickey.

10. Mickey sleeps _____ hours than Brian.

11. Mickey gets _____ exercise than Brian.

12. Brian eats _____ donuts than Mickey.

Exercise 23. INTERVIEW. Complete the questions. Ask a classmate your questions.

1. Do you eat more _____ than _____ ?

2. Does _____ eat less _____ than _____ ?

3. Do you drink more _____ ?

4. Does _____ drink as much _____ as _____ ?

5. Does _____ get _____ sleep _____ ?

6. Do you and _____ get more exercise _____ ?

7. Are you as _____ as _____ ?

8. Do you have fewer _____ than _____ ?

9. _____ less _____ ?

10. _____ more _____ ?

Too and *either*

Examples:

My sister **is** a teacher, and my brother **is too**.
My sister **isn't** an English teacher, and my brother **isn't either**.

My brother **teaches** math, and my sister **does too**.
My brother **doesn't** teach in a public school, and my sister **doesn't either**.

My sister **studied** in the United States, and my brother **did too**.
My sister **didn't** go to graduate school, and my brother **didn't either**.

My brother **can** speak English very well, and my sister **can too**.
My brother **can't** speak German, and my sister **can't either**.

FORMULA 11-3

(…, **and**)	subject	form of **be** auxiliary	**too** .

Formula 11-3 is used for repetition of an affirmative statement.

Example: *(write one from above)* _____

FORMULA 11-4

(…, **and**)	subject	form of **be** + **n't** auxiliary + **n't**	**either** .

Formula 11-4 is used for repetition of a negative statement.

Example: *(write one from above)* _____

Exercise 24.   Complete the sentences. Use *too* and *either*.

1. You should study tonight, and I should _____ .
2. My mother doesn't drive, and my aunt doesn't _____ .
3. My parents speak two languages, and my grandparents do _____ .
4. I'm going on vacation next week, and my boss is _____ .
5. I won't be in town next week, and my boss won't _____ .

Exercise 25.   Complete the sentences. Use *too* and *n't either*. Also include correct auxiliaries or forms of *be*.

1. Ottawa is in Ontario, and Toronto _____ .
2. Saudi Arabia has a lot of oil, and Mexico _____ .
3. Columbus didn't travel to Asia, and Balboa _____ .
4. Churchill couldn't speak Russian, and Roosevelt _____ .
5. The United States won't send a space ship to Jupiter soon, and the Soviet
   Union _____ .
6. Peru isn't on the Atlantic coast, and Ecuador _____ .
7. Many Moroccans speak Arabic and French, and many Algerians _____ .
8. Nelson Rockefeller wasn't president of the United States, and Robert Kennedy _____ .
9. Miami and Chicago aren't state capitals, and New York City _____ .
10. Malaysia was a British colony, and India and Pakistan _____ .
11. Last semester my roommate took a history course, and I _____ .
12. I should study for the geography exam, and you _____ .

Exercise 26.   MINI CONVERSATIONS.

Examples: Do you like pizza?   (Yes)   Are you hungry now?   (No)

A: <u>Do you like pizza?</u>   A: <u>Are you hungry now?</u>.
B: Yes, I <u>do</u>.   B: No, I'm <u>not</u>.
A: I <u>do</u> too.   A: I'm <u>not</u> either.

1. Do you eat meat? (Yes)
2. Do you eat pork? (No)
3. Can you speak Russian? (No)
4. Can you speak English? (Yes)
5. Did you study English last year? (No)
6. Will you study English next semester? (Yes)
7. Do you walk to class? (No)
8. Do you have a car? (Yes)
9. Are you going to go out of town next weekend? (Yes)
10. Were you out of town last weekend? (No)
11. _____ ? (Yes)
12. _____ ? (No)

Exercise 27.

Complete the sentences. Write about classmates and family members. Each sentence should end with *too* or *either*.

1. I like _____ , and _____ too.
2. _____ can't _____ , and _____ either.
3. _____ didn't _____ , and _____ .
4. I'm _____ , and _____ .
5. _____ should _____ , and _____ .
6. _____ doesn't _____ .
7. _____ too.
8. _____ either.

Activities

A. RIDDLES. What are the answers?

1. What's as big as an elephant, but doesn't weigh anything?
2. How are the letter "a" and "noon" similar?
3. What animal can jump as high as a tree?
4. What is taller when it sits up than when it stands?
5. The more it dries, the wetter it becomes. What is it?

B. DISCUSSION. Discuss the similarities and differences between two places (cities or countries). In your discussion include some of the following topics: food, clothing, prices, buildings, climate, population, government, customs. Use some of the following comparative forms: *more … than, less … than, similar to, different from, (not) as … as, the same as.*

C. WRITING.

1. Compare two places. Use the topics and comparative forms in section B. Discussion.

2. Describe the life of a parent, a grandparent, or an ancestor.

D. PUZZLE.

Part 1. Answer the questions. The letters of the correct answers fit in the spaces after the questions.

1. What ocean borders Peru and Ecuador? *The* __ Ⓞ __ __ __ __ __ *Ocean*
2. What island is both a nation and a continent? __ __ __ __ __ __ __ Ⓞ __ __
3. In what American city is Waikiki Beach? __ __ __ __ Ⓞ __ __ __
4. What country sold Alaska to the United States? __ __ __ __ __ Ⓞ
5. Of what nation were India, Malaysia and Pakistan colonies?
   __ __ __ __ __ __ Ⓞ __ __ __ __
6. What river extends 1885 miles and separates the Republic of Mexico from the state of Texas? *The* __ __ Ⓞ __ __ __ __ __ __

7. What South American city is larger in population than Rio de Janeiro?

__ __ __   __ __ O__ __

8. What Texas city, home of the Johnson Space Center, is the fourth largest city in the United States?   __ __ __ __ __ __ O

9. What British university is older than Cambridge University?

__ __ __ __ __ O *University*

10. How many states are there in the United States?   __ __ __ O __

11. What building in Washington, D.C. is at 1600 Pennsylvania Avenue?

The __ O__ __ __   __ __ __ __ __

12. What Asian mountain is higher than Mount Fuji? *Mount* __ __ O__ __ __ __

13. What British airport is larger and busier than London Gatwick Airport?

London __ __ __ __ __ __ __ O *Airport*

14. In what city is Lincoln Center, a famous performing arts center?

__ __ __   __ O__ __

15. What mountains extend from Alaska to New Mexico?

The O__ __ __ __ *Mountains.*

16. What South American country is larger in size than Argentina? __ __ __ __ __ O

17. What jet is faster than the Boeing 747 Jumbo Jet? *The* __ __ __ __ __ __ O__

Part 2. To answer the question below, write the letters in circles in Part 1 in the order in which they appear.

Where do the historical and geographic facts in Part 1 come from?

__ __ __   __ __ __ __ __ __   __ __ __   __ __ __ __ __

E. DICTATION. You will hear each sentence two times. Write exactly what you hear.

1. _____

2. _____

3. _____

4. _____

5. _____

6. _____

7. _____

Review Quizzes

A. LISTENING COMPREHENSION: SENTENCES

For each problem, you will hear a short sentence once. After you hear a sentence, read the four choices. Decide which written sentence is the closest in meaning to the spoken sentence. Circle the letter of the correct answer.

1. (A) I sold it to him.
   (B) He sold it to me.
   (C) He bought it from me.
   (D) I bought them from him.

2. (A) My sister has the same number of children as my brother.
   (B) My sister has only one child, and my brother does too.
   (C) My sister and my brother are too small.
   (D) My sister and my brother are small children.

3. (A) Susie's sister bathed herself.
   (B) Susie bathed her sister.
   (C) Susie's sister gave Susie a bath.
   (D) Susie gave herself a bath.

4. (A) My uncle is as heavy as my father.
   (B) My uncle is shorter than my father.
   (C) My uncle is the same height as my father.
   (D) My uncle is taller than my father.

5. (A) She must speak Spanish.
   (B) She should speak Spanish.
   (C) She can speak Spanish.
   (D) She might speak Spanish.

B. LISTENING COMPREHENSION: CONVERSATIONS

You will hear short conversations between two people. At the end of each conversation, a third person will ask a question about the conversation. You will hear the question only once. After you hear the conversation and the related question, read the four possible answers. Decide which answer is the best response to the question. Circle the letter of the best answer.

1. (A) go to the park
   (B) park the car right there
   (C) look for a park
   (D) find a different place to park

2. (A) He mailed it to her.
   (B) He gave it to her.
   (C) She sent it to him.
   (D) She gave it to him.

3. (A) It's a very large store on Mason Street.
   (B) It only sells shoes.
   (C) He doesn't remember its name.
   (D) He didn't forget to buy shoes.

4. (A) go shopping now
   (B) go shopping tonight
   (C) go shopping the next morning
   (D) go shopping tomorrow at 10 p.m.

5. (A) how hot the man was
   (B) the temperature
   (C) the percent of humidity
   (D) the score of the volleyball game

C. STRUCTURE: SENTENCE COMPLETION

Choose the *one* word or phrase that best completes the sentence. If none of the choices correctly completes the problem, choose (D) *None of the above*. Circle the letter of the correct answer.

1. Her class schedule is -------- his.

   (A) different
   (B) different that
   (C) different as
   (D) different from

2. Our car isn't -------- your car.

   (A) as new
   (B) new as
   (C) new than
   (D) *None of the above*

3. My television is -------- yours.

   (A) the same
   (B) as same as
   (C) the same as
   (D) the same like

4. They gave -------- for his birthday.

   (A) Tom a watch
   (B) a watch Tom
   (C) to Tom a watch
   (D) *None of the above*

5. -------- I please have some more ice cream?

   (A) Should
   (B) Would
   (C) Must
   (D) Could

6. I have -------- homework than you.

   (A) few
   (B) fewer
   (C) less
   (D) *None of the above*

7. I explained --------.

   (A) the homework to him
   (B) to him the homework
   (C) him the homework
   (D) the homework him

8. They fed --------.

   (A) their
   (B) theirself
   (C) theirselves
   (D) *None of the above*

9. My car isn't -------- as yours.

   (A) the same size
   (B) the same big
   (C) same
   (D) similar

10. Could he -------- me a ride home?

    (A) give
    (B) gives
    (C) gave
    (D) giving

11. I'm not very tall, and my sister isn't very tall --------.

    (A) too
    (B) either
    (C) also
    (D) *None of the above*

12. This math exam was -------- the last one.

    (A) as hard
    (B) harder
    (C) more hard
    (D) *None of the above*

D. STRUCTURE: ERROR IDENTIFICATION
Each sentence has four underlined words or phrases. Circle the *one* underlined word or phrase that is not correct. Then correct the sentence.

1. <u>Did</u> you <u>cut</u> <u>you</u> <u>with</u> that sharp knife?
     A   B   C   D

2. She <u>doesn't</u> <u>smoke,</u> and I <u>don't</u> smoke <u>too.</u>
          A   B   C   D

3. <u>May</u> you please <u>tell</u> <u>me</u> <u>the correct answer</u> ?
     A   B   C   D

4. My cousin and I <u>couldn't</u> <u>build</u> a house <u>by</u> <u>ourself.</u>
                  A   B   C   D

5. He <u>must</u> <u>being</u> <u>tired</u> after his <u>long trip.</u>
       A   B   C   D

6. I am <u>the</u> <u>same</u> <u>tall</u> <u>as</u> my brother.
         A   B   C D

7. I have <u>to study</u> for <u>an exam</u> tonight, and you <u>have</u> <u>too.</u>
         A   B   C   D

8. My <u>little brother</u> <u>fell down</u> the stairs, but he <u>didn't hurt</u> <u>hisself.</u>
          A   B   C   D

9. <u>Is</u> his sister <u>work</u> <u>at the</u> restaurant every weekday <u>from seven to three?</u>
   A   B   C   D

10. <u>Could</u> you please <u>lend</u> <u>to me</u> <u>some money</u> until tomorrow?
        A   B   C   D

11. <u>Is</u> your <u>history class</u> this semester <u>interesting</u> <u>as</u> your geography class?
    A   B   C   D

12. My sister <u>lives</u> <u>in the</u> United States, and my parents <u>does</u> <u>too.</u>
            A   B   C   D

13. My friends <u>didn't</u> <u>enjoy</u> <u>theirselves</u> <u>on</u> their vacation.
            A   B   C   D

14. <u>Could</u> you please <u>explain</u> <u>me the answers</u> <u>today</u> after class?
        A   B   C   D

15. Terry <u>went</u> <u>to</u> school by <u>himself,</u> and Pat <u>didn't</u> either.
         A   B   C   D

CHAPTER 12

Reading

Death Over the Pacific   (Part One)

Passengers are boarding Transpacific Airlines flight #936 from Asia to North America.

Captain Drake:	Good morning, ma'am. Welcome aboard.
Jessica Fleming:	Thank you. This is my first flight over the Pacific, and I'm a little nervous.
Captain Drake:	Our flight crew is very experienced, and the flying conditions are excellent today. Your flight on Transpacific Airlines will be calm and smooth.
Flight Attendant Pike:	Ma'am, may I see your boarding pass, please? (*Jessica Fleming presents her boarding pass.*) You're in seat 15A in Business Class. This aisle.
Jessica Fleming:	Thank you.
Flight Attendant Pike:	Sir, your boarding pass, please. (*Arthur Burton presents his boarding pass.*) You're in seat 15B, next to that woman. Just follow her.
Arthur Burton:	Thank you.

Jessica Fleming and Arthur Burton take their seats in row fifteen.

A few hours later during the flight.

Jessica Fleming:	Was this your first trip to Asia?
Arthur Burton:	No, ma'am. I've been to Asia many times.
Jessica Fleming:	This was my first visit to the Orient. I took a ship from Los Angeles to Hong Kong six weeks ago, and I traveled to five different countries in Asia. Have you ever visited Hong Kong?
Arthur Burton:	Yes, I have.
Jessica Fleming:	I love Hong Kong! Were you vacationing in Asia or were you there on business?
Arthur Burton:	I was there on business.
Jessica Fleming:	Excuse me, I haven't introduced myself. I'm Jessica Fleming.
Arthur Burton:	I'm glad to meet you, Miss Fleming. I'm Arthur Burton.
Jessica Fleming:	It's Mrs. Fleming, but I've been a widow for several years. I'm a bit nervous about this flight. This is the longest flight that I've ever taken, and I've never flown over the Pacific before.
Arthur Burton:	Just sit back and relax, Mrs. Fleming. The movie is about to begin.

Later during the movie.

Flight Attendant Pike:	Here's your coffee, sir.
Arthur Burton:	I didn't order anything to drink.
Flight Attendant Pike:	Oh, you didn't? Oh, well, would you like this cup of coffee or something else to drink?
Arthur Burton:	I'll have the coffee. Thanks.

Arthur Burton drinks the cup of coffee. He continues to watch the movie. Twenty minutes later he begins to feel sick. He puts his head down, and he breathes heavily. Jessica Fleming takes off her headphones and turns to Arthur Burton.

Jessica Fleming:	Is something wrong?
Arthur Burton:	I can't breathe!

Jessica Fleming pushes the button to call the flight attendant. Arthur Burton takes a small red container out of the pocket of his suit coat.

Arthur Burton: Mrs. Fleming, please take this and hide it in your purse. It has top secret photographs on microfilm. When you land, call Joe. His number is 459-5112, 459-51 … .

Arthur Burton's head falls onto his tray table. Two flight attendants arrive.

Flight Attendant Jones: What's wrong?
Jessica Fleming: He's having difficulty breathing.
Flight Attendant Pike: Let's take him to the First Class upper deck. He can lie down there, and we'll look for a doctor on the plane.

The flight attendants help Arthur Burton to the front of the plane and up the stairs to the upper deck. Jessica Fleming begins to follow them.

Flight Attendant Pike: Ma'am, please return to your seat. We'll take care of this.
Flight Attendant Jones: Don't worry. He'll be okay.

Jessica Fleming sits down. She reaches into her purse. She looks at the small container from Arthur Burton. "Microfilm," she says to herself. "459-5112, Joe." A few minutes later Jessica Fleming walks to the stairs. She begins to climb the stairs. The pilot, Captain Drake, is coming down the stairs.

Captain Drake: Ma'am, don't go up there.
Jessica Fleming: I must speak to Mr. Burton.
Captain Drake: You can't. He had a heart attack, and he's dead.

To Be Continued

Exercise 1. Answer the questions based on the story.

1. Was this Jessica Fleming's first trip to Asia?
2. How did Jessica Fleming travel to Asia?
3. Where did Jessica Fleming go in the Orient?
4. Has Jessica Fleming flown over the Pacific Ocean before?
5. Why was Arthur Burton in Asia?
6. Does Arthur Burton order a cup of coffee during the movie?
7. What does Arthur Burton give Jessica Fleming?
8. What does Arthur Burton tell Jessica Fleming?
9. Where do the flight attendants take Arthur Burton?
10. What happens to Arthur Burton?

Exercise 2. Make guesses to answer the questions related to the story. (The answers are not in the story.)

1. What was Arthur Burton doing in Asia?
2. Who does he work for?
3. What did Arthur Burton take photographs of?
4. Why does Arthur Burton give the container to Jessica Fleming?
5. Who is Joe?
6. What is Jessica Fleming going to do with the small red container?

Pronunciation of [r]

Exercise 3.   A. Listen to the pronunciation of [r]. Then repeat the words.

were	purse	worry	drink	room
sir	art	very	trip	reach
are	turn	borrow	breathe	rain
your	aboard	forest	price	wrong
order	earth	tourist	street	red

B. Listen to the sentences. Then repeat the sentences.

1. Jessica Fleming worried about her return trip over the Pacific.
2. She and Arthur Burton traveled aboard Transpacific Airlines from the Orient to North America.
3. Arthur Burton did not order a drink, but he was very thirsty.
4. Jessica put Arthur Burton's red microfilm container in her purse.

Present Perfect: Continuation from Past to Present

Dialog

Student: How long **have** you **lived** here?
Teacher: I **have lived** here since 1985.
Student: How many years **have** you **taught** English?
Teacher: I've **taught** English for six years.
Student: How long **have** you **spoken** English?
Teacher: I've **spoken** English all my life!

The present perfect is used for a situation that began in the past and continues into the present. The present perfect consists of *has* or *have* and the past participle of the verb.

FORMULA 12-1

Subject	have has	(not)	verb [past participle]	(complement) .

Write two example sentences from the dialog:

_____

_____

In affirmative present perfect statements, the subject pronoun and *has* or *have* often form contractions. Other singular subjects can also form contractions with *has*.

Exercise 4.   Complete the list of affirmative contractions in the present perfect.

I have studied	= *I've studied*		**he has** studied	= *he's studied*
you have studied	= _____		**she has** studied	= _____
we have studied	= _____		**Pat has** studied	= _____
they have studied	= _____		**My cousin has** studied	= _____

In the present perfect *have* and *has* often combine with *not* to form negative contractions.

Examples: Pat **has not** studied. = Pat **hasn't** studied.
              I **have not** studied. = I **haven't** studied.

For most verbs in English, the past participle form is the same as the simple past form.

Examples:

BASE FORM	SIMPLE PAST AND PAST PARTICIPLE FORM
attend	attended
enjoy	enjoyed
have	had
teach	taught
try	tried

Irregular Past Participles

Some common English verbs have irregular past participles (different from their simple past tense forms).

BASE FORM	PAST PARTICIPLE FORM
be	been
drive	driven
give	given
go	gone
know	known
speak	spoken
take	taken

Exercise 5.   Use the phrases to write complete sentences in the present perfect.

1. My wife and I / be married for thirty years.
   My wife and I have been married for thirty years.

2. We / know each other for thirty-three years.

   _____

3. Our children / live here all their lives.

   _____

4. Pat / not go to school for two years.

   _____

5. She / work in a bank since last year.

   _____

6. Tom / be in the army for eleven months.

   _____

7. He / not visit us since last summer.

_____

8. Chris / drive a car for six months.

_____

9. He / not have any accidents.

_____

10. He / give his friends rides to school.

_____

In present perfect sentences, *for* is followed by an amount of time:

for	{	ages a long time many years four months two weeks a day five hours thirty minutes

In present perfect sentences, *since* is followed by a specific time expression relating to the past:

since	{	1985 last year (last) spring (last) January (last) Saturday yesterday (this) morning seven a.m.

Exercise 6.   Write *for* or *since* before each time expression.

Example: I've been here __*since*__ last month.

1. _____ July
2. _____ last night
3. _____ half an hour
4. _____ ten thirty
5. _____ a day
6. _____ several years
7. _____ 1979
8. _____ yesterday
9. _____ 9:00

10. _____ New Year's Day
11. _____ about a week
12. _____ Monday morning
13. _____ July fourth
14. _____ a little while
15. _____ September
16. _____ a minute or two
17. _____ three months
18. _____ a very long time

Exercise 7.   Complete the sentences. Use the present perfect forms of the verbs in parentheses. Add *for* or *since*.

1. I _____ (work) at Atlas Petroleum Company _____ 1982.

2. Mark Mendez _____ (be) my boss _____ four years.

3. I _____ (know) him _____ about six years.

4. I _____ (want) to find a new job _____ a long time.

5. The company _____ (not, give) me a raise _____ three years.

6. I _____ (not, have) much free time _____ a year.

7. I _____ (have) to work every day _____ two months.

8. I _____ (not, go) out of town _____ February.

9. My wife and I _____ (not, take) a vacation _____ last year.

Exercise 8. Use the phrases below to write true sentences in the present perfect. Complete each sentence with a time expression.

1. I / attend this school since   _____

2. I / study English for   _____

3. My teacher / teach English since   _____

4. My teacher / work here for   _____

5. We / not have an English exam for   _____

Exercise 9. MINI CONVERSATIONS.

Examples: you live here   Susan live here
              1986   several years

Lee: How long <u>have you lived here?</u>   Jan: How long <u>has Susan lived here?</u>
Pat: <u>I've lived here since 1986.</u>   Kim: <u>She's lived here for several years.</u>

1. you attend this school
   September

2. your brother be sick
   five days

3. you have stomach problems
   yesterday

4. Carmen play the guitar
   a long time

5. Ali speak English
   a year

6. Tom's parents be married
   1946

7. Ron take dance lessons
   last month

8. you drive a car
   four years

9. Mary's father work at General Hospital
   1972

10. Mary's father be a doctor
    thirty years

11. your grandparents own their house
    many years

12. you know how to play chess
    six years

13. Mrs. Bergman have a cat
    three months

14. you feel tired
    Saturday

15. you and your friend be here
    nine o'clock

16. you be in this English course
    _____

17. you know your teacher
    _____

18. you _____

19. your _____

20. _____
    _____

Note: In present perfect sentences, *all* is followed by a specific amount of time in a singular form without an article.

I have been here **all** {
my life.
year.
semester.
month.
week.
day.
afternoon.
}

Exercise 10.

INTERVIEW. Use a term from each column to make questions in the present perfect. Ask a classmate your questions. Answers should include *for, since,* or *all*.

| How long
How many years
How many months
How many weeks

_____ | have
has | you
you and your _____
you and _____
(name)
your _____
_____
(name)
_____ and _____
(name)   (name)
_____ | attend
be
drive
have
know
like
live
own
play
speak
study
take
work
____ | this school
here
a car
soccer
English
a guitar
in _____
at _____
with _____
_____ |

Examples: How many years has your family lived here?
How long have you studied English?

Indirect Objects with *for*

FORMULA 12-2 | Subject | verb | direct object | **for** | indirect object |

Examples: Could you please translate **this letter for Mr. Mason**?
The bilingual secretary prepared **a translation for him**.
The secretary also answered **the letter for him** in Spanish.

The verbs in the box can have direct objects and indirect objects.

answer	close	open	repeat
change	fix	prepare	translate

With these verbs the word *for* goes before the indirect object. These verbs can function with only a direct object. They can not function with only an indirect object.

Exercise 11. MINI CONVERSATIONS.

Example: answer the phone / me

Les: Could you <u>answer the phone</u> for <u>me</u>?
Terry: Sure. I'd be glad to <u>answer it</u> for <u>you</u>.

1. change the lightbulb / me
2. repeat the story / the children
3. close the door / us
4. prepare the meal / Grandma
5. translate this letter / the boss

6. answer the telephone / me
7. fix _____ / _____
8. open _____ / _____
9. answer _____ / _____

Exercise 12. MINI CONVERSATIONS.

Example: fix your bicycle / you
             Paul and Al / it / me
             last weekend

Sandy: Who <u>fixed your bicycle</u> for <u>you</u>?
Kazumi: <u>Paul and Al fixed it</u> for <u>me</u>.
Sandy: When <u>did they fix it</u> for <u>you</u>?
Kazumi: They <u>fixed it</u> for <u>me</u> last weekend.

1. answer the letter / Mr. Rogers
   his secretary / it / him
   two days ago

2. open the presents / the baby
   his sister / them / him
   on his birthday

3. close the windows / Dad
   Jim / them / him
   last night

4. fix your television / you
   Charles / it / us
   last weekend

5. translate the contract / the lawyer
   Mrs. Ito / it / her
   last week

6. change the tire / Grandma
   Uncle Tom / it / her
   on Sunday

7. prepare the package / Mr. Lopez
   Jim and Maria / it / him
   yesterday morning

8. fix _____ / _____
   _____ / _____ / _____

Exercise 13. Complete the sentences with a verb from the first box, a direct object from the second box, an indirect object from the third box, and *for*.

answer	open	this song	the window	me	the boss
change	prepare	a letter	the answer	us	the teacher
close	repeat	the car	the channel	Mom	the students
fix	translate	the tire	the question	my dad	the president
		the door	_____	everyone	_____

Example: Hassan and Ali *translated this song for us* .

1. Could you _____ ?
2. The students _____ .
3. The teacher _____ .
4. Could you please _____ ?
5. The mechanic _____ .
6. My brother _____ .
7. Can your sister _____ ?
8. The professor _____ .
9. The clerk _____ .
10. _____ .

Death Over the Pacific (Part Two)

Several hours later.

Max Kilgore:	Excuse me, ma'am. May I sit here?
Jessica Fleming:	Well, yes, if you want to.
Max Kilgore:	Thank you.

Max Kilgore sits down in Arthur Burton's seat.

Max Kilgore:	My name is Max Kilgore. I'm a sky marshall. Here's my identification badge. I've been in the coach section of this plane. May I ask you a few questions?
Jessica Fleming:	Yes.
Max Kilgore:	A tall man was sitting here a few hours ago. Did you talk to him?
Jessica Fleming:	Yes, I did. We talked for a short while.
Max Kilgore:	What did you talk about?
Jessica Fleming:	We talked about our travels in the Orient.
Max Kilgore:	What did he tell you about his visit to Asia?
Jessica Fleming:	He was there on business, and he was very familiar with Asia. That's about all. I did most of the talking.
Max Kilgore:	Did he tell you anything else?
Jessica Fleming:	Well, he didn't say very much.
Max Kilgore:	What did he eat?
Jessica Fleming:	He had the chicken dinner.

Max Kilgore:	Did he drink any alcohol?
Jessica Fleming:	No, he only had a few cups of coffee.
Max Kilgore:	Did he take any medicine?
Jessica Fleming:	I don't think so. Mr. Kilgore, is Mr. Burton really dead?
Max Kilgore:	Yes, he is. He died of a heart attack upstairs. Thank you for your help.
Jessica Fleming:	You're welcome.

Max Kilgore walks to the stairs of the upper deck and goes up the stairs.

A while later Captain Drake comes to Arthur Burton's seat. He begins to look around the seat.

Captain Drake:	Ma'am, may I talk to you for a few minutes?
Jessica Fleming:	Yes, of course.
Captain Drake:	This has not been a calm flight. Mr. Burton's death was very sudden, wasn't it?
Jessica Fleming:	Yes, it was.
Captain Drake:	Did he have any luggage with him on board?
Jessica Fleming:	No, I don't think so.
Captain Drake:	Did you see a small container?
Jessica Fleming:	A small container? Why do you ask?
Captain Drake:	Before he died, Mr. Burton said that he had lost a small container.
Jessica Fleming:	Really?
Captain Drake:	Yes, it contains a roll of film of his last family photos. If you find the container, please let me know.
Jessica Fleming:	Of course.
Captain Drake:	Excuse me, I must check on my co-pilots.

A short while later.

Max Kilgore:	Hello, again, Mrs. Fleming. (*Max Kilgore sits down in seat 15C.*) I've just called our office in San Francisco on the air telephone. Someone will be here to meet the airplane and to take Mr. Burton's body. I have a few more questions. Mr. Burton had trouble breathing, didn't he?
Jessica Fleming:	Yes, he did.
Max Kilgore:	Could he talk at all?
Jessica Fleming:	Yes, he could.
Max Kilgore:	Did he call for help?
Jessica Fleming:	No, I saw him, and I pushed the button. A male and a female flight attendant came. Oh, here comes the woman now.
Flight Attendant Pike:	Ma'am, here's your tea. Do you care for any cream or sugar?
Jessica Fleming:	Well, I didn't order any tea, but thank you. I'll have some sugar, please.

The flight attendant leaves. Jessica Fleming puts the cup to her lips. Then she sets it down on the tray.

Max Kilgore:	Who took Mr. Burton to the upper deck?
Jessica Fleming:	The two flight attendants.
Max Kilgore:	Did Mr. Burton complain of any chest pains before he had the heart attack?
Jessica Fleming:	No, he didn't. Mr. Kilgore, could you call the police on the air telephone? They should meet the airplane. Mr. Burton did not die of a heart attack. Someone murdered him, and I know who did it.

To Be Continued

Exercise 14.

Answer the questions based on Part Two of *Death Over the Pacific*.

1. Who is Max Kilgore?
2. Where was he sitting when Mr. Burton began to feel ill?
3. Did Mr. Burton drink any alcohol?
4. Did Mr. Burton take any medicine?
5. Did Mr. Burton have any luggage on board the plane?
6. Who lost a small container?
7. Who was looking for the container?
8. Who did Max Kilgore call?
9. Who served Jessica Fleming some tea?
10. According to Jessica Fleming, who should Max Kilgore call? Why?
11. According to Jessica Fleming, did Arthur Burton die of a heart attack?
12. According to Jessica Fleming, what happened to Arthur Burton?

Present Perfect: Indefinite Time

Dialog

Robin:	Have you ever been to England?
Courtney:	No, I haven't. You've been there, haven't you?
Robin:	Yes, I have.
Courtney:	How many times have you traveled to England?
Robin:	I've gone there three times.
Courtney:	Where have you been in England?
Robin:	I've been to London, Oxford, and Dover. Why haven't you ever gone to England?
Courtney:	I've never had enough time or money.

The present perfect is used to refer to a past situation at an indefinite time.

Implications:

1. The situation may still occur.

or

2. The situation may occur again.

Examples:

Have you ever been to Canada?
No, I haven't ever been there.

How many times have you been to New Zealand?
I've been there once.

Irregular Past Participles

BASE FORM	PAST PARTICIPLE FORM
break	broken
drink	drunk
eat	eaten
fly	flown
ride	ridden
see	seen
swim	swum

Exercise 15. PAIRWORK. Work with a classmate. Ask each other the questions. Give short answers.

Questions

Have _____ ever _____ ?

Has _____ ever _____ ?

Answers

Yes, _____ have.

No, _____ haven't.

Yes, _____ has.

No, _____ hasn't.

Examples: your father / be to Africa

A: Has your father ever been to Africa?
B: No, he hasn't.

you / eat turkey

A: Have you ever eaten turkey?
B: Yes, I have.

1. you / drink iced tea
2. you / work in an office
3. you / live alone
4. your mother / study psychology
5. you / swim in the Pacific Ocean
6. you / ride an elephant
7. it / snow in your hometown
8. you / see a tornado
9. you / eat pumpkin pie
10. our teacher / be in England

11. you / drive a truck
12. your parents / meet our teacher
13. you / speak to a famous person
14. your father / fly an airplane
15. you / have a pet
16. your family / travel to Ireland
17. you / break your leg
18. you / go ice skating
19. you / _____
20. your _____ / _____

Exercise 16. MINI CONVERSATIONS.

Example: you / be on TV
              twice

A: Have you ever been on TV?
B: Yes, I have.
A: How many times have you been on TV?
B: I've been on TV twice.

1. you / take the TOEFL
   once

2. your brother / have a car accident
   twice

3. you / break your arm
   once

4. your parents / fly in an airplane
   several times

5. _____ (*name*) / give a large party
   a couple of times

6. your sister / ride on a snowmobile
   a few times

7. your family / visit Disneyland
   twice

8. _____ (*name*) / see a movie in English
   many times

9. you / eat Chinese food
   many times

10. your mother / go to Hawaii
    a couple of times

11. your teacher / be late for class
    once

12. your father / make spaghetti
    many times

13. you / swim in the Atlantic Ocean
    once

14. you / _____
    _____

15. your _____ / _____
    _____

16. _____ (name) / _____
    _____

The present perfect can refer to a recent indefinite time. You can use the present perfect with the words *recently* and *today*. You can also use the present perfect with time expressions with *this*, for example, *this morning, this week, this month, this semester, this year*.

Examples: I have been busy today.
             I have been busy this week

Note: You cannot use the present perfect with past tense time expressions (for example, *yesterday, last week, last month*) without the word *since*.

Examples: I was busy yesterday.   I've been busy since yesterday.
             I was busy last week.   I've been busy since last week.

Irregular Past Participles

BASE FORM	PAST PARTICIPLE FORM
begin	begun
come	come
do	done
get	gotten
run	run
write	written

Exercise 17.   INTERVIEW. Work with a classmate. Use the phrases to make questions in the present perfect.

Example: write any letters today

A: Have you written any letters today?
B: Yes, I have (written some letters today).   *or*
     No, I haven't (written any letters today).   *or*
     Yes, I've written three letters today.

1. come to class late recently
2. do your homework for today
3. begin to study for the next grammar test
4. get good grades in this course this semester
5. be sick recently
6. write any letters this week
7. get any mail this week

8. see a good movie recently
9. read a good book this month
10. go to a concert recently
11. go out for dinner this month
12. run in a marathon race this year
13. _____ recently
14. _____ this year

Exercise 18.

Complete the dialog between a doctor and a patient with present perfect forms of the verbs in parentheses.

Doctor: I'm sorry I'm late. There was an emergency at the hospital.

_____ (you, be) here for a long time?

Patient: No, I _____ (not, be) here very long.

Doctor: How _____ (you, feel) recently?

Patient: I _____ (have) a headache for three days.

Doctor: What medicine _____ (you, take)?

Patient: I _____ (take) some aspirin, but it _____ (not, help).

Doctor: _____ (you, have) a fever too?

Patient: No, I _____ .

Doctor: _____ (your stomach, hurt)?

Patient: Yes, it _____ .

Doctor: What _____ (you, eat) recently?

Patient: I _____ (be) on a grapefruit diet for week. I _____ (not, eat) anything else for seven days. I _____ (lose) eight pounds.

Doctor: I think that the grapefruit diet _____ (cause) your headache. I'll recommend a better diet for you.

Superlative Forms of Adjectives

Examples:

French Guiana is **the smallest** country in South America.
Brazil is **the largest** of the thirteen South American countries.
São Paulo, Brazil is **the biggest** city on the continent.
It's also **the most crowded** city.

The Amazon River is **the longest** river in South America.
Mt. Aconcagua in Argentina is **the highest** point on the continent.
The farthest point from North America is in Chile.
What's **the prettiest** place in South America? Ask a South American!

Superlative Forms of Adjectives: Using *-est* and *most*

Use the superlative to compare *more than two* people, places, or things.

	ADJECTIVE	SUPERLATIVE
1. Add **-est** to one-syllable adjectives.	high long	the highest the longest
2. If a one-syllable adjective ends in a single consonant preceded by a single vowel, double the final consonant and then add **-est**. (Exceptions: adjectives ending in **w** or **y**.)	big wet low	the biggest the wettest the lowest
3. If a one-syllable adjective ends in **e**, add only **st**.	large wide	the largest the widest
4. If a one-syllable adjective or a two-syllable adjective ends in a consonant +**y**, change the **y** to **i** and add **-est**.	dry heavy	the driest the heaviest
5. Use **most** with adjectives that have two syllables (but do not end in **y**), and with adjectives that have more than two syllables.	famous beautiful	the most famous the most beautiful
6. Exceptions:	good bad far	the best the worst the farthest

Exercise 19. Write the superlative forms of the adjectives.

1. cold _____
2. hot _____
3. careful _____
4. nice _____
5. noisy _____
6. sad _____
7. bad _____

8. modern _____
9. pretty _____
10. handsome _____
11. far _____
12. fat _____
13. thin _____
14. gray _____

15. dirty _____
16. expensive _____
17. good _____
18. lazy _____
19. popular _____
20. clean _____
21. easy _____

Exercise 20. MINI CONVERSATIONS.

Example: hard test
             take

Sue: This is a hard test.
Jim: It certainly is. It's the hardest test that I've ever taken.

1. long book
   read

2. slow train
   take

3. beautiful lake
   see

4. dangerous road
   drive

5. clean city
   see

6. funny joke
   hear

7. big party
   give

8. large steak
   have

9. bad movie
   see

10. good pizza
    eat

11. difficult homework assignment
    do

12. boring play
    attend

13. modern hotel
    see

14. _____

    _____

Exercise 21.   Complete the sentences. Use *the* and the superlative form of each adjective in parentheses. For sentences 7–19 also write a subject.

(tall)   1. Abraham Lincoln was ___*the tallest*___ president in American history.

(long)   2. Franklin Roosevelt's term as president was _____ presidential term in U.S. history.

(young)   3. John Kennedy was _____ president of the United States.

(old)   4. Ronald Reagan was _____ American president.

(intelligent)   5. Albert Einstein was one of _____ people of this century.

(serious)   6. Hunger is one of _____ problems on earth.

(popular)   7. _____ was one of _____ leaders in my country.

(expensive)   8. _____ is _____ car.

(rich)   9. _____ is one of _____ people alive.

(important)   10. _____ is one of _____ languages in the world.

(good)   11. _____ is _____ movie I've ever seen.

(friendly)   12. _____ is one of _____ people I know.

(nice)   13. _____ is _____ city I have visited.

(bad)   14. _____ is _____ food I've ever eaten.

(great)   15. _____ is _____ singer of all time!

(powerful)   16. _____ is one of _____ people in the world.

(difficult)	17. _____ is _____ subject in school.
(funny)	18. _____ is _____ comedian I know.
(beautiful)	19. _____ is _____ actress from my country.
( )	20. _____

Exercise 22. MINI CONVERSATIONS.

Example: tall building / world
  the Sears Tower in Chicago
  the Empire State Building

Jan: What did you see during your vacation?
Kim: I saw the tallest building in the world.
Jan: What is the tallest building in the world?
Kim: It's the Sears Tower in Chicago.
Jan: Is it taller than the Empire State Building?
Kim: Yes, it is.

1. old university / United States
   Harvard University
   Yale University

2. large cathedral / world
   St. Peter's in Rome
   Notre Dame in Paris

3. popular amusement park / United States
   Disney World
   Disneyland

4. high mountain / world
   Mt. Everest
   Mt. Fuji

5. low point / United States
   Death Valley in California
   the Grand Canyon in Arizona

6. big department store / world
   Macy's in New York City
   Harrods in London

7. small country / world
   Vatican City
   Monaco

8. good zoo / United States
   San Diego Zoo
   San Antonio Zoo

9. long river / United States
   the Mississippi River
   the Missouri River

10. fast train / world
    the French TGV train
    the Japanese Bullet train

11. large passenger ship / world
    the Norway
    the Queen Elizabeth II

12. busy port / United States
    the port of New York and New Jersey
    the port of Los Angeles and Long Beach

Exercise 23. INTERVIEW. Complete the opinion questions with *What* or *Who*, the verb *be*, and superlative forms of the adjectives in parentheses. Ask and answer the questions with a classmate.

(great)	1. *Who is the greatest* singer alive today?
(good)	2. *What is the best* _____ song you've ever heard?
(intelligent)	3. _____ person in your family?
(funny)	4. _____ person you know?
(nice)	5. _____ person you've ever met?

(important)   6. _____ day in your life?

(bad)   7. _____ movie you've seen?

(interesting)   8. _____ subject you've studied in school?

(enjoyable)   9. _____ trip you've taken?

(far)   10. _____ place you've been from home?

(beautiful)   11. _____ place you've ever been to?

(interesting) 12. _____ place you've visited?

(famous)   13. _____ person you've ever seen?

(good)   14. _____ book you've ever read?

(important)   15. _____ thing in life?

(serious)   16. _____ problem in the world today?

Exercise 24.   WRITING. Answer one of the questions from Exercise 23 in a paragraph.

Exercise 25.   Complete the sentences with comparative or superlative forms of the
adjectives in parentheses. Remember to include *than* with comparatives
and *the* with superlatives.

1. (small)   Connecticut isn't __*the smallest*__ state in area in the United States. Rhode Island
   is __*smaller than*__ Connecticut. It's also __*smaller than*__ Delaware.

2. (large)   The State of Texas is _____ California, but it isn't
   _____ Alaska. Alaska is _____ state.

3. (cold)   Alaska is _____ state in the United States. It's
   _____ North Dakota.

4. (hot) The American state with _____ annual average temperatures isn't Hawaii. The average temperatures in Arizona are _____ in the United States.

5. (dry) Arizona is _____ state in the southwestern United States. It's also _____ state in the entire country.

6. (wet) Florida isn't _____ state in the United States. Alabama is _____ Florida.

7. (populated) California is _____ New York State. It's _____ state in the country.

8. (crowded) New York State isn't _____ state. New Jersey is _____ New York State, but New York is _____ California.

9. (large) New York City is _____ city in population in the United States. It's _____ Los Angeles, and it's also _____ Chicago.

10. (far) Honolulu, Hawaii is _____ from the nation's capital _____ Juneau, Alaska. It's _____ state capital from Washington, D.C. It's also _____ state capital from Denver, Colorado.

Indirect Objects with *for*

Dialog

Liz: Did you make **Jeff and Jean a chocolate birthday cake**?
Pam: No, I didn't make **them a chocolate cake**, but I made **a vanilla cake for them.**
Liz: Did you buy **any presents for them**?
Pam: I bought **Jean a necklace,** and I bought **Jeff a watch.**

With some verbs the indirect object can go before or after the direct object.

FORMULA 12-2

Subject	verb	direct object	**for**	indirect object

Example: I bought a necklace for Jean.

FORMULA 11-2

Subject	verb	indirect object	direct object

Example: I bought Jean a necklace.

With the verbs in the box the indirect object can go before or after the direct object.

bake	build	buy	cook	get	make

Exercise 26. MINI CONVERSATIONS.

Example: make you that sweater
             my grandmother

Ann: Who <u>made you that sweater</u>?
John: <u>My grandmother made it</u> for <u>me</u>.

1. buy you the birthday gift
   my classmates

2. cook your grandfather supper
   I

3. bake the teacher the birthday cake
   one of the students

4. get me this cup of coffee
   I

5. get your mother the flowers
   her parents

6. build you that bookcase
   my brother

7. buy your sister the diamond ring
   her boyfriend

8. make us the sandwiches
   my mother

9. buy _____

   _____

Exercise 27.   Rewrite each sentence about the family picnic using the other form.

Example:
Uncle Ed found a good picnic site for us.

Uncle Ed found us a good picnic site.

1. _____

2. Dad built a fire for Mom.

3. _____

4. _____

5. Ed bought soda pop for us.

6. Dick brought candy for the children.

He got Dad some firewood.

_____

Mom cooked us hamburgers.

Dick made everyone a salad.

_____

_____

Exercise 28.   VERB TENSE REVIEW. Complete the sentences with the correct forms of the words in parentheses. Add auxiliary words where necessary. Verb tenses included in this passage are present, present continuous, present perfect, simple past, past continuous, and future.

London Bridge

Where _____ (be) London Bridge? It _____ (not, be) in London, England. It _____ (be) in the southwestern United States since 1971.

The Thames River _____ (divide) London into two parts. London Bridge _____ (connect) the two parts of London from 1831 to 1968. Modern traffic on the bridge _____ (be) very heavy. In the 1960s London Bridge _____ (fall) down when city officials _____ (decide) to save it. They _____ (not, want, destroy) this famous bridge. They _____ (sell) the bridge to a Los Angeles corporation. The McCulloch Corporation _____ (buy) the bridge in 1968 for $2,460,000. The bridge _____ (consist) of 10,000 tons of stones. In London, workers _____ (take) the bridge apart and _____ (put) a number on each stone. The stones _____ (travel) 10,000 miles by ship to Long Beach, California. Then they _____ (go) 330 miles by truck to Lake Havasu City, Arizona. The shipment of the stones from England to Arizona _____ (cost) seven and a half million dollars.

In Lake Havasu City, workers _____ (rebuild) London Bridge on dry land with the original stones. Then they _____ (cut) a channel under the bridge from Lake Havasu. The governor of the state of Arizona and the lord mayor of London _____ (dedicate) the bridge on October 10, 1971. London Bridge _____ (not, fall) down any more. Since 1971 many tourists _____ (see) the bridge. An English village at the east end of the bridge also _____ (attract) tourists. Thousands of tourists from around the world _____ (visit) the bridge and the village next year. Would you _____ (like, visit) London Bridge? For more information, you _____ (can, write) to this address:

Chamber of Commerce
1930 Mesquite Avenue
Lake Havasu City, Arizona 86403
U.S.A.

Exercise 29. Write a letter to the Chamber of Commerce in Lake Havasu City. In your letter you might say that you have never visited Lake Havasu City. Ask for tourist information.

Activities

A. RIDDLES. What are the answers?

1. What's the smallest room in the world?
2. What are the largest ants in the world?
3. What are the tallest buildings in the world?
4. What is the longest word in the English language?
5. What's the hardest thing about learning to ice skate?

B. PUZZLE. Participle Hunt. In the puzzle there are past participle forms of the verbs in the box. They are read in a straight line (from left to right, right to left, vertically up or down, or diagonally). Circle the participles. The arrows before the verbs indicate the direction of the participle in the puzzle. *Examples:* participles for *say* and *sell* are circled.

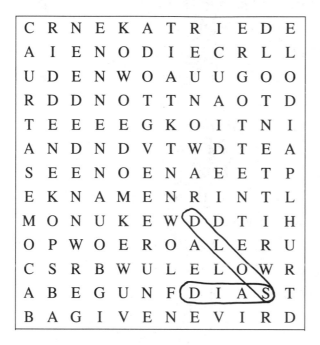

↘ add	↑ fly	← say			
↗ be	↓ get	→ see			
→ begin	→ give	↖ sell			
↗ break	↖ go	↑ sit			
↑ come	↓ hurt	↑ speak			
↙ cut	↘ know	↗ swim			
↑ die	↗ meet	← take			
← do	↓ need	↑ tell			
↙ drink	← own	→ try			
← drive	↑ pay	↑ win			
↙ eat	↓ ride	↑ write			
↗ feel	↓ run				

C. DISCUSSION TOPICS. Work with your classmates.

1. Changes that have occurred in the last year in my city / in my country / in the world
2. The best way to learn a foreign language
3. The best place to live
4. The most important invention

D. PAIRWORK. The sentences are about the story, "Death Over the Pacific." Fill in the blanks to complete the sentences with information from the two parts in this chapter. Then to the left put the fifteen sentences in order (____) from 1 for the first sentence to 15 for the last sentence.

(____) The flight attendant serves Arthur Burton a cup of _____ .

(____) _____ asks Jessica Fleming about Mr. Burton's container.

(____) Max Kilgore introduces _____ to Mrs. Fleming, and he asks her a few questions.

(____) Two flight attendants take Arthur Burton to the _____ .

(____) _____ begins to breathe heavily.

(____) Jessica Fleming and Arthur Burton board a Transpacific Airlines _____ .

(____) _____ examines the container from Arthur Burton.

(____) "Someone _____ Mr. Burton," Jessica Fleming tells Max Kilgore.

(____) Mrs. Fleming and Mr. Burton discuss their trips to _____ .

(____) _____ makes his first call on the air telephone.

(____) Mrs. Fleming pushes _____ to call for help.

(____) _____ welcomes Jessica Fleming aboard the flight.

(____) Arthur Burton gives Jessica Fleming a small _____ .

(____) _____ serves Jessica Fleming a cup of tea.

(____) Captain Drake says to Mrs. Fleming, "He had a _____ , and he's dead!"

E. ROLE PLAYS. Work with a classmate.

1. Detective Investigation. The conclusion to "Death Over the Pacific" follows in Section F. With a classmate play the roles of detectives. Make guesses about the conclusion of the story before you read it. Discuss how Mr. Burton *really* died. Answer the questions *who, how, why, when, where,* etc.

2. Job Interview. With a classmate play the roles of an employer and a job applicant. The first words of some of the employer's questions are below:

Have you ever _____ ?

How long have you _____ ?

(Wh-_____) did you _____ ?

What (is, was) the best _____ ?

F. READING.

Death Over the Pacific   (Conclusion)

Flight Attendant Pike: Welcome to California. We have landed at San Francisco International Airport. Please stay in your seats until we arrive at the gate.

A few minutes later the airplane arrives at the gate. The front door of the plane opens. Six police officers enter.

Police Officer: Where's the body?
Flight Attendant Pike: Upstairs.

Several police officers run up the stairs. Captain Drake and Flight Attendant Pike quickly leave the plane.

Jessica Fleming: Police! Catch that flight attendant! She poisoned Arthur Burton. Stop the pilot too! He's also responsible!

Two police officers run out of the plane after Captain Drake and the flight attendant.

G. WRITING. Think about the story *Death Over the Pacific*. Create answers for these questions. Then use your answers and your other ideas about the mystery story to write a conclusion to the story.

1. Do the police catch Captain Drake and the flight attendant?
2. Did they really murder Mr. Burton? If yes, why? If no, how did he die?
3. What happens to Captain Drake and the flight attendant?
4. How do the passengers react to the situation in the airplane?
5. What does Mrs. Fleming tell the police?
6. What does Jessica Fleming do with Arthur Burton's container?
7. Does Mrs. Fleming call Joe? If yes, who is he, and what does he tell her?

H. DICTATION. You will hear each sentence two times. Write exactly what you hear.

1. _____
2. _____
3. _____
4. _____
5. _____
6. _____
7. _____
8. _____
9. _____

Review Quizzes

A. LISTENING COMPREHENSION: SENTENCES

For each problem you will hear a short sentence. You will hear each sentence one time. After you hear a sentence, read the four choices. Decide which written sentence is the closest in meaning to the spoken sentence. Circle the letter of the correct answer.

1. (A) His brother's been weak.
   (B) His brother got sick one week ago.
   (C) His brothers spent a week in bed.
   (D) His brother Ben is sick.

2. (A) Some of the houses are larger than our house.
   (B) We live in the longest house.
   (C) Our house is bigger than the other houses.
   (D) Our house isn't the biggest house.

3. (A) She bought toys for her brother.
   (B) She bought toys for her brothers.
   (C) She bought a toy for her brother.
   (D) She bought a toy for her brothers.

4. (A) Susan is the oldest.
   (B) Pat is the oldest.
   (C) Mary is the oldest.
   (D) Pat and Susan are older than Mary.

5. (A) They have made two meals for him.
   (B) They made him two meals a week ago.
   (C) She has made two meals for him recently.
   (D) She made him two meals a week ago.

6. (A) John is shorter than Bill.
   (B) Bill is the shortest.
   (C) John is taller than Jim.
   (D) John is the tallest.

B. LISTENING COMPREHENSION: CONVERSATIONS

You will hear short conversations between two people. At the end of each conversation, a third person will ask a question about the conversation. You will hear the question only once. After you hear the conversation and the related question, read the four possible answers. Decide which answer is the best response to the question. Circle the letter of the best answer.

1. (A) She started a computer company.
   (B) She has been there for four weeks.
   (C) She's been at the company for a long time.
   (D) She began four days ago.

2. (A) The college game was worse than some high school games.
   (B) It was the worst game he has ever seen.
   (C) College games are the best football games.
   (D) College games are usually worse than high school games.

3. (A) She doesn't want to ski.
   (B) She should teach the man to ski.
   (C) The man should find a different ski instructor.
   (D) She is a very good skier.

4. (A) His mother has lived in France for many years.
   (B) His mother hasn't lived in France for a long time.
   (C) His mother has learned English very well.
   (D) His mother speaks both French and English.

5. (A) It's bigger than her old house.
   (B) It's not as large as the old house.
   (C) It's the same size as her old house.
   (D) It's yard is not as big as the yard of the old house.

C. STRUCTURE: SENTENCE COMPLETION

Choose the *one* word or phrase that best completes the sentence. If none of the choices correctly completes the problem, choose (D) *None of the above*. Circle the letter of the correct answer.

1. I have -------- my homework.
   (A) to did
   (B) to done
   (C) did
   (D) done

2. Scott answered -------- .
   (A) me the question
   (B) to me the question
   (C) the question to me
   (D) *None of the above*

3. Bonnie has worked here -------- a year.
   (A) since
   (B) for
   (C) all
   (D) *None of the above*

4. Yesterday was the -------- day of the year.
   (A) hottest
   (B) hotter
   (C) most hot
   (D) more hot

5. I -------- with Linda at ten o'clock today.
   (A) speak
   (B) spoke
   (C) spoken
   (D) have spoken

6. This restaurant -------- many interesting dishes.
   (A) to have
   (B) having
   (C) has
   (D) have

7. Jim -------- ten letters to his girlfriend last month.
   (A) has written
   (B) have written
   (C) wrote
   (D) have wrote

8. I'll make -------- .
   (A) some coffee to you
   (B) you some coffee
   (C) for you some coffee
   (D) *None of the above*

9. Tomorrow afternoon I -------- along the beach in Acapulco.
   (A) will be walk
   (B) will walking
   (C) will be walking
   (D) will to walk

10. Could you please open -------- ?
    (A) for me the window
    (B) me the window
    (C) the window to me
    (D) *None of the above*

11. We -------- that movie twice.
    (A) are seeing
    (B) have seen
    (C) have been seen
    (D) *None of the above*

12. The Soviet Union is -------- country in the world.
    (A) bigger
    (B) biggest
    (C) the bigger
    (D) the biggest

13. -------- when you fell?
    (A) Were you running
    (B) Have you run
    (C) Did you run
    (D) Did you running

14. My cousin -------- here since last month
    (A) lives
    (B) lived
    (C) is living
    (D) *None of the above*

15. Their children are -------- mine.
    (A) the youngest
    (B) as young
    (C) younger than
    (D) *None of the above*

16. She's -------- here all day.
    (A) being
    (B) been
    (C) has been
    (D) having been

D. STRUCTURE: ERROR IDENTIFICATION
Each sentence has four underlined words or phrases. Circle the *one* underlined word or phrase that is not correct. Then correct the sentence.

1. Pablo's roommate hasn't come to class yesterday morning.
      A   B   C   D

2. That was worst movie I have seen this year.
          A   B   C   D

3. How long she has wanted to have her own apartment?
         A   B   C   D

4. The prime minister is the more important person in that country.
                  A   B   C   D

5. We haven't wrote any compositions since last week.
       A   B   C   D

6. The Nile River is the most long river in Africa.
     A   B   C   D

7. I have traveled on the most biggest ship in the world several times.
       A   B   C   D

8. She has studied at the best high school in town since two years.
        A   B   C   D

9. Paul is the taller man she's ever met.
         A   B   C   D

10. She didn't buy any groceries since last Friday.
        A   B   C   D

11. Bill and Susan are the most intelligents people I know.
               A   B   C   D

12. Maria's English professor's translated her several letters since last semester.
     A   B   C   D

13. I have spoken to him twice last weekend.
        A   B C   D

14. Your uncle is the youngest than your aunt, isn't he?
           A   B   C   D

15. Our daughter hasn't gone to school for three week.
             A   B   C   D

Appendixes _____

Appendix 1. Verb Forms

Base	Present (third person, singular)	Present Participle	Simple Past	Past Participle
be	is	being	was / were	been
begin	begins	beginning	began	begun
break	breaks	breaking	broke	broken
bring	brings	bringing	brought	brought
build	builds	building	built	built
buy	buys	buying	bought	bought
catch	catches	catching	caught	caught
choose	chooses	choosing	chose	chosen
come	comes	coming	came	come
cost	costs	*	cost	cost
cut	cuts	cutting	cut	cut
do	does	doing	did	done
drink	drinks	drinking	drank	drunk
drive	drives	driving	drove	driven
eat	eats	eating	ate	eaten
fall	falls	falling	fell	fallen
feed	feeds	feeding	fed	fed
feel	feels	feeling	felt	felt
fight	fights	fighting	fought	fought
find	finds	finding	found	found
fly	flies	flying	flew	flown
forget	forgets	forgetting	forgot	forgotten
get	gets	getting	got	gotten / got
give	gives	giving	gave	given
go	goes	going	went	gone
grow	grows	growing	grew	grown
have	has	having	had	had
hear	hears	*	heard	heard
hide	hides	hiding	hid	hidden
hit	hits	hitting	hit	hit
hold	holds	holding	held	held
hurt	hurts	hurting	hurt	hurt
know	knows	*	knew	known
leave	leaves	leaving	left	left
lose	loses	losing	lost	lost
lend	lends	lending	lent	lent
make	makes	making	made	made
meet	meets	meeting	met	met
pay	pays	paying	paid	paid
put	puts	putting	put	put
read	reads	reading	read	read

*The present participle form is omitted for verbs not commonly used in this form.

Base	Present (third person, singular)	Present Participle	Simple Past	Past Participle
ride	rides	riding	rode	ridden
ring	rings	ringing	rang	rung
run	runs	running	ran	run
say	says	saying	said	said
see	sees	*	saw	seen
sell	sells	selling	sold	sold
send	sends	sending	sent	sent
shake	shakes	shaking	shook	shaken
sing	sings	singing	sang	sung
sit	sits	sitting	sat	sat
sleep	sleeps	sleeping	slept	slept
speak	speaks	speaking	spoke	spoken
spend	spends	spending	spent	spent
stand	stands	standing	stood	stood
steal	steals	stealing	stole	stolen
swim	swims	swimming	swam	swum
take	takes	taking	took	taken
teach	teaches	teaching	taught	taught
tell	tells	telling	told	told
think	thinks	thinking	thought	thought
throw	throws	throwing	threw	thrown
understand	understands	*	understood	understood
wake	wakes	waking	woke	woken
wear	wears	wearing	wore	worn
win	wins	winning	won	won
write	writes	writing	wrote	written

*The present participle form is omitted for verbs not commonly used in this form.

Appendix 2. Continents, Regions of the World, Nations, and Related Adjectives

Continent / Region	Adjective
Africa	African
Antarctica	Antarctic
Asia	Asian
Australia	Australian
Central America	Central American
Europe	European
Latin America	Latin American
Middle East	Middle Eastern
North America	North American
Orient	Oriental
Scandinavia	Scandinavian
South America	South American

Nation	Adjective	Nation	Adjective
Algeria	Algerian	Hungary	Hungarian
Argentina	Argentinian / Argentine	Iceland	Icelandic
		India	Indian
Australia	Australian	Indonesia	Indonesian
Austria	Austrian	Iran	Irani(an)
Bahrain	Bahraini	Iraq	Iraqi
Belgium	Belgian	Ireland, (the) Republic of	Irish
Bolivia	Bolivian		
Brazil	Brazilian	Israel	Israeli
Canada	Canadian	Italy	Italian
Chile	Chilean	Jamaica	Jamaican
Colombia	Colombian	Japan	Japanese
Costa Rica	Costa Rican	Jordan	Jordanian
Cuba	Cuban	Kenya	Kenyan
Cyprus	Cypriot	Korea[3]	Korean
Denmark	Danish	Kuwait	Kuwaiti
(the) Dominican Republic	Dominican	Lebanon	Lebanese
		Libya	Libyan
Ecuador	Ecuador(i)an	Malaysia	Malaysian
Egypt	Egyptian	Mexico	Mexican
El Salvador	Salvador(i)an	Morocco	Moroccan
England[1]	English / British	(the) Netherlands	Dutch
Finland	Finnish	New Zealand	New Zealand
France	French	Nicaragua	Nicaraguan
Germany[2]	German	Nigeria	Nigerian
Greece	Greek	Norway	Norwegian
Guatemala	Guatemalan	Oman	Omani
Haiti	Haitian	Pakistan	Pakistani
Honduras	Honduran	Panama	Panamanian

Nation	Adjective	Nation	Adjective
Paraguay	Paraguayan	Syria	Syrian
(the) P.R.C.[4] (China)	Chinese	Taiwan[5]	Taiwanese
Peru	Peruvian	Thailand	Thai
(the) Philippines	Philippine	Tunisia	Tunisian
Poland	Polish	Turkey	Turkish
Portugal	Portuguese	(the) U.S.S.R.[6]	Russian / Soviet
Romania	Romanian	(the) United Arab	
Qatar	Qatari	Emirates	Emirati
Saudi Arabia	Saudi (Arabian)	(the) United Kingdom[1]	British / English
Singapore	Singaporean	(the) U.S.A.[7]	American
South Africa	South African	Uruguay	Uruguayan
Spain	Spanish	Venezuela	Venezuelan
Sweden	Swedish	Vietnam	Vietnamese
Switzerland	Swiss	Yemen	Yemeni

[1] England (or Great Britain) = the United Kingdom of Great Britain and Northern Ireland
[2] Germany = the Federal Republic of Germany (West Germany) or the German Democratic Republic (East Germany)
[3] Korea = the Republic of Korea (South Korea) or the Democratic People's Republic of Korea (North Korea)
[4] P.R.C. = the People's Republic of China
[5] Taiwan = the Republic of China
[6] U.S.S.R. = the Union of Soviet Socialist Republics or the Soviet Union
[7] U.S.(A.) = the United States (of America)

Appendix 3. First Names

English

When more than one name is listed, the first name (or given name) is the most common legal name. The other name or names that follow the /, such as Alexander / Alex and Margaret / Maggie / Margie, are often nicknames. The names that follow in parentheses ( ), such as Bill (William) and Betty (Elizabeth), are the common formal names for the previous one, which is often a nickname.

Some of the English names are also found in other languages with the same or similar spelling. Some are originally from other languages, but are now common in English.

Male	Male/ Female	Female	Male	Male/ Female	Female
Abraham					Diana
Adam			Dick (Richard)		
		Agatha			Donna
Albert					Dorothy
Alexander/Alex		Alexis	Edward/Ed		
Alfred					Elizabeth/Beth/ Betty/Liz
		Alice			Ellen
		Amanda			Elsa
		Amy			Emily
Andrew					
		Angela	Eric		
		Ann or Anne or Anna			Faith
				Fran	
Arthur			Franklin/Frank		
		Barbara/Barb	Gary		
		Beth (Elizabeth)	George		
		Betty (Elizabeth)	Glenn		
Bill (William)			Hector		
Bob (Robert)					Holly
Bobby (Robert)			Ian		
Ben			Isaac		
		Bonnie	Jack (John)	Jackie	Jacqueline
Brad			James/Jim		
Brian				Jan	
Carl					Jane
		Carol		Jean	
		Carry	Jeff		
Charles					Jennifer/Jenny
		Cher	Jerry		
Christopher	Chris			Jess	Jessica
		Cindy			Jill
Clyde					Joan
	Courtney				Joanne
Dan (Daniel)			John		
David			Joe/Joey		

Male	Male/Female	Female	Male	Male/Female	Female
		Judy	Nelson		
		Karen			Nina
		Kathleen/Kathy/			Nora
		Kate/Kay			Olga
Keith					Pam
Ken			Paul		
	Kim		Patrick	Pat	Patricia
		Laura			Pearl
	Lee		Peter		
Leon			Phil		
	Les		Ray		
		Lilly	Richard/Rick/		
		Linda	Dick		
		Lisa			Rita
		Liz (Elizabeth)			
		Lola	Ronald/Ron		
Lou		Louise	Robert/Bob/		
		Lucille/Lucy	Bobby		
	Lynn			Robin	
Mac			Roger		
Mark					Sally
			Sam		
		Marcia		Sandy	Sandra
		Margaret/			Sarah
		Maggie/	Scott		
		Margie	Sid		
		Marie			Silvia
		Martha			Sophia
Martin					Sonia
		Mary			Stella
Matthew			Steven/Steve		
Max					Susan/Sue/Susie
		Megan	Ted		
		Melissa		Terry	
Michael/Mike			Tim		
Mickey					Tina
Mitch					
		Mona	Tom/Tommy		
		Nancy	Tony		
Nicholas/Nick	Nicky		Victor		
Neil			Wallace		
			William/Bill		

Other Languages (Several of these names are used in English.)

Male	Male/Female	Female	Male	Male/Female	Female
Abdulla/Abdul			Marcos		
Akiro					Maria
Ali					Marie
		Ana			Marta
Angel			Massoud		
Antonio					Mayumi
Arnoldus					Mimi
Carlos			Mohamed*		
		Carmen	Nabil		
		Elena	Najib		
		Fatima	Nicolas		
Hamid					Olea
Hans			Pablo		
		Harda	Paco		
Hassan			Pepe		
Hussein			Pierre		
		Indira	Saleh		
Ivan			Sigmund		
Jamal					Silvia
		Jamila			Susana
Jose			Talal		
	Kazumi		Tatsuo		
Khalid			Toshio		
		Kiyomi			Yumi
		Lin			Yoko
		Lupe	Yoshi		
		Machiko			

*Alternate spellings = Mohammad, Mohammed, Muhammad

Appendix 4. Map of the United States of America

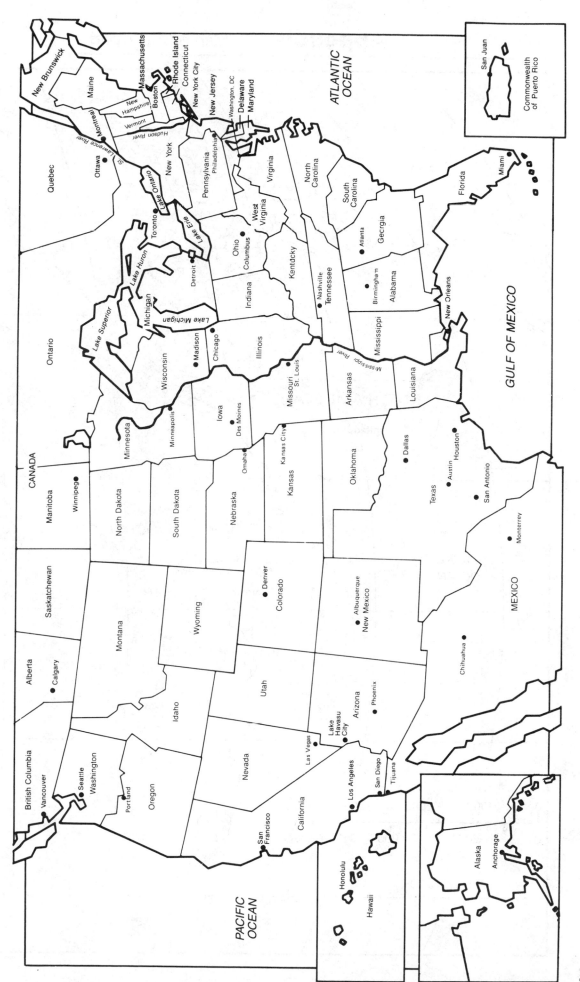

Appendix 5. Map of the World

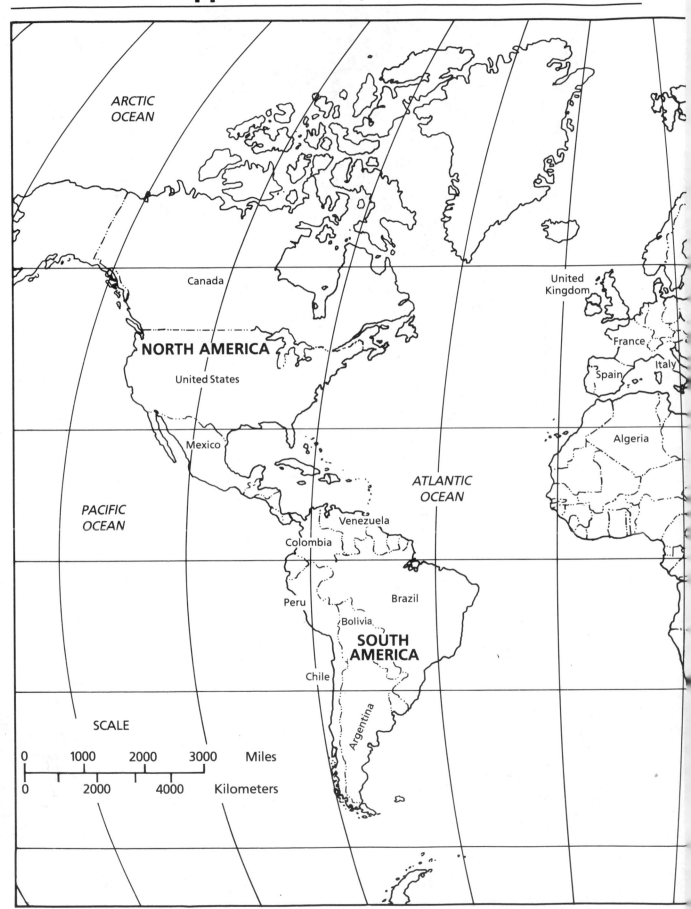

ARCTIC OCEAN

Canada

United Kingdom

France

NORTH AMERICA

Spain

Italy

United States

Algeria

Mexico

ATLANTIC OCEAN

PACIFIC OCEAN

Venezuela

Colombia

Peru

Brazil

Bolivia

SOUTH AMERICA

Chile

Argentina

SCALE

0	1000	2000	3000	Miles
0	2000		4000	Kilometers

ARCTIC OCEAN

ASIA

Union of Soviet Socialist Republics

EUROPE

Mongolia

Turkey

China

South Korea

Japan

Israel Iraq Iran

Libya

Egypt

Saudi Arabia

India

Thailand

Sudan

Philippines

AFRICA

PACIFIC OCEAN

Ethiopia

Malaysia

Indonesia

INDIAN OCEAN

AUSTRALIA

New Zealand

ANTARCTICA

Index _____